VOLCANIC WINES

jacqui
small

VOLCANIC WINES
SALT, GRIT AND POWER

JOHN SZABO, MS

FOREWORD BY ANDREW JEFFORD

Quarto is the authority on a wide range of topics.
Quarto educates, entertains and enriches the lives of
our readers—enthusiasts and lovers of hands-on living.
www.QuartoKnows.com

First published in 2016 by
Jacqui Small LLP
An imprint of Aurum Press
74-77 White Lion Street
London N1 9PF
www.jacquismallpub.com

Publisher: Jacqui Small
Senior Commissioning Editor: Fritha Saunders
Managing Editor: Emma Heyworth-Dunn
Commissioning/Project Editor: Hilary Lumsden
Designer: Namkwan Cho, gradedesign.com
Production: Maeve Healy
Picture credits are listed on p.251

British Library Cataloguing-in-Publication Data
A catalogue record for this book is available from the British Library.

10 9 8 7 6 5 4 3 2 1

ISBN 978-1-910254-00-4

Printed in China

CONTENTS

FOREWORD
BY ANDREW JEFFORD

Those who enjoy wine soon come to ask a simple, child-like question. (The best questions are simple and child-like.) Why do wines smell and taste as they do? This is the point of departure for all wine study, and the attempt to answer it fills bookshelves and working lives. It matters not just for those who love wine, but to all of those interested in the relationship between plants and environment, and in questions of agricultural quality.

If you believe that wines smell and taste as they do because of the way in which their agricultural raw materials are processed (winemaking), then you don't need this book. Consult oenological handbooks; read winemaker profiles.

Talk to most winemakers, though, and you will find them a self-effacing lot. They know, of course, that they can perform well or badly with their raw materials – and this is a source of anxiety to them, since they only get one chance a year to practice their craft. But they will also point out that what they can achieve depends entirely on the quality of those raw materials. Should we call it a cliché or an eternal verity? I don't know, but this is what you will hear, repeatedly: 'wine is made in the vineyard'. Viticulturalists (those who grow the vines) echo their winemaking counterparts. Their job, too, is to maximize potential, though they can never exceed it. To point this out is not to denigrate the extraordinary complexity of each set of tasks, but to understand its parameters.

That potential is derived from the relationship between a particular vine variety and rootstock to a physical and temporal environment: a place and a season.

This is an extraordinarily complex matter. What might matter most: the soil and stones in which are vine's roots are buried? The position and aspect of a vineyard on a hill? The welter of inputs which adds up to what we call a 'climate'? The particular meteorological phenomena of that year? Of course they all matter, but we have as yet no accepted procedure for weighing their relative importance. What we must do, for the time being, is ask the questions.

John Szabo's ambitious thematic addition to terroir studies assays the potential of wine creation in areas of the world whose soils are derived, to a greater or lesser extent, on volcanic materials. This is timely, for two reasons. First, because the approach is a new one: most wine books look at wine creation via a regional or national (administrative or political) approach rather than beginning with one of the fundamental themes of terroir. Second, because soils derived from other origins, and in particular limestone, have been extensively assayed in this respect in the past; it was time for a volcanic contribution.

Szabo has a gift for describing geological processes at work, and he has been assiduous in travelling through those wine regions of the world with 'volcanic soils', and talking to those wine craftsmen and women who know them most intimately. He realizes that this is no more than a single strand of a complex picture, and relates soil to topography and climate. He tastes with curiosity; he describes with passion. He has asked the simple, child-like questions that matter, and the result is both informative and innovative.

OPPOSITE *Water vapour streams from Mount Etna, Europe's, and one of the world's, most active volcanos. Grey or black smoke are more alarming signs.*

INTRODUCING VOLCANOES
THEIR BRIGHTER SIDE

Volcanoes are most often seen in the light of their destructive forces. Angry red-glowing fountains of lava, thunderous landslides, fiery clouds of poisonous gasses snuffing out all life within their grasp; towering columns of smoke and ash stretching into the stratosphere, disrupting air traffic, altering climate and causing crop losses nearby and on the other side of the world – these are the vivid Hollywood-style images conjured up by volcanoes. It's an unfairly bad rap. Truly cataclysmic volcanic eruptions are like shark attacks or airplane crashes: exceedingly rare (much more so, in fact). But when they do happen, they're admittedly catastrophic and decisive, which creates a disproportionate measure of fear that belies their statistical insignificance. In a list of the 40 most expensive and lethal natural disasters since 1970, no volcanic eruptions feature at all. Yet, since the beginning of time, volcanoes have nourished countless myths and fuelled superstitions of vengeful gods and destructive beasts lurking beneath the earth's surface.

Volcanism's almighty dark side hides an essentially constructive purpose: the constant renewal of the earth and a rebalancing of the internal forces that make our planet a livable habitat. Volcanoes have been around since the Earth coalesced from interstellar dust some 4.5 billion years ago. Volcanic eruptions created the atmosphere and oceans – the very essences of life support.

The ash and lavas emitted from ongoing eruptions renew soils with a heady mix of minerals, further supporting agriculture and sustaining life. Paradoxically, their often steep slopes, and threateningly damaging potential, have discouraged equally destructive human encroachment, preserving habitats for rare plant and animal species. In some spectacular instances, the fall out of calamitous eruptions has frozen time itself, as at Pompeii and Akrotiri, preserving a vivid record of life in the distant past for us to see.

FATAL ATTRACTION

Humankind since the dawn of time has been attracted to volcanoes. It's not for the thrill of putting one's life in peril, but rather the magical things that happen around them. Tracking the expansion of Roman civilization, for example, is like a join-the-dots drawing of thermal hot springs that arise in volcanic zones across Europe. Such baths have long been held to have healing properties, and it was also soon realized that drinking the water from these highly mineralized sources did wonders for your health.

But it's the superlative things that grow on or near volcanoes that have led me to write this book. Volcanic soils nurture the world's most prized coffee shrubs and intensely flavoured vegetables, and, to get to the point, wine grapes. In a unique twist, the challenging topography and phylloxera-inhospitable soils of many volcanic regions have had the unexpected consequence of conserving a vast number of rare, indigenous grape varieties that might otherwise have been sacrificed to the Gods of easy commercialism, not to mention fascinating farming practices that would be more familiar to a Renaissance painter than a 21st century vintner. But perhaps more importantly, and key to this work, many wines that grow on or near volcanoes happen to be particularly good.

It was this realization that inspired this book, which in turn ensued from a banal question: what is my favourite wine? As I struggled to respond to my editor's request for a short paragraph, feeling acutely uncreative – Champagne? Barolo? Burgundy? – I began to consider some of the more remarkable oddities I had stumbled across: Santorini, Etna, Badacsony came to mind. Others followed. Soon, a picture crystallized: the one thing these regions had in common was their volcanic soils. That was it: my favourite wine grows on a volcano!

The idea erupted, and brought me here. I am not trying to prove that volcanic wines are the world's best, however; I have soft spots

OPPOSITE *The magnificent Pico stratovolcano on the island of Pico, Azores.*

for many. Instead, I'd like to share my belief that volcanic wines represent a worthy collection of highly distinctive, individual expressions – stubborn holdouts in a world of merging flavours. Along the way I'll shed some light on some of the darker basaltic corners of planet wine, and cast a slightly different glow on long-admired regions – from the bedrock up. Most importantly, I'll share some of the remarkable stories of the people who toil in these strange, antique, backbreaking vineyards, scratched from barren rock and occasionally perched beneath a potentially lethal vent, and the wines they craft.

Setting the Limits

Although volcanic soils account for only around one per cent of the world's surface, grapes seem to occupy a disproportionate share. Some limits on the scope of this work had to be imposed, and since I'm not a geologist or soil scientist, I allowed myself to draw rather broad lines around my definition of volcanic soils: soils that formed from parent volcanic material. For the most part that means soil formed from extrusive igneous rocks – lava in all of its colourful variations – plus all of the rest of the fragmented materials that regularly get ejected from volcanoes, collectively called tephra. I include soils heavily laced with volcanic ash, even if they're not on a volcano, and also, where appropriate, vines grown on volcanic alluvium and colluvium, volcanic rocks that

washed or tumbled down hills into valleys. Considering where these conditions coincided with commercially relevant production and commendable quality, I drew up my list.

Regretfully, many qualified regions did not make it into these pages for more mundane constraints, familiar to anyone who has written a book on a vast subject. Southern Austria and Slovenia, Japan, New Zealand's North Island, British Columbia, France's Auvergne region, and a multitude of other volcanic AVAs in California and DOCs in Italy are just some of the regions remorsefully not covered. Other places, like Cape Verde's fascinating, tiny wine-producing Fogo Island was both too remote and production too limited, while the wines of lonely Château deFay, dropped seemingly straight out of Normandy onto the eastern slopes of the Agua volcano in Guatemala, were, well, too experimental. Lastly, for similar reasons, it was not possible to visit every winery in every region covered, so take the list of producers recommended as representative, not exhaustive.

It's been an amazing journey, one that hasn't ended. I hope you enjoy it, too.

John Szabo MS, Toronto

INTO THE HEART OF THE VOLCANO
WHERE & HOW VOLCANOES FORM

Volcanism is a staggeringly complex subject, still imperfectly understood, with much ongoing debate, conjecture and speculative modelling. The precise details of how and why volcanism occurs are far beyond the scope of this book (and even some of the theories I've outlined are controversial). But to broadly understand where and roughly why volcanic regions arise, and the major types of rocks you'll encounter in volcanic wine regions, read on. See also the Glossary, p.248.

Volcanoes are essentially vents on the earth's surface that allow often highly pressurized gasses, and molten and solid rock, to escape from the earth's crust or mantle below, temporarily restoring equilibrium. The earth's crust and upper mantle, technically called the lithosphere, is not one solid spherical piece, but rather fractured into a number of tectonic plates, like a jigsaw puzzle (how many pieces the puzzle has depends on which geologist you ask, but most agree on around eight to nine major plates, and dozens of microplates).

These plates are not stationary; they drift atop the underlying, more fluid asthenosphere like rafts on ocean currents. The vast majority of volcanoes form along the edges of these plates, which can be moving towards one-another (convergent boundaries), drifting apart (divergent boundaries), or sliding laterally past one-another (transform boundaries), such as along the San Andreas Fault (see p.54). Divergent plate boundaries are also the sites of trench formation (rift zones), while mountains are often crumpled up along convergent plate boundaries, and generate 80 per cent of the world's seismic energy – the cause of earthquakes.

TYPES OF VOLCANISM

There are three main types of volcanism: rifting, subduction and hotspots. **Rifting** of oceanic plates at divergent boundaries results in submarine volcanism, such as along the Mid-Atlantic Ridge (see p.98). Magma escaping though the fissures left by the spreading plates forms new sea crust and undersea mountain chains. Occasionally the submarine volcanoes break the surface and form islands – Iceland and the Azores are classic examples. Continental rifting can also lead to volcanism, as occurred in the Upper Rhine Graben in southern Germany and Alsace, where a sinking trench (*graben*) between two parallel faults provided the opportunity for magma to escape to the surface in isolated weak spots, notably, for the purpose of this book, at the Pechsteinkopf (Pfalz), Rangenkopf (Alsace) and the Kaiserstuhl Volcanic Complex in Baden.

Less important in terms of volume of magma released, but far more spectacular, is the volcanism that arises along convergent plate boundaries where continents and oceans drift together, such as around the margins of the Pacific Ocean, which gives rise to the so-called Pacific Ring of Fire (see pp.18, 54, 88). The heavier oceanic plate is dragged under the continental plate in a process called **subduction**. The sinking slab of oceanic lithosphere eventually melts and releases water, which in turn lowers the melting point of the overlying crust. Building pressure from the injection of magma is eventually able to find release through the weakened continental crust above, often erupting in memorably deadly fashion.

A chain or 'arc' of mostly picturesque stratovolcanoes forms parallel to the actual offshore subduction zone. The Cascade Volcanic Arc, the Andean Volcanic Belt and the Campanian Volcanic Arc (see pp.21, 88, 172) are classic examples of this type of volcanism. The amount of oceanic crust that vanishes each year into the earth is about equal to the amount of new crust formed at spreading margins, keeping the size of the earth's surface stable.

Another less violent source of volcanic material resulting from subduction is reclaimed oceanic crust, accumulated in coastal areas. Like a bulldozer riding a conveyor belt, the leading edge of the continental plate scrapes off taller bits of the sea floor (composed of basalts with overlying sediments), as the oceanic plate subducts beneath it, adding to the continental mass. Much of the western edge of North America is composed of accreted sea crust, some of which makes for prime vineyard land, as in Oregon's coastal hills (see p.18).

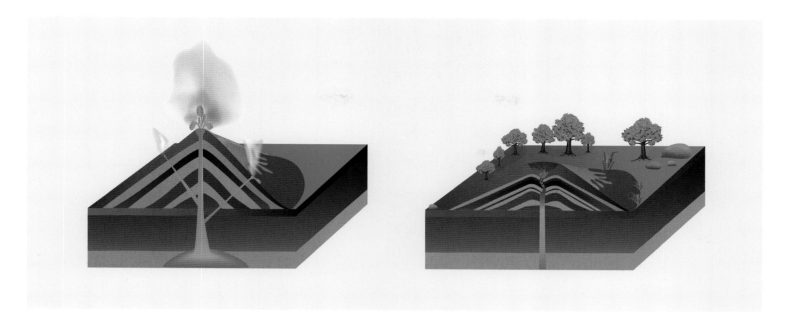

Hotspots are a third, if controversial and not universally accepted, cause of volcanism. The theory pertains to areas on the earth's surface above mantle plumes – upwellings of unusually fiery molten rock from the mantle. Hotspots are found at or near plate boundaries, such as in the Azores, in the middle of oceanic plates, as in the Canary Islands and Hawaii, as well as under continents. A hotspot for example was responsible for the massive floods of Columbia River Basalts (see p.21), now under Yellowstone National Park. Hotspots appear to be fixed relative to the motion of overlying tectonic plates, accounting for the time progression of volcanism observed; as a hotspot volcano drifts past the mantle plume that created it on its tectonic raft, it becomes extinct and a new, younger vent behind is formed above the plume.

Types of Lavas

Volcanoes emit a wide variety of lavas, the precise chemical composition of which (and thus of soils they eventually weather into) depends on a great many factors. Lavas are categorized by their relative proportions of silica (silicon dioxide), the most abundant surface mineral, as well as other major elements like iron, magnesium, potassium, calcium and sodium. Basalt has the lowest silica content, usually less than 50 per cent, with high proportions of iron and magnesium, which also form the minerals olivine and pyroxene to give basalt its characteristic dark colour. Andesite, dacite and rhyolite are the other major types of lava,

in order of increasing percentages of silica, potassium and sodium, and decreasing iron and magnesium. Rhyolite is generally the palest-coloured volcanic rock thanks to its high silica content. The composition of airborne materials emitted during an eruption, collectively called pyroclastics or tephra, as well as ash, mirrors closely the main type of lava, since it forms from the same magma. Most volcanoes specialize in one type of lava, but to add to vineyard soil complexities, the same volcano can erupt different lavas at different times due to changing composition in the magma below.

Types of Eruptions

Eruptions fall into two main categories: effusive are relatively mild, with gentle lava flows or fountaining, also called Strombolian or Hawaiian eruptions after the common nature of eruptions on those islands. They emit mostly basalts, the most fluid of lavas that can be spurted out with ease. Explosive are the most feared, caused by the sudden and violent expansion and depressurization of gases trapped in more viscous magmas like rhyolite beneath the vent. The more silica, the more viscous the magma – silica is like the cornflour (cornstarch) that thickens the sauce. Thicker magmas trap and contain more gases, and are thus more likely to erupt explosively. Plinian eruptions are highly explosive, producing a huge plume of smoke and ash that can rise many miles into the stratosphere – so-named for Pliny the Younger, the Roman statesman who described in frightening detail the volcanic eruption of Vesuvius in 79AD.

ABOVE *Classic stratovolcano formation: successive layers of viscous lava from multiple eruptions form a cone-shaped mountain. Erosion later re-shapes its profile.*

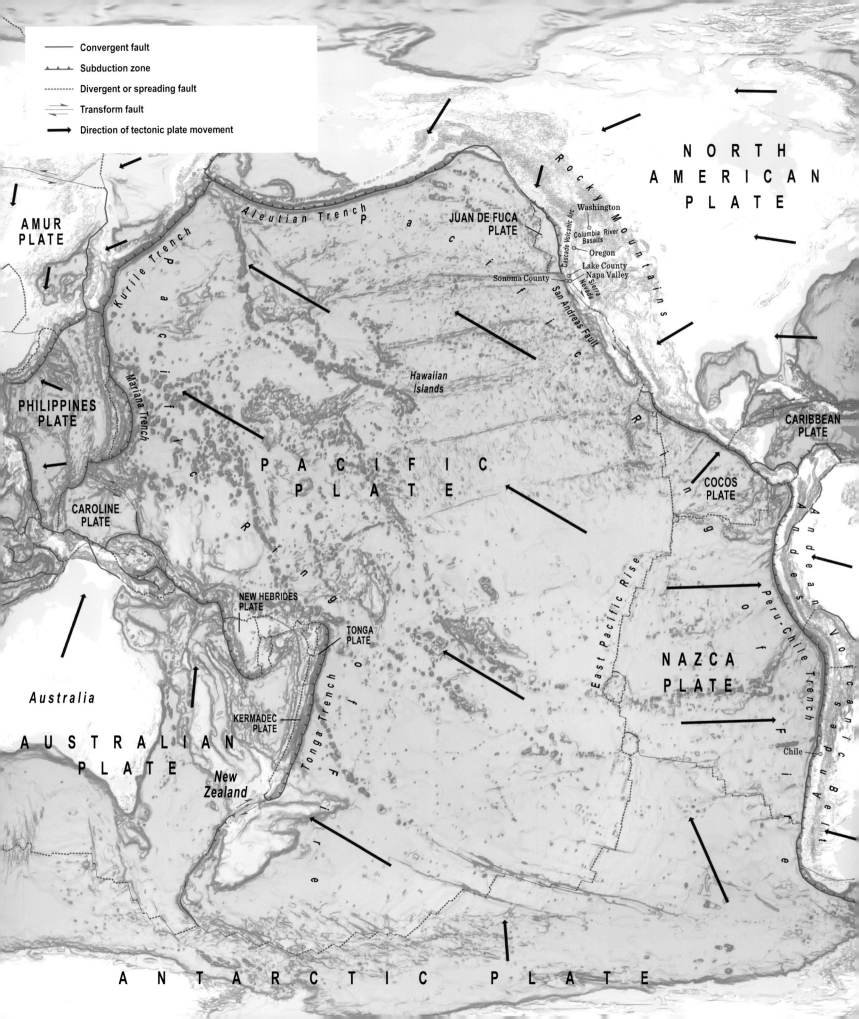

Greenland

Iceland

EURASIAN PLATE

British Isles

Ahr/Mittlerhein
Mosel
Nahe/Rheinhessen
Pfalz
Alsace
Soave
Baden
Somlo
Tokaj
Badacsony
Alps
Pannonian Basin

The Azores

Gloria Fault

Pitigliano
Campania
Basilicata
Mt Etna

Santorini
South Aegean Volcanic Arc

Madeira
Canary Islands

ANATOLIA PLATE

AEGEAN SEA PLATE

Zagros Mountains

Himalayas

YANGTZE PLATE

Mid-Atlantic Ridge

ARABIAN PLATE
Arabian Peninsula

INDIAN PLATE

SUNDA PLATE

AFRICAN PLATE

Great Rift Valley

BURMA PLATE

SOUTH AMERICAN PLATE

SOMALIA PLATE

Madagascar

AUSTRALIAN PLATE

Mid-Atlantic Ridge

Southwest Indian Ocean Ridge

Southeast Indian Ocean Ridge

SCOTIA PLATE

ANTARCTIC PLATE

Scale (along equator) 1:75 000 000

VOLCANIC SOILS & WINES
LINKING IT ALL TOGETHER

Let's be clear: there is no such thing as 'volcanic wine'. There are, however, wines grown on volcanic soils that come in a radiant, infinitely nuanced rainbow of colours, tastes and flavours. What I mean is that there is no volcanic *wine* in the singular, but a great and varied many. Terroir is a complex system of which soils (and their parent geologies) are an important part, but of course not the only part. Comparable characteristics exist, but volcanic wine regions around the world have even more unique features. Before discussing some of the similarities between volcanic wines, let's look at what makes them individual.

First, leaving behind the other components of terroir, 'volcanic soil' is only slightly more descriptive than 'cheese'. Cheese is made from milk, as volcanic soil derives from parent volcanic materials. There are hundreds of different types of soils that might be called volcanic, even according to my relatively limited definition. In obvious places such as Vesuvius, Etna, Santorini or the isles of Macaronesia – places formed by volcanoes – the volcanic-ness of the dirt is unquestionable. But even there, soil composition varies astonishingly. Even pure lavas come in Technicolor variations. They range from a few days to tens of millions (billions) of years old, and have different chemical and physical structures – from pure rock to volcanic sand or weathered old clays.

That's just the tip of the volcano. I haven't even mentioned human interference on soil chemistry and structure. And once you move outside of the obviously volcanic areas into regions of mixed geology, where seismic and tectonic activity have sliced and diced the bedrock, and wind, water, glaciers, gravity and bulldozers have inconveniently mixed and moved soils around, the complications for scientists (and volcanic wine writers and their mapmakers), looking to link wines and soils on such a macro level, are impossible to contend with.

Connections between wine chemistry and soil chemistry have been found, and we know scientifically and empirically that soils do influence wine. But these observations are only applicable on a micro scale. And at best, they only hint at the possible relation to the actual *taste* of wine. Indeed, it seems a dangerously reductionist line of inquiry. It's a great challenge for scientists to explain subjective taste and flavour experiences in a meaningful way. And there is no universal, measurable connection between all volcanic wines.

WHAT VOLCANIC WINES SHARE

But despite grand variations, there are nevertheless a couple of features that appear with enough regularity in wines grown on volcanic soils (even if they are not exclusive to them) to lead to anecdotal, if not rigorously scientific, conclusions. These features loosely sketch the picture that is then completed by the infinite subtleties of every region and every wine and every vintage.

Number one is that wines from volcanic soils hinge on a common mouthwatering quality, sometimes from high acids, almost always from palpable saltiness, sometimes both. Mineral salts involving elements present in wine – like potassium, magnesium and calcium, along with their acid-derived molecular partners like chloride, sulphate and carbonate – have been implicated (although in seaside vineyards it's often plain old sodium chloride from sea spray, not soils). Mineral salts may also explain the vague but pleasantly bitter taste found in some wines.

Number two is their savoury character. Volcanic wines have fruit, of course, but it's often accompanied, if not dominated by non-fruity flavours in the earthy and herbal spectrums of flavour, along with all of the nuances covered under the magnificently useful, multi-dimensional term *minerality* and all of its varied definitions. Minerality and volcanic wines walk hand-in-hand.

OPPOSITE *Luis Felipe Edwards' 'LFE 900' project in Colchagua Valley, Chile (up to 900 metres/2953 feet).*

The best examples, like all great wine, seem to have another, or at least different, dimension, a common sort of density that can only come from genuine extract in the wine, not alcohol or glycerol, or just tannin and acid. It's a sort of weightless gravity, intense, heavy as a feather, firm but transparent, like an impenetrable, invisible force shield of flavour that comes out of nowhere but doesn't impose itself, it's just there and you have to work your tongue around it. It can be gritty, salty, hard, maybe even unpleasant to some, but unmistakable.

The Volcanic Family of Soils

These characteristics have their roots at least partly in the soils. And although extremely varied, there are properties shared by many soils in the volcanic family that make them particularly suitable for high-quality wine.

For one, especially young volcanic 'soils' (formed on lavas) are often more rock than soil – they have not had time to weather into water-retentive clays. Since low water availability is the single most important growing factor to produce quality grapes, this is an obvious advantage. Soils derived from ash, sand and tephra (also with little clay) likewise tend to drain like sieves (strainers). Finally and obviously, the volcanic soils most often exploited for vineyards are almost always on hillsides, where gravity ensures that water is limited.

Paradoxically, volcanic soils, at least the best ones for wine-growing, are relatively infertile. Despite lavas generally having a generous amounts of the major macro and micronutrients required by plants (potassium, calcium, magnesium, sulphur, iron, etc), they're not readily available to root systems. They must first be weathered into an available form, and then made soluble

ABOVE *Viña Koyle's biodynamic volcanic-andesitic vineyard in Los Lingues, Colchagua-Andes DO, Chile.*

in water to be taken up by root systems. But water, as we've just seen, is not often available, and young soils/rocks are not ready to give up their nutrients just yet. The situation is compounded by the fact that little else can grow in dry, rocky, infertile soils, so there's very little build up of organic matter that could otherwise store water and harbour nutrients.

In the end, vines get a broad and balanced diet, but in small quantities (low fertility but without particular deficiencies), which triggers them to focus on ripening fruit – the *raison d'être* of a vine – rather than grow shoots and leaves. Simply put, semi-parched, semi-starved vines produce less fruit, smaller bunches, thicker grape skins (where most aromas and flavours are stored), and result in more deeply coloured, concentrated, structured and age-worthy wines with a broader range of flavours.

Still within the family, especially old, highly-weathered volcanic soils have the contrasting property of water retention (lots of clay), which, when matched to a dry growing season (eg. Willamette Valley or Monte Vulture) keeps vines moist, unstressed and able

to focus on even, steady ripening. And on dry and sunny Lanzarote, the thick covering of yesterday's volcanic ash (geologically speaking) is what makes grape-growing possible, acting like moisture-retaining mulch over the older soil. Similarly, the water-absorbent pumice of Santorini drinks in night-time moisture and shares it with the vines.

The chemistry of specific volcanic soils, too, has interesting effects on parts of the collection, some direct, but most indirect. Potassium levels are key in Badacsony, the Azores and Santorini; iron influences Soave and Washington State, measurable mineral ash plays its part in perceived minerality in Alsace, while a link between soil and wine chemistry, and wine aroma/flavour and taste, has been found in Germany. See each chapter for more details on this.

These are just a few examples of the shared and varying properties of volcanic soils, which, together with the right combination of climate, grape and human intervention – in a word 'terroir' – give rise to a collection of some of the world's most singular wines.

Do volcanic wines exist? You bet. Read on.

THE PACIFIC NORTHWEST
THE COLUMBIA RIVER BASALTS
& THE CASCADE VOLCANIC ARC

The Pacific Northwest is an area as rich in geological events as a 19th century Russian novel, recounting a complex past of volcanic hotspots and arcs, repeated lava and glacial flooding, tectonic rifts and mountain building, wind sculpting and weathering. Over eons, all of these events have woven together to create the present tapestry of Oregon and Washington State's wine-growing regions.

The entire northwest strip of North America is a region of 'active geology', and in particular, volcanism. The Pacific Northwest lies along the much broader Pacific Rim Volcanic Arc that follows the edge of the Pacific tectonic plate – the planet's largest – around the Pacific Ocean where it meets surrounding plates. This horseshoe-shaped belt of earthquake-prone rift zones and fiery volcanic arcs stretches some 40,000 km (25,000 miles) from southern Chile around to New Zealand. Three-quarters of the world's active and dormant volcanoes, and nine out of ten of the planet's earthquakes occur along the Ring of Fire.

Some of the region's first volcanic soils came literally out of the sea. About 50 million years ago, the leading edge of the Pacific's Farallon Plate (see p.54) drifted into the North American plate and was forced beneath it. The continent began scraping crust off of the Pacific plate like a spatula, essentially marine sediments and ancient basalts from submarine volcanoes along the Juan de Fuca Ridge, adding them to its plate. The western edge of North America grew, extending further westward as more material was accreted. Still today the Pacific Northwest gains a little landmass every year.

Then around 17 million years ago, when the coast had made much progress in reclaiming land from the sea, the western edge of the North American Plate drifted over a hotspot. The upwelling pressure caused by the magma plume created weaknesses in the overlying continental crust, eventually fracturing it open into long irregular fissures. Unimaginable quantities of pressurized lava were thus liberated, spewing into the air like a fiery curtain, a volcanic flood.

ONE LARGE IGNEOUS PROVINCE
Basaltic lava flows poured periodically for ten million years through river valleys and across plains, some following the ancient Columbia Gorge and reaching as far as the Pacific and spilling down into the Willamette Valley in northwestern Oregon. Each

OPPOSITE *The tectonically upthrust, grass-covered basalt hills of eastern Washington.*

episode added another layer of hardened lava onto the one beneath like a giant layer cake, creating what geologists call a Large Igneous Province, or LIP. In the areas of greatest accumulation in the central Columbia Basin, the basalt bedrock is hundreds of metres thick (thousands of feet), and occasionally even deeper. Under the Rattlesnake Hills of eastern Washington, for example, geologists have drilled more than 3.2 km (2 miles) without finding the bottom.

The immense weight of so much accumulated lava – an estimated 174,000 cubic km (miles) – was enough to cause a giant bowl-shaped depression in the earth's crust, centred around the town of Pasco, Washington. This impressive formation is called the Columbia River Basalts, and it extends from Idaho to the Pacific in an area larger than England and Wales combined. Incidentally, the same hotspot that caused this activity is no less active today; it has tracked relentlessly southeastward as North America drifts over it north-westward. You can visit the potentially lethal subterranean magma plume in the northwest corner of Wyoming over 600 km (370 miles) away, in Yellowstone National Park.

ABOVE LEFT *Domaine Serene's Grace vineyard in Dundee Hills AVA, Willamette Valley, Oregon.*

ABOVE RIGHT *Snow-covered Mt Hood volcano from Carabella vineyard at the top of Chehalem Mountains AVA, Willamette Valley, Oregon.*

Not long after Columbia River Basalts ceased flowing some six million years ago, renewed subduction of the Pacific Plate under North America lifted the ancestral Cascade Mountains even higher. This created the Cascade Volcanic Arc, a chain of young stratovolcanoes and shield volcanoes, lava domes and cinder cones, stretching from northern California to southern British Columbia. The central part of the Cascade Arc in Washington State and northern Oregon is the youngest and most active, with most volcanoes less than two million years old and the highest peaks less than 100,000 years old. Many potentially deadly cones are visible from both city centres and vineyards: Mt Rainier, Mt St Helens and Mt Adams in Washington, and Mt Hood, Mt Jefferson and Three Sisters in Oregon, among many others. But counter-intuitively, Cascade volcanism (so far) has had only minor impact on the wine regions of the Pacific Northwest, mainly in the Columbia Gorge and in the eastern foothills of the Cascades in Washington.

Ice Age Floods

If the story ended there, the entire Pacific Northwest would be nothing but volcanoes and basalt flood plains. But more recently, a mere 18,000 to 12,000 years ago during the last Ice Age, great continental ice sheets occasionally advanced and retreated from the north, creating vast, ice-dammed lakes. The dams would periodically fail as water pressure built up behind it. The largest of these, Lake Missoula in Montana, gives its name to the cataclysmic cycle of Ice Age floods that released as much as ten times the combined flow of all modern rivers worldwide in a single event, scouring the Columbia Basin, stripping, carving and eroding, and depositing incalculable amounts of flood sediments all the way from Montana to northwestern Oregon. This cycle occurred as many as 62 times, laying the foundation for much of the rich agricultural land in the Columbia Basin.

In the process, the basalt bedrock was covered in stratified deposits in all but the highest hills, up to 300 metres (1000 feet) in eastern Washington, slightly lower by the time the floods reached the Willamette Valley. Thus, although the underlying geology of the wine regions of eastern Washington, and many parts of northern Oregon is almost exclusively Columbia basalt, only hillside sites can rightly be called volcanic. Additionally, wind would later sculpt the landscape further, blowing some of the flood sediment and other eroded material back up the Columbia Gorge into Washington and depositing it as the soil type called loess, covering more of the basalts.

This brief run through of many millions of years of history explains the unique and complex mix of marine sediments, flood sediments, loess, Columbia River basalts and more ancient Pacific sea crust basalts found in the wine regions of the Pacific Northwest. But considering that a major earthquake is long overdue, and another major eruption is a question of when, not if, the lay of the land could well change again at a moment's notice, and I will have to rewrite this chapter.

ABOVE (FROM LEFT TO RIGHT) *Wilridge Winery, Naches Heights; Blue Mountains, North Fork, Walla Walla; Red Mountain; Horsepower Vineyard, Rocks District;* *Force Majeure, Red Mountain; Pacific Rim Solstice vineyard, Yakima Valley; Wilridge Naches Heights (twice); Horsepower Vineyard, Rocks District;* *Columbia River flowing through basalt; Blue Mountains, North Fork, Walla Walla; Wilridge, Naches Heights.*

WASHINGTON STATE

Washington State, like neighbouring Oregon, traces its modern wine-growing history back about half a century. The arrival in 1967 of outside consulting expertise in the form of California winemaking legend André Tchelistcheff, hired by American Wine Growers to help guide the nascent fine wine industry, heralded a new era. From barely a half-dozen commercial wineries in 1970, Washington has grown to over 850 registered wineries, and is now the second largest wine producer in the USA: spectacular growth for a single generation.

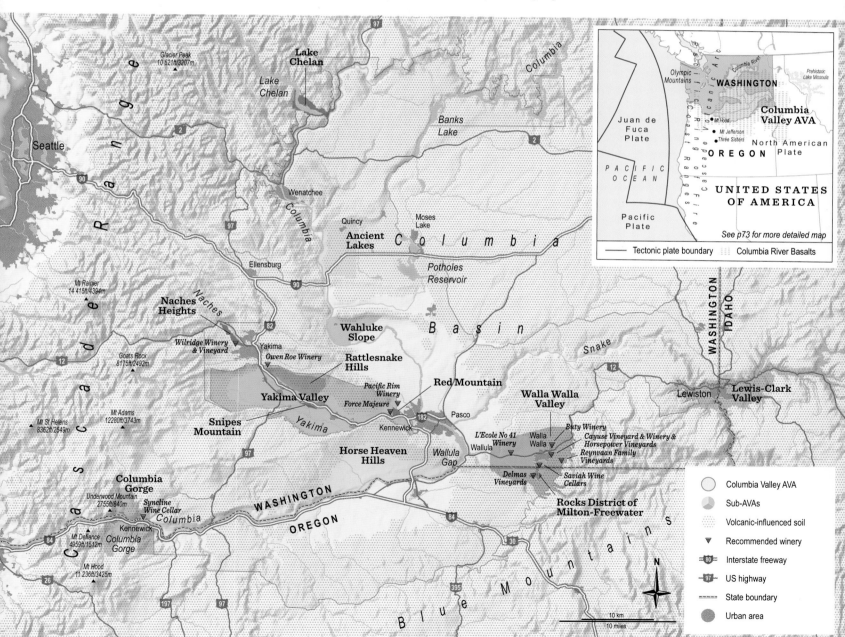

All of Washington's wine regions (tiny Puget Sound excluded), lie on the eastern side of two parallel mountain ranges: the coastal Olympic Mountains, and the more formidable volcanic arc known as the Cascade Mountains, whose highest peak, Mt Rainier, reaches 4392 metres (14,409 feet). The mountains act as an effective barrier against Pacific moisture, and grapes grow in a semi-desert. Geologically, Washington's vineyards sit atop one of the world's most impressive Large Igneous Provinces, the massive accumulation of formerly molten rocks known as the Columbia River Basalts. Yet for the reasons outlined in the chapter introduction, most of the state's vines root in deep flood sediments and wind-blown loess; only basalts above nature's arbitrary flood crest remain exposed enough to harbour vine roots. But although few of these uplands have been planted thus far, they are the future. So much of the smart money is currently heading to the hills, literally, where these beautiful basalts have stood defiantly for at least six million years, barely weathered in the desert climate, waiting to make vines struggle in the pursuit of world-class wine. The future of Washington wine will be far more volcanic.

CLINGING TO THE RING OF FIRE

Those living around the aptly named Pacific Ring of Fire are well aware of the occasional catastrophic consequences of inhabiting the edge of active tectonic plates, endlessly rifting, sinking, crashing and scraping against one another, causing reliably recurrent earthquakes and volcanic eruptions. These devastating forces work both independently, and occasionally, in synchronicity, as happened on May 18, 1980, when a sudden earthquake caused the weakened north face of Mt St Helens in Washington State to crumble, creating the largest landslide ever recorded.

Highly pressurized molten magma contained within the volcano was thus suddenly exposed to the atmosphere, and erupted in spectacular Plinian fashion, captured in images that shocked the

ABOVE *Owen Roe's Union Gap vineyard overlooking the Yakima Valley.*

OPPOSITE ABOVE *The Blue Mountains on the North Fork of the Walla Walla River, potentially some of Washington State's best future vineyard land.*

OPPOSITE BELOW *The exploratory trench dug by Force Majeure atop the Red Mountain AVA, showing virtually no topsoil over pure volcanic rock.*

world. The foaming, blazing hot mix of lava, pulverized rock and gas was ejected so fast it overtook the avalanche. Snow and glacial ice on the volcano liquified instantly, mixing with the lava to form thunderous lahars (volcanic mudslides) that gathered mass and momentum, accumulating more debris along their destructive descent. The lahars flowed as far as the Columbia River over 80 km (50 miles) to the southwest. A plume of volcanic ash rose 24 km (15 miles) into the atmosphere, eventually falling like powdery grey snow over the entire northwest corner of North America.

Heading to the Hills

'This is where I would plant,' Kevin Pogue tells me as we wind our way up the valley on the North Fork of the Walla Walla River near the Washington/Oregon border. I look at the surrounding Blue Mountains covered with pale-green wild grasses, framed by the occasional outcrop of black basalt bedrock breaking the surface on the thin hillsides and peaking out on the ridge crests in surprising geometric precision. Aside from a few isolated patches of young vines that have yet to yield their first crop, vineyards are notably

absent. I say notably, because that's what Pogue is strangely referring to. This is where he would plant grapevines, if he were ever to establish a vineyard. Pogue is a professor of geology at Whitman College in Walla Walla and a respected vineyard consultant – he's dug pits and analyzed soil structure and chemistry throughout the region, and advised many of the top producers on what, and especially where, to plant. So it's telling that he's pointing to virgin hillsides as the promised land for fine wine – land with no history, no track record to prove its suitability. He has more than a hunch that these hills are destined for greatness. He knows.

Why Pogue can say this with confidence is not exactly a mystery. Hillsides have been considered prime terroir for fine wine production since long before Roman times. So what, exactly, makes hillsides so well suited to fine wine? In a word, it's *drainage* – mostly water drainage, but air drainage is also important, especially in frost-prone areas like eastern Washington that are blasted regularly by arctic air. Cold air drains off hills and pools, like water, in the lowest spots it finds. In cold climates, this is

---

ABOVE *Mid-slope of Red Mountain AVA cleared for planting, showing thick covering of wind-blown loess and flood sediments. Volcanic soils found higher up.*

*Pogue, K.R., 2010, *Influence of basalt on the terroir of the Columbia Valley American Viticultural Area: Proceedings of the 8th International Terroir Congress, Centro di Ricerca per la Viticoltura, Soave, Italy, v.1, p.4-50–4-55.*

where you get the most vine damage, which is inconvenient to say the least, even if it doesn't affect quality directly.

But water drainage on the other hand, does affect quality *directly*. Indeed, water availability is considered the single most important quality parameter for grape-growing by most experts. Vines of course need water, but less is better if you're a wine-grower in pursuit of excellence. Rocky hillsides have other physical benefits. Not only do they hold less water, they also promote faster and more complete ripening thanks to the solar radiation that surface rocks absorb and radiate back to grape bunches. Energy also radiates downward into soils and heats ground moisture, which stays warm long after sunset. Pogue speculates that the warmer ground water enables more efficient nutrient absorption by vine roots, leading ultimately to greater complexity in wines (see also p.45–6).

But there's more. Pogue has also recommended planting in Washington's exposed fractured basalts not just for their advantageous physical characteristics, but also for their unique chemistry. It's clear that the particular composition of these basalts makes for distinctive wines, even if the precise mechanisms of how are not fully understood. According to Pogue's research, 'vineyard soils in the Columbia Valley AVA that incorporate basalt bedrock or basalt alluvium show substantial increases in available iron relative to the more widely planted loess-based soils'.* Pogue measured an increase of up to 233 per cent more available iron in basalt-

influenced soil samples than in pure loess (as well as higher magnesium and calcium carbonate). Considering that iron is an important nutrient for grapevines, and, continues Pogue, 'unlike most elements, the concentration of iron in grapes and vineyard soils has been demonstrated to be directly related,' it stands to reason that wine chemistry, and by extension, texture and flavour, are affected by the higher iron concentration, however circuitously. Proving that scientifically, however, is another matter altogether. But in any case, the taste differences are self-evident.

Economics is the main reason why so few of these potentially great volcanic sites have been planted so far. Most of them are logically found on steep slopes and hilltops and are thus more expensive to farm (and irrigate). And yields are naturally lower. They'll never produce commodity wines. But now that Washington wines have earned critical acclaim, and the higher price that accompanies it, the economics make more sense, and more of these sites will be developed.

Rising Above the Tide

I witness evidence of this future atop Red Mountain, a 430-metre-high (1410-feet) mound of upthrust basalt just west of the Tri-Cities that lends its name to one of Washington's most illustrious AVAs. The mountain was directly in the path of the repeated Ice Age Missoula floods that pushed through the Wallula Gap to the

southeast and roared across the flatlands before slamming into it. Each successive flood's load of gravel, sand and silt carried down from Montana settled out of the swirling slack waters in the back eddy on the southwest side of the hill, blanketing the lower three-quarters of the mountain and the entire valley at its feet.

Red Mountain's crown, however, is pure exposed fractured basalt. The AVA's dual terroir was laid bare for me thanks to Paul McBride of Force Majeure, who had just cleared land for a new vineyard planting about two-thirds of the way up the mountain. A cut had been made in the hillside to lessen the slope angle and make way for the upper rows of vines, and it was clearly below the crest of the Missoula floodwaters: the exposed soils looked as much like a thick sandy-silty beach as a future vineyard site. But a trough dug higher up the hill for another prospective vineyard is definitely above the highwater mark; large pieces of fractured basalt rock protrude almost immediately from the meagre covering of wind-blown dust that coats the upper quarter of Red Mountain – there's virtually no soil – it's almost pure rock.

The pattern on Red Mountain is repeated throughout Washington: virtually every vineyard in the Columbia Basin under 350 metres (1150 feet) takes root in thick sediments left behind by multiple flood episodes or blown by wind, while the few, though increasing number of vineyards planted above can rightly be called volcanic.

Washington State's (Partially Volcanic) AVAs

Washington counts 13 American Viticultural Areas (AVAs), the largest of which is the Columbia Valley AVA into which all others are nestled, with the exception of Puget Sound, the sole AVA on the west side of the Cascades, and the Columbia Gorge AVA, which is essentially an extension of the southwestern ridge of the Columbia Valley AVA. The five most prominently volcanic are highlighted here. Although the new (2015), uniformly volcanic Rocks District of Milton-Freewater AVA is often associated with Washington (most producers have Washington addresses) it lies entirely within Oregon (see p.45).

First planted in 1975 by John Holmes and John Williams of Kiona Vineyards, **Red Mountain AVA** lies at the eastern end of the Yakima Valley at the confluence of the Horse Heaven Hills and Rattlesnake Mountain where the Yakima River snakes between them. It's Washington State's smallest AVA (in terms of total available area, though it has more acreage planted than others) and most exclusive, reveered for its muscular, age-worthy reds. A veritable who's who of Washington wineries either have vineyards in or buy grapes – both Rhône and Bordeaux varieties – from Red Mountain. Most of the truly volcanic soils on the upper quarter of Red Mountain have yet to be exploited. Grand Rêve and Force Majeure are the current exceptions, with more plantings on the way. Shaw and Quintessence Vineyards are also eying up

ABOVE LEFT *Geologist Dr. Kevin Pogue at L'Ecole Nº 41's Ferguson vineyard.*

ABOVE RIGHT *James Mantone of Syncline Cellars above the Columbia River.*

OPPOSITE ABOVE *Andesite plateau of Naches Heights AVA*
OPPOSITE BELOW *Columbia River flows through the Wallula Gap between basalt anticlines.*

Red Mountain's volcanic soils, with vineyards planned for the upper elevations. The key to Red Mountain fruit, according to Paul McBride, is managing the considerable tannins. The short, sunny, intense growing season – Washington's warmest – and constant winds build thick skins, often resulting in astringent wines if not handled delicately

The **Yakima Valley AVA**, as the name implies, is a relatively low-lying stretch of land on either side of the Yakima River directly east of Mt Adams. It's the state's oldest AVA granted in 1983, with the oldest vines (Cabernet Sauvignon was planted as early as 1957) and the most acreage. It's one of Washington's cooler growing areas, especially in the western half of the valley close to the foothills of the Cascades, previously considered a hindrance, though today a treasured advantage in the quest for more refined wines.

Most of the AVA's vineyards are on flood sediments and loess, save for a few elevated parcels such as the Red Willow Vineyard, which sits on a relatively steep slope mostly above the flood crests, and thus is heavily influenced by volcanic material. Two-dozen wineries purchase grapes from Red Willow. Owen Roe Winery's high-elevation monopole Union Gap vineyard is likewise mostly on stony volcanic soils, as is Pacific Rim's Soltice vineyard.

Far up the Yakima River to the northeast in the foothills of the Cascades lies the recent (2011) **Naches Heights AVA**. It's unique in the Columbia Valley in that vineyards lie on a plateau over a relatively recent flow of andesitic lava (as opposed to the more ancient basaltic lava that underlies the rest of the Columbia basin). 'We're standing on the world's longest andesite flow,' Paul Beveridge of Wilridge Vineyards tells me. About a million years ago, an eruption of the Goat Rocks series of volcanic peaks in the Cascade Range spewed forth what's called Tieton andesite – named after the nearby town and river. Following the ancient riverbed, the lava flowed eastward over 80 km (50 miles) before finally hardening into solid rock where U.S. 12 now crosses the Naches River. Wind-blown material has filled in depressions on the andesite plateau, so vines root in both loess and straight into the rock where the soil is shallower. At 350 to 700 metres (1150 to 2300 feet) elevation, appropriately-named Naches Heights is one of the coolest regions in eastern Washington. 'Certain grapes like Petit Verdot and Cabernet Sauvignon struggle to ripen in some

vintages,' reveals Beveridge. Also uniquely for Washington, the entire, albeit still relatively small AVA, is certified either LIVE (Low Input Viticulture and Enology) or biodynamic.

The town of Walla Walla in the southeastern corner of the state is eastern Washington's most stylish and wine-tourist-friendly centre, and the **Walla Walla Valley AVA** is likewise one of the state's most recognized. Again, the vast majority of vineyards root in thick loess, though there has been a great deal of recent interest in higher-elevation volcanic soils, particularly in the foothills of the Blue Mountains in the area referred to as the 'North Fork', where shallow topsoil quickly reveals the basalt bedrock. Cayuse Vineyard, Tertulia and Maison Bleu already have vines in the ground, and another large plantation is in the works. The AVA also spills over into Oregon, where some of its finest, and certainly most volcanic, vineyards are found (see p.45).

The **Columbia Gorge AVA** is also shared between Washington State and Oregon. The Washington side lies above a particularly scenic stretch of the majestic Columbia River, framed by the twin volcanic peaks of Mt St Helens and Mt Adams to the north, and Mt Hood to the south in Oregon. But the key volcanic influence comes from the less-spectacular-looking Underwood Mountain just 2 km (1.2 miles) north of the river – a shield volcano, born from an extension of the Casacade Arc. It erupted less than a million years ago, sending thick streams of basalt lava into the Columbia Gorge and across the river into Oregon.

The main volcanic vineyards of the region thus lie on the south-facing slopes below the mountain but above flood crests, one of the oldest and best known of which is Celilo Vineyard, first planted in 1972 on a gently sloping bluff overlooking the Columbia River. Officially belonging to the Chemawa soil series (formed in volcanic ash and basalt alluvium, found on terraces and hills), locals refer to Celilo's soils as 'shot soils', owing to the abundance of granular bits of fused volcanic ash and pyrolclastic material resembling buckshot. The climate is distinctively cooler and wetter than anywhere else in eastern Washington. With close to 1.2 metres (47 inches) of rain annually irrigation is not necessary and cool-climate-loving varieties like Riesling, Grüner Veltliner, Gewürztraminer, Chardonnay and Pinot Noir perform well. Celilo sells grapes to over two-dozen wineries in Washington and Oregon.

OPPOSITE *Basalt skyscrapers that line the Columbia Gorge.*

WASHINGTON STATE – THE WINES & THE PEOPLE

Buty Winery

535 E Cessna Ave
Walla Walla
WA 99362
butywinery.com

Nina Buty started her winery in 2000 with a vision for blended wines from organic vineyards made with a natural aesthetic, an extension of her background in art and geology. The young Rockgarden estate, planted in 2008 on a former apple orchard in the highest section of the Rocks District AVA, is already producing an uncommonly pure and focused, old-wood-aged, ethereal Syrah blend (with Cabernet Sauvignon and Mourvèdre) Rediviva of the Stones. 'We waited years to buy only here. Anywhere else further out in the cobblestones would have been a compromise,' Buty affirms. A winery to watch.

Cayuse Vineyard & Winery
& Horsepower Vineyards ★★★

PO Box 1602 (Cayuse) / 1622 (Horsepower)
Walla Walla
WA 99362
cayusevineyards.com
horsepowervineyards.com

Frenchmen Christophe Baron, who earned the nickname 'bionic frog' while working in Australia, is one of Washington's (and Oregon's) most admired wine-growers, and his wines some of the most sought after in the USA since he discovered and planted in The Rocks in 1997. All vineyards are farmed biodynamically. Syrah from the original Cailloux vineyard manages an impossible balance between density and finesse, with smoky, meaty, blood and iodine flavours and a floral lift from co-fermented Viognier. Coccinelle Vineyard Bionic Frog Syrah is the darkest, most opulent and voluptuous in the Cayuse Cellar. Distinctive Armada vineyard,

the latest ripening, yields an even meatier, more tannic and burly Syrah, the last to be released. Sister company Horsepower Vineyards produces Grenache and Syrah from high-density Rocks District AVA vineyards, farmed by horse, in a relatively more elegant, refined style, also brilliant. Wine from new plantings in the basalts of Walla Walla's Blue Mountains is highly anticipated.

Delmas Vineyards ★★

SJR Vineyard
Lower Dry Creek
Milton-Freewater
OR 97862
delmaswines.com

Steve Robertson was one of the driving forces behind the creation of The Rocks District AVA, inspired by the unique character of the wines he observed right out of the gate from his SJR vineyard, planted in 2007. His interpretation of this terroir is more finely detailed and less savage than many – a beautiful, elegant style. SJR vineyard also supplies fruit to other wineries.

Force Majeure ★

50207 Antinori Road
Benton City
WA 99320
forcemajeurevineyards.com

Paul McBride started planting this small, premium-focused Red Mountain estate in 2006. Early wines made in collaboration with Ciel du Cheval have been phased out, and all wines are now from estate fruit. Initial releases of Cabernet, and especially Syrah, are impressively ripe, deeply fruity and firmly structured. New plantings of Grenache, Syrah, Roussanne and Picpoul among others in the volcanic upper part of the mountain are eagerly awaited. Winemaker

Todd Alexander, formerly at Bryant Family Vineyard in Napa, heads up production, with ambitious plans.

L'Ecole N° 41 Winery ★★

41 Lowden School Rd
Lowden
WA 99360
lecole.com

Founded in 1983 in a refurbished, 1915 Frenchtown schoolhouse, L'Ecole N° 41 is one of Walla Walla's most prominent wineries run by the second generation of the Clubb family. The newest addition to their large collection of sites is the spectacular monopole Ferguson vineyard (entirely in Oregon), planted in 2008 on the fractured rock of the Vansycle Basalt Ridge. 'Mixed layers of multiple lava flows are woven together in a puzzle-like pattern, intersected with deep veins of calcium carbonate leaching deep into the basalt,' Marty Clubb describes, yielding wine with 'deep iron minerality'. Ferguson Vineyard Bordeaux blend is indeed brilliant, with a sanguine note. It exploded from the first release with international success, and will surely only get better.

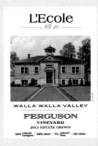

Owen Roe Winery

309 Gangl Road
Wapato
WA 98951
owenroe.com

Irish ex-pat David O'Reilly made the first vintage under his Owen Roe label in 1999 (a homage to the Irish rebel who fought against Cromwell), and now runs smart operations in both Oregon's Willamette Valley and Washington State. The Union Gap vineyard, planted in 2005, surrounds the Washington winery – named for the cut in the Rattlesnake Hills through which the Yakima River flows – and is in the warmest corner of the otherwise cool Yakima Valley, above the flood crests with exposed volcanic rock. Pearl Block Cabernet Franc, from a raised circular mound of particularly stony soils, is on the softer side, generous and polished; flagship Union Gap Red Blend (equal parts Merlot, Cabernets Franc and Sauvignon with a splash of Malbec) is more structured, sandy and gritty, with mix of red and black fruit and a touch of currant leaf.

Pacific Rim Winery ★

8111 Keene Road
West Richland
WA 99353
pacificrimwines.com

Revered American wine industry iconoclast Randall Grahm launched Pacific Rim in 1992 with the intention of making great Riesling, something he felt he couldn't do in his native California. Success was swift and enormous. Although Grahm sold in 2011 to the Mariani Family of Banfi Vintners, Pacific Rim continues the legacy, making mainly Riesling (also Chenin Blanc and Gewürztraminer) including excellent Solstice Vineyard Riesling from a parcel of deceptively flat land – although it appears to be quite low near the Yakima Valley floor, it sits on a syncline at nearly the same elevation

as the top of the Rattlesnake Hills. Planted in 1980, there is barely half a metre (2 feet) of topsoil over basalt bedrock, yielding one of Washington's best, essentially dry, full-bodied and lime-tinged Rieslings.

Reynvaan Family Vineyards ★★★

6309 Cottonwood Rd
Walla Walla
WA 99362
reynvaanfamilyvineyards.com

Mike and Gale Reynvaan own this small family winery at the top quality level, with a long waiting list for allocations. Christophe Baron of Cayuse Vineyard consults. 'Foothills in the Sun' vineyard in the foothills of the Blue Mountains is one of Washington's highest elevation sites, planted to Syrah, Cabernet Sauvignon and Viognier in 2007. 'In the Rocks' vineyard, logically in the Rocks District AVA, was planted two years earlier, and is the origin of the outstanding Stonessence Syrah, an exotic amalgam of black olive tapenade, sesame oil, pepper and smoked meat. All wines are worth tracking down.

Saviah Wine Cellars ★

1979 JB George Road
Walla Walla
WA 99362
saviahcellars.com

Montanans Richard Funk and wife Anita moved to Walla Walla in 1991, and planted their first vines a decade later in partnership with the local Brown family, expanding since. Prized Funk vineyard in the Rocks District AVA, planted in 2007, is the source of a fine pair of Syrahs: The Funk, co-fermented with Viognier to soften and add a floral lift, and pure The Stones Speak in the more typically tarry and meaty idiom. According to Funk, 'the aromatic profiles for Rocks District Syrah tend to be more savoury (briny, olive, cured meats) than any of the other Syrahs I work with from the Columbia Valley or other areas in

the Walla Walla Valley. In a blind tasting they really shine. The soils play a huge part.'

Syncline Wine Cellars ★★

111 Balch Road
Lyle
WA 98635
synclinewine.com

James and Poppy Mantone make an excellent range of sensible, infinitely drinkable wines in a collection of concrete vats, eggs and old barrels using a feather-light winemaking touch. Rhône variety focused estate vineyards in the Columbia Gorge are planted in flood sediments, though volcanic grapes are purchased from Celilo Vineyard, in which Mantone takes an active farming role. Memorable sparkling Scintillation from Pinot Noir and Chardonnay has zero dosage and no added sulphur. Straight, still Celilo Vineyard Pinot Noir is vibrant and crunchy, and at under 13% ABV is radically lighter and fresher than most others in Washington State. Celilo Grüner Veltliner intrigues.

Wilridge Winery & Vineyard

2830 Naches Heights Road
Yakima
WA 98908
wilridgewinery.com

Considering his past as an environmental lawyer, it's not surprising that Paul Beveridge's Wilridge Vineyard, on a cool, andesite plateau in the Naches Heights AVA, is farmed organically/ biodynamically. Everything from Bordeaux to Rhône and Italian grapes are planted, bottled both individually and in blends in a style meant for happy, honest quaffing, priced fairly. Nebbiolo is pleasantly firm and fresh. Syrah/Mourvèdre offers up fleshy dark fruit with appealing weight and minimal wood influence. Zweigelt is dangerously drinkable with a light chill.

OREGON

At just 50 years young, small but mighty Oregon has carved a firm niche within national and international circles of devoted wine drinkers. Less than 20 years ago wines from Oregon were still regarded with scepticism. Today, no serious wine list is complete without representation from the Beaver State. Nearly two-thirds of vineyards are dedicated to just one grape, Pinot Noir, which makes Oregon rather unique in the New World. Whereas recently tapped wine-growing regions invariably experiment with a wide range of grapes in the hopes of discovering what works best, Pinot Noir has been the mainstay in Oregon from the very earliest days of wine production. Did the unswerving devotion to a single grape pay off? It seems so. Is there still more to discover? You bet.

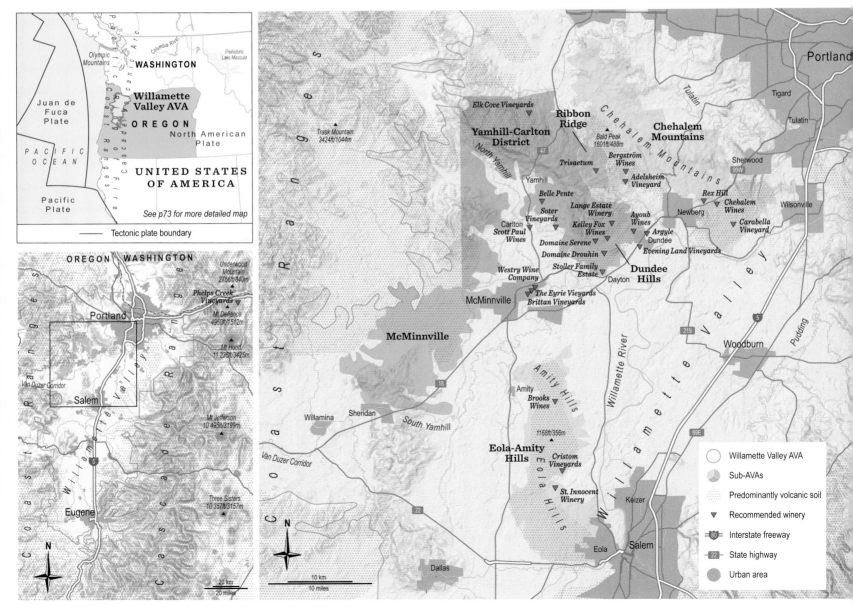

See p73 for more detailed map

Tectonic plate boundary

Willamette Valley AVA

Sub-AVAs

Predominantly volcanic soil

Recommended winery

Interstate freeway

State highway

Urban area

ABOVE (LEFT TO RIGHT) *Bergström Wines; Mt Hood from Dundee Hills; Cristom Vineyards; Soter Vineyards, Eola-Amity Hills; Chehalem Wines; Belle Pente; Elk Cove Vineyards; Westrey's winery-vine nursery; Evening Land's high-density vineyards; Cristom Vineyards; Phelps Creek Vineyards under Mt Hood; Brittan Vineyards.*

Oregon, and more specifically the Willamette Valley, is not uniformly volcanic – so much is evident from the complex geological history of the Pacific Northwest (see p.18). Here, adjacent vineyards are planted on such radically different soils as marine sediments, wind-blown loess and variations on volcanics. And Pinot Noir is the perfect medium to express their nuances, like a geological microscope, not least because Pinot Noir makers on the whole tend to be minimalists in the winery, or at least they apply the same techniques to all lots precisely to be able to express the differences that arise solely from the growing site. It's the curse, or the blessing, of Pinot producers to be utterly subservient to the vineyard. Eastern Oregon is also home to the most uniformly volcanic appellation in the Americas – The Rocks District of Milton-Freewater AVA, while Oregon's portion of the rising Columbia Gorge AVA lies in the volcanic shadows of Mt Hood and Mt Defiance.

WHERE & WHEN THE RAIN FALLS

The Pacific Northwest often conjures up images of thickly forested hills, the deep green of Douglas firs setting off the more translucent greens of mosses and grasses, which in turn gently contrast with the pastel reds and browns of soils, the dark blue of the Pacific, and the slick black of wet basalt rock. And the image is fitting. From around October through to June, over two metres (80 inches) of rain falls on the Oregon coast, a strip of largely deserted beaches protected by a near-continuous chain of state parks. This west side of the Coastal Range is fully exposed to the Pineapple Express, an atmospheric river of warm, wet air that streams in from the waters around Hawaii with the reliability and regularity of a Swiss train. On the other side of these low coastal hills in the Willamette Valley, the rainfall is slightly less, though it's still significant.

By contrast, on the east side of the much more imposing Cascade Mountain Range, past the stratovolcano Mt Hood – Oregon's tallest peak at 3,429 metres (11,250 feet) – rainfall is negligible. This area, like the vineyards of eastern Washington, lies in a remarkably effective rain shadow, a semi-desert. Rainclouds drop virtually all of their precipitation on the western flanks of the mountains as they rise, cool and condense, wrung out as it were by the tall peaks.

But back in the Willamette the rain is sufficient to have resulted in one of the valley's most influential features of terroir: beautifully weathered Columbia River Basalt. Oregon's particularly wet

OPPOSITE ABOVE *Misty morning in the Dundee Hills, with Mt Hood awakening on the horizon.*

OPPOSITE BELOW *Brittan Vineyards in the McMinville AVA.*

ABOVE *Winter pruning in the Dundee Hills.*

winters have sped up the weathering of exposed layers of basalt that flowed 550 km (350 miles) through the Columbia Gorge from Washington and Idaho, grinding them into deep, iron-rich red clay soils that yield utterly original Pinot Noir.

What is probably less well known to anyone outside of Oregon, however, is how warm and dry the summers are. The current record, from 2012, is 104 straight days without a drop of rain during the critical growing season. Temperatures can, and regularly do exceed 30°C (86°F) in the warmer pockets of the valley, and full ripeness is almost always achievable before the Pineapple Express rolls in, with conscientious farming and modest yields. This is another climatic feature of the region that makes these particular volcanic soils useful for great Pinot Noir: the ability to retain moisture during long periods of drought.

Such critical observations did not escape Oregon Pinot Noir pioneer David Lett when searching for the right spot to establish a vineyard. After months of research, he found that the northern end of the Willamette Valley had exactly the climate he was looking for,

despite the prevailing, mostly Californian wisdom of the time that Oregon was too cold and too wet to make palatable wine of any kind. But Lett believed that a grape's finest expression would be found at the outer limits of its viable ripening zone, and Oregon was certainly at the limit for Pinot Noir. He knew that soil, too, matters, and makes the difference between good and great Pinot even within the same climate.

With an auger packed in the back of his car he travelled around the northern end of the valley, stopping here and there at interesting spots to dig holes and inspect the dirt. The valley-floor flood sediments were too heavy and waterlogged; the marine sedimentary soils around Yamhill-Carlton and Ribbon Ridge were conversely not water-retentive enough, considering the dry summers and shortage of irrigation water. The strikingly red volcanic soils of the Dundee Hills were relatively deep, water retentive, but not overly heavy, nutrient-rich or exceedingly fertile. Just right. He pulled up the Pinot vines in his Corvallis nursery and, along with Pinot Gris, Pinot Meunier, Chardonnay and Melon de Bourgogne (mistaken at

ABOVE *Cristom's Jessie vineyard in the Eola-Amity Hills.*

OPPOSITE ABOVE *Phelps Creek Vineyards in the Columbia Gorge.*

OPPOSITE BELOW *Elk Cove's volcanic Clay Court vineyard, Chehalem Hills.*

the time for Pinot Blanc) and planted them in the Dundee Hills as The Eyrie Vineyard. The year was 1966, and the Dundee Hills and its volcanic soils, called Jory after a local family, would become the epicentre of the Oregon Pinot Noir success story. Jory would even become the official state soil of Oregon.

Oregon has since gone through many phases of development from those early pioneer years, and Pinot Noir has been planted all over the valley in other soil types: principally Willakenzie and its variations on sedimentary soils, Laurelwood (wind-blown loess overlying basalt) and more volcanic Jory and its shallower variation called Nekia, among other more nuanced classifications. Each in time would reveal a different face of Pinot Noir, a true patchwork of complementary styles, and provide endless opportunity for comparison and discussion.

Tasting the Difference: Pinot Noir on Marine Sediment vs. Volcanic

For any generalization many exceptions can be found, and myriad factors other than soil, like elevation, sun exposure and wind patterns, can have a dramatic impact on style, not to mention the human factors. But the principal differences in wine style observed in Pinot Noir grown on Willakenzie soils and Jory soils are related to water holding capacity. Jory soils are deeper and more clay rich, and thus absorb more water and retain it for longer than the free-draining (sandy) sedimentary soils. Given Oregon's generally dry summers, vines in sedimentary soils often experience drought stress towards the end of the growing season as the soil completely dries out. Grapes thus stressed don't ripen their polyphenols (tannins) as completely as a vine provided with adequate (not excessive) moisture, and skins tend to become thicker to protect the seeds within. Sugar concentration also increases more quickly, and all things being equal, vines grown on sedimentary soils are harvested up to a week earlier than those on deeper volcanic soils.

The net result is that Willakenzie Pinot Noir often has a deeper colour, darker, black-fruit flavours and more burly tannins. These wines take more time to unfurl. David Autrey of Westry Wine Company describes them as 'more structured', while James Cahill of Soter says, 'it's pretty easy to see in the glass. They're darker, denser'.

Pinot Noir in volcanic soils, on the other hand, ripens later, and so fruit stays in the vibrant red berry spectrum, usually accompanied by an appealing range of spice, sometimes downright exotic. Tannins tend to be lighter and finer, and acids more pronounced and juicy. 'Volcanic soils provide a more pleasant, generous root environment for the vines – more moisture, nutrients, etc,' explains Mark Vlossak, winemaker at St. Innocent Winery. 'What you see is more red fruit, more heady, engaging perfume.' The consensus among others on the style of volcanic Pinots is striking, 'they're lighter in colour, with more elegance, beauty and finesse, and perfume,' declares Mo Ayoub of Ayoub Wines. According to Autrey, they're 'higher acid, with more red fruit', while Adam Campbell describes them as having 'a core of sweet red fruit, like red cherry.'

The Science of Soil & Wine

Linking soil chemistry to wine chemistry and sensory profile is the holy grail of wine research, cutting straight to the heart of the concept of terroir. But the challenges in connecting the dots are formidable. In Oregon, however, Professor Dr. Scott Burns PhD, head of Geology at Portland State University, and PhD student Kathryn Barnard, set out to do just that – outlined in a thesis defended in late 2015. Burns and Barnard first endeavoured to 'fingerprint' the soils of the Willamette Valley, using both physical (particle size, structure, consistence, horizon depths, organic carbon and level of soil profile development) and chemical (pH, macro and micro-nutrient composition, trace elements and clay mineralogy) measurements. They found that Jory soils had consistently higher levels of phosphorus, sulphur, iron, manganese and cobalt, and lower measures of magnesium, potassium and sodium when compared to Willakenzie and Laurelwood soils. Chemical differences were also reflected in the grapes and the wines made from them. Quite how these small chemical differences account for such large sensory profile changes is the next step in the research. But it's abundantly clear that soils have a lot to say when it comes to the aroma and taste of wine.

Oregon's Other Grapes

Oregon's most planted white variety is Pinot Gris, a grape that was planted alongside Pinot Noir in 1965. The conditions in the Willamette are not dissimilar to Alsace, so it's not surprising that it performs well here. Riesling, too, is one of the state's best secrets – try examples from Brooks, Trisaetum, or Chehalem grown on different soils for fascinating terroir comparisons.

OPPOSITE ABOVE *Slick road leading to the Eola-Amity Hills.*

OPPOSITE BELOW *Stately Domaine Serene atop the Dundee Hills.*

Chardonnay got off to a rough start in Oregon, due in large part to the planting of the wrong clones – late-ripening Californian clones. The resulting wines were searingly acidic and generally uninteresting. But the arrival of vine material from Burgundy (Dijon clones) widely available from the early 1990s thanks to the efforts of David Adelsheim, changed the scene completely. The Dijon clones ripen earlier are thus are better suited to Oregon's cool climate (and ironically are not suited to California's warmth), and quality has risen steadily. Try Domaine Serene or Evening Land Vineyards for examples of the Willamette's volcanic best, or Columbia Gorge's Phelps Creek.

Rhône varieties, too, give world-class results, albeit not in the Willamette Valley. The Rocks District of Milton-Freewater AVA is the source of some of the world's most original Syrah and Grenache (see p.45). These are wines of genuine smoky, meaty intensity and complexity, which raise eyebrows back in the Rhône Valley itself.

Oregon's Volcanic AVAs

Oregon currently has 18 official AVAs, though volcanic soils are found mainly in the Willamette Valley and Columbia Gorge AVAs, and eastern Oregon's Walla Walla and Rocks District of Milton-Freewater AVAs.

The **Willamette Valley AVA** has six sub-AVAs, of which four have consequential distribution of volcanic soils. The **Dundee Hills AVA** is the most uniformly volcanic, a clenched-fist-shaped, contiguous landmass that lies above the valley floor, the result of tectonic up-thrust. The area is effectively protected from major climatic variations in a mini rain shadow, and sees slightly less rain than other parts of the Willamette. The 'knuckles' of the hill run in a north to south ridge with the rounded thumb forming the southern end, and the fingers facing east towards the Cascade Mountains. On a clear day, Mt Hood and Mt Jefferson are clearly visible on the eastern horizon. The majority of vineyards are on

ABOVE *Sunset over Soter's Eola-Amity Hills vineyards.*

the top, south and east-facing flanks of the hills, carved by several creeks running eastward from the top of the ridge down to the Willamette River, like the valleys between your fingers. Elevation and slope mean less frost damage, warmer nights and less fog than vineyards closer to the valley floor. The soils here are purely volcanic Jory, deep (one to three metres/three to ten feet down to the sandstone and basalt bedrock) and intensely red-coloured from oxidized iron liberated from the basalt during weathering. Only those vineyards above the 60-metre (200-foot) contour line, up to the highest point at 325 metres (1000 feet), are included in the appellation; the vineyards below, composed of both eroded volcanic soils and flood sediments, are excluded. It's here that David Lett planted Oregon's first Pinot Noir vines in 1966, and where today many of the finest and most elegant, supple and succulent Pinot Noirs of Oregon are grown. Many top producers have vineyards or source grapes here.

The **Eola-Amity Hills AVA** is likewise almost purely volcanic for vineyards above around 75 metres (250 feet) up to the ridge top at 215 metres (700 feet), though Pinot Noir differs in style from the Dundee Hills. This north-to-south oriented ridge lies west of the Willamette River and runs some 20 km (12 miles) north from Salem, putting the western side directly in the face of the Van Duzer Corridor, Oregon's equivalent to Sonoma County's Petaluma Gap. Cold Pacific air funnels into the valley through a break in the Coast Range (Highway 18/22 follows the corridor out to the coast) every summer afternoon, dropping temperatures dramatically and allowing grapes to retain high acidity. Temperance Hill, one of the Eola-Amity Hills' most celebrated vineyards, receives the brunt of the cool winds, and each year many fingers are crossed to help grapes reach full maturity. Argyle sources grapes here for sparkling wine. The harvest at Temperance Hill is always among the latest in the Willamette, but when it goes well, it produces some of Oregon's edgiest, most compellingly spicy and firm Pinot Noir. Soils in the upper elevations quickly thin out. Referred to as Nekia, such shallow (less than 50 cm/20 inches deep), free-draining volcanic soils are some of the most sought after, combining the finesse and red-fruit character of Jory soils with the ripeness, power and structure of sedimentary Willakenzie soils. 'Eola Hills wines tend to have much more spice – cinnamon, clove, nutmeg, ginger – and more of a balance between red and dark fruit,' explains Mark Vlossak.

The **Chehalem Mountains AVA** and the **McMinnville AVA** are both highly varied, mixed soil appellations. Lying on the east and southeast slopes of the Coast Range, McMinnville in particular is a geological hotch-potch (hodgepodge) consisting of uplifted marine sediments and, uniquely for Oregon, 45-million-year-old marine basalts (called the Nestucca Formation, a 650-metre (2000-feet) thick bedrock formation of ocean floor basalt), which are much older and more weathered than Columbia River Basalts. The shallow volcanics result in highly structured wines, also influenced by the low rainfall (McMinnville sits in the protective weather shadow of the Coast Range) and, in the case of the vineyards in the southern end of the appellation, by the cooling influence of the Van Duzer Corridor.

The Chehalem Mountains is a southwest-to-northeast oriented series of hilltops and ridges that rise to just below 500 metres (1600 feet) at Bald Peak, the highest in the Willamette Valley. Only vineyards above 75 metres (250 feet) are included in the AVA. The northeast flank of the mountains is covered by a thick layer of wind-blown loess soil called Laurelwood. The southwest flank is

dominated by Willakenzie marine sediments, while the central ridge and southeastern edge of the AVA are dominated by volcanic Jory soils. There can be up to three weeks difference in harvest time between sites.

Across the Cascades in the eastern part of the state, the **Columbia Gorge AVA** is shared with Washington State, straddling the mighty Columbia River on either side of the spectacular gorge carved through the basalt bedrock of the Cascade Range, in the shadow of Mt Hood volcano. It's via this sea-level passage through the Cascades that immense rivers of lava once flowed, and several million years later, the floods of Ice Age lakes. Sheer cliffs of basalt rise almost straight out of the river in places; elsewhere you'll find more gently terraced land scoured and sculpted by water and wind. This is easily the Pacific Northwest's most climatically varied AVA, ranging from cool and wet in the west to high desert in the east. The most widely planted section of the AVA is in the Hood River Valley due north from Mt Hood, which has similar precipitation and heat summation as the Willamette Valley, though over a slightly shorter,

OPPOSITE *Stoller Family Estate at the southern end of the Dundee Hills.*

ABOVE *Deep mounds of basalt cobbles in Cayuse Vineyards' Cailloux vineyard (see p.32).*

more intense growing season. As elsewhere, lower elevations have mostly Missoula flood sedimentary soils, though higher up are Columbia River Basalts as well as soils formed on more recent deposits from weathered volcanic mudflows and basalt/andesite lavas from Mt Defiance and Mt Hood (Oak Grove and Hood soil series) and Underwood Mountain on the Washington side (Chemawa soil series). These low-nutrient soils are favoured for high-quality grape-growing. The volcanic Pinots from the Gorge tend to more refinement and elegance and, although are less well-known than Willamette Pinot, show terrific potential.

The **Walla Walla Valley AVA** in eastern Oregon is likewise shared with Washington State, though Oregon has the lion's share of planted volcanic vineyards, such as L'Ecole N° 41's Ferguson vineyard on the Vansycle Basalt Ridge. Nestled within the Walla Walla Valley, entirely on the Oregon side, is the state's newest (2015) **The Rocks District of Milton-Freewater AVA**. 'The Rocks', as it is known colloquially, is the USA's most geologically homogenous appellation. The AVA petition was put together by geologist Kevin Pogue, who drew the boundaries around an alluvial fan of the Walla Walla River, consisting entirely of volcanic debris carried down from the Blue Mountains and deposited on the valley floor.

It was the sight of the heaps of dark-coloured basalt cobblestones that first caught the attention of Frenchman Christophe Baron in the mid-90s. While driving near the town of Milton-Freewater, Baron spotted the unusual soils, unlike anything else in the Pacific Northwest. They reminded him of Châteauneuf-du-Pape in the Southern Rhône Valley, famous for its mounds of pudding stones. It was mostly fruit orchard land at the time, but Baron suspected it would be special for grapes. He purchased what land he could and started planting his Cailloux (pebbles) vineyard in 1997. Soon after, he launched Cayuse Cellars (American deformation of *cailloux*), and the wines garnered immediate critical acclaim. It kicked off a sort of land grab in the region. Rhône varieties, and especially Syrah from The Rocks, are some of the best, not just from the Pacific Northwest, but anywhere in the world, and deserve to be included among the very top examples.

As in the Southern Rhône, or any stony-gravelly vineyard, the soil is very well drained, which encourages vines to root deeply. The cobblestones absorb solar radiation, increasing daytime grape bunch temperatures, which, in turn, promotes faster and more complete ripening. But perhaps even more importantly, as Pogue speculates, the stones also radiate heat into the soil, heating up ground water, which stimulates more efficient nutrient

absorption by vine roots – all chemical reactions are sped up at higher temperatures – and also leads to better ripening and overall vine health. It stands to reason that vines, and thus grapes, have a more complete collection of macro- and micro-elements derived from the soil, adding, at least indirectly to greater complexity in their wines.

A challenge in The Rocks wines is high pH (low acid); it's unclear whether soil chemistry (high potassium), or the high ripeness promoted by the basalt cobbles, or both, are responsible. Most wines from the AVA require an acid addition to stabilize them.

Pinot's Home Away from Home

Today there are over 600 registered wineries in Oregon. In an ironic twist, the old world, and specifically Burgundy, the physical and spiritual home of Pinot Noir, now looks to Oregon for new inspiration. Robert Drouhin and his daughter Veronique were the first Burgundians to set-up shop in Oregon in the late 80s, but many more have since pressed Oregon Pinot Noir in consulting roles, including Patrice Rion (Chehalem Wines), Louis-Michel Liger-Belair (Chapter 24 Vineyards), Dominique Lafon (Evening Land Vineyards) and Alexandrine Roy (Phelps Creek). The venerable Maison Louis Jadot purchased Resonance Vineyard in 2013 and installed the legendary Jacques Lardière as winemaker, while others have entered into joint ventures such as Jean-Nicholas Méo of Méo-Camuzet with music executive Jay Boberg.

Yet despite the spotlight, there's still very much a rural farming community feel throughout the Willamette Valley. Wineries are sprinkled along unpaved country roads and hidden in mountain foothills, many with little more than a shingle hung out to declare their presence. The feeling of new discovery is still strong, and that there's more to prove. As Adam Campbell of Elk Cove says, 'there's lots of institutional knowledge today, but you still feel like an explorer. The best vineyard in Oregon probably hasn't been planted yet.'

ABOVE *Harvesting at Phelps Creek Vineyards in the Columbia Gorge AVA, under imposing Mt Hood.*

OPPOSITE ABOVE *Vansycle Basalt Ridge with L'Ecole Nº 41's Ferguson vineyard above (see p.32).*

OPPOSITE BELOW *Evening Land's Seven Springs vineyard, Eola-Amity Hills.*

ABOVE *Morning over Cristom Vineyards,*
Eola-Amity Hills

OREGON – THE WINES & THE PEOPLE

Adelsheim Vineyard ★★★

16800 NE Calkins Lane
Newberg
OR 97132
adelsheim.com

David Adelsheim is one of the pillars of the Oregon wine industry, having settled with his wife Ginny in 1971. He quickly realized after a trip to Burgundy in 1974 that the vine material available in the USA would be a hindrance to quality, and set about the lengthy process of importing Burgundian clones (aka the 'Dijon' clones) into Oregon. Over a decade later Adelsheim finally succeeded, enabling a much broader spectrum of Pinot Noir styles in the Willamette Valley, and also making fine Chardonnay a possibility by replacing unsuitable California clones. Adelsheim's style has evolved over the years to more elegance and transparency, helped by Dave Paige who joined as winemaker in 2001. Of the estate's volcanic Pinots, Boulder Bluff Vineyard from the Chehalem Mountains is sweet-fruited, fresh and pretty; Bryan Creek, also from Chehalem Mountains but at a higher elevation, is more ashy, smoky and stony; Temperance Hill from the Eola-Amity Hills, with its shallower soils and reliable winds, is the most distinctive, gamey, leafy and peppery. Dundee Hill's Winderlea Vineyard, which dives into savoury territory, is a favourite.

Argyle

691 Highway 99W
Dundee
OR 97115
argylewinery.com

Argyle, the first foreign-owned winery in Oregon, was established by Aussie Brian Croser of Petaluma (Adelaide Hills, South Australia)

and Texan Rollin Soles in the Dundee Hills in 1987. The sole *raison d'être* was sparkling wine, as Bollinger Champagne was also partnered with Petaluma. 'We knew we could do it every year,' Allen Holstein says, Argyle's wine-grower. But the introduction of the Dijon clones, and new viticultural techniques in the late 80s, brought still wines into the portfolio. Argyle's production (including the Nuthouse and Spirithouse brands) is now split 60:40 still to sparkling, even if the estate's reputation still rests on the latter. Estate vineyards are predominantly volcanic: Knudsen at the top of the Dundee Hills is the original parcel; Lone Star and Spirit Hill in the Eola Amity-Hills were purchased later. Knudsen Vineyard Blanc de Blancs is a sparkling wine of quivering, razor-sharp acidity and gentle yeasty-biscuity (cookie) character, with the potential to age a decade or more.

Ayoub Wines ★★

9650 NE Keyes Lane
PO Box 127
Dundee
OR 97115
ayoubwines.com

Mohamad (Mo) Ayoub worked as both an engineer and a chef before falling in love the Willamette Valley. Instead of opening a restaurant, he 'ended up with this money pit instead' (laughs). His prime Dundee Hills estate vineyard, planted in 2001, yields a gracious and refined Pinot Noir, picked early like all of his wines to preserve freshness. Brittan Vineyard Pinot Noir with its shallow volcanic soils in the McMinnville AVA delivers a tighter, leaner, sharper expression, trading fruit for more exotic spice, ash, herb and smoke. Also excellent Estate Chardonnay, lean and minerally.

Belle Pente ★

12470 NE Rowland Road
Carlton
OR 97111
bellepente.com

It's hard to miss the dramatically steep vineyard of Belle Pente ('beautiful slope') hanging off the coastal hills as you approach the winery. Owners Jill and Brian O'Donnell focus on wine, not appearances; the sign announcing that you've arrived hangs on an ancient *foudre* that looks as though it has been sitting out since the winery was established in 1994. O'Donnell it seems, has left the computer business in Silicon Valley far behind. Pinot vineyards are split between Belle Pente, on sedimentary soils, and Murto in the volcanic Dundee Hills, planted in 1978. Each is bottled separately, with a Reserve also blended from both. Murto is usually the first to open and reveal its delicate red fruit, while Belle Pente takes more time to evolve. The wines have a gentle, appealing honesty, with the natural feel of minimal winemaking intervention.

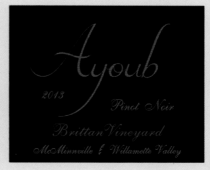

Bergström Wines ★★★

18215 NE Calkins Lane
Newberg
OR 97132

bergstromwines.com

It's a shame for volcanic wine-lovers that Portland native Josh Bergström doesn't make more Pinot Noir, as these are some of the most impressive examples in the state. Josh and father John have farmed biodynamically from the start in 1999, though style has evolved significantly from oaky and powerful to far greater delicacy. Bergström credits a trip to Burgundy in 2011 as one of the main catalysts for change, 'my wines were too ripe,' he confesses. 'Earlier harvest, less extraction and sparing new wood have made the wines far prettier, and more age-worthy.' Bergström is also out to produce Oregon's best Chardonnay and he's close with Sigrid, his flagship, a beautifully detailed wine with tension and energy (although it's from sedimentary, not volcanic soils). Pinot from Temperance Hill in the Eola-Amity Hills is superb, with white pepper, herbal spice and crunchy berry fruit. Estate Pinot from the Dundee Hills has a jolt of the ferrous quality provided by red, iron-rich volcanic soils.

Brittan Vineyards ★

829 NE 5th Street
Suite 700
McMinnville
OR 97128 (winery shop)

brittanvineyards.com

Former California winemaker Robert Brittan was searching for a cool site and, specifically, 'recent volcanic soils, red, with high iron content, and a lot of large rocks, where the root system will reach the basalt bedrock'. He found the right combination in the McMinville AVA in 2004. From the first vintage in 2006, Brittan began bottling two separate lots of Pinot from his estate,

noting the distinct character that arose from variations on the volcanic soil theme. Basalt Block from parcels on marine basalts, much older than Columbia River Basalts, is dark and meaty, firm and tannic. Gestalt Block Pinot from younger Columbia basalts is even darker, with serious cut, pronounced salty minerality and more on the back end. A third Pinot, yet to be named, is planned from a section of 'intrusion' basalt.

Brooks Wines ★★

21101 SE Cherry Blossom Lane
Amity
OR 97101

brookswine.com

Jimi Brooks tragically passed away in 2004 at the age of 38, but the local wine community rallied to keep the vineyard going. Jimi's sister Janie stepped in to manage affairs on behalf of Jimi's young son Pascal, now sole owner, and winemaker Christopher Williams has remained since. All vineyards are farmed biodynamically. Riesling is a rare focus, led by the exceptional Estate bottling, made dry. Multiple cuvées of Pinot Noir offer variations on the theme of grace: new wood is rare and extended ageing is the norm. Old vines Temperance Hill is especially floral; Estate Rastaban shows plenty of earth and smoke, and cool, wind-buffeted York Hill from young Pinot vines in Columbia Gorge AVA volcanic soils under sister Terue label shows the terrific promise of rarified delicacy.

Carabella Vineyard ★

PO Box 2180
Wilsonville
OR 97070

carabellawine.com

Recovering geologist Mike Hallock spent 12 years searching for his ideal vineyard, which he found high up on Parrett Mountain in the Chehalem Mountains AVA. Ironically, Hallock's speciality

was sedimentary soils, but he was searching for Jory – volcanic – believing them to be superior. 'The Pinots exhibit elegance over power, complexity, brilliant colour, high-toned aromatics and a palate that emphasizes the red fruit sector of the spectrum,' he says with characteristic precision. A large basalt boulder gave rise to Carabella's second label, Plowbuster. Inchinnan Pinot Noir is the 'concession' to the commercial market, a bigger, more impressive style; house pride Eve's Garden Pinot Noir is lighter and leaner, with exotic Indian spice, zesty and firm, a textbook example of Oregonian volcanic Pinot. Particularly fine, crisp, saline Chardonnay 'Dijon 76' comes from the highest, thinnest soils on the property called the North Block.

Chehalem Wines

31190 NE Veritas Lane
Newberg
OR 97132

chehalemwines.com

Estate co-owner Harry Peterson-Nedry has a background in hi-tech manufacturing, hot superalloy castings to be accurate, so it's no surprise that Chehalem wines are technically precise and consistent. Peterson-Nedry first started 'dabbling' in wine in 1980 'to seek utter fulfillment' when he purchased the Ridgecrest property in the Ribbon Ridge AVA with its sedimentary soils. 1990 marked the first commercial release, and Bill Stoller (of Stoller Family Estate) became a partner in 1993, injecting cash and eventually fruit from his Dundee Hills vineyard. A third site, Corral Creek Vineyards on wind-blown loess over basalt in the Chehalem Mountains AVA, rounds out the portfolio. Whites are a speciality led by Riesling, of which the Three Vineyard blend is the most satisfying, playing to Peterson-Nedry's view that blends make for more complex wine. Stoller Vineyards Pinot Noir is the only (very good) purely volcanic wine in the portfolio, gentle, perfumed, with intriguing curry spice.

Cristom Vineyards ★★★

6905 Spring Valley Road NW
Salem
OR 97304
cristomvineyards.com

Pittsburg-based engineer Paul Gerrie bought an abandoned winery and vineyard in the Eola-Amity Hills in 1992 and hired winemaker Steve Dorner and vineyard manager Mark Feltz, the team still in place today. The unwavering house style featuring depth and ageability (with proven track record) shows through in four single-vineyard Pinots from the predominantly volcanic estate. Majorie Vineyard is plummy and exotically spiced; Jessie Vineyard, with its more variable soil depth, higher organic matter and more favourable pH and calcium levels, yields even more grip and structure. Both need time. Fine-value Mt Jefferson and Sommers Reserve multi-vineyard cuvées are restaurant wine list regulars.

Domaine Drouhin Oregon ★

PO Box 700
Dundee
OR 97115
domainedrouhin.com

Domaine Drouhin Oregon (locally 'DDO'), is the US outpost of Burgundy-based Maison Joseph Drouhin, a prime property at the top of the Dundee Hills. It was a moral boost for the Oregon wine industry when Robert Drouhin and daughter Véronique arrived in 1987, having been sufficiently convinced the Willamette Valley was suitable for Pinot Noir and Chardonnay. Véronique made wine from purchased fruit the following year and construction of the winery and planting began immediately. The estate's Dundee and Eola-Amity Hills vineyards are all volcanic – a big leap for a terroir-obsessed family familiar only with the limestone-marls of Burgundy. The wines show unsurprising old world firmness, with restraint and elegance. Pinot Noir Cuvée Laurène is the company's flagship, a selection of top barrels from the Dundee estate aimed at longevity. In its youth it can be lean and angular, but shifts into beguiling exotic spice and ferrous-sanguine notes with age.

Domaine Serene ★★★

6555 NE Hilltop Lane
Dayton
OR 97114
domaineserene.com

Ken and Grace Evenstad built one of the Willamette Valley's most eye-catching properties in 1990, set high in the Dundee Hills surrounded by manicured vineyards. Although Domaine Serene looks like a Spanish villa with its terra cotta roof and warm yellow walls, wine influence is clearly continental-French; the Evenstads were inspired by Burgundy. Winemaker Erik Kramer, with a degree in geology and a minor in math and chemistry, approaches wine-growing rigorously and attention to detail is evident. Variations on finessed and understated Pinot Noir and Chardonnay (including some of the oldest Dijon clones in Oregon) are produced from the Jory soils of the estate vineyards. Generously proportioned 'Côte Sud' Chardonnay from a south-facing parcel is considered the most opulent in the range, but in an international context is still balanced and fresh. Grace Pinot Noir epitomizes both house and appellation: elegant, silky and perfumed.

Elk Cove Vineyards ★

27751 NW Olson Road
Gaston
OR 97119
elkcove.com

The Campbell family was among the initial dozen to make wine in the Willamette, planting their first vineyards in 1974. Six estate vineyards represent the major soil types, a blend of which is Elk Cove's Pinot calling card. Purely volcanic Clay Court in the Chehalem Hills AVA yields Pinot with vibrant red-berry-cherry character, all finesse; sedimentary Mt Richmond in Yamhill-Carlton has more blue fruit and typically harder tannins. Overall these are polished wines, crafted for early enjoyment.

Evening Land Vineyards ★★

1326 N Hwy 99W
Suite 100
Dundee
OR 97115 (winery shop)
elvwines.com

The company, which also has vineyards on the Sonoma Coast and in Burgundy, is led by sommelier Rajat Parr and winemaker Sashi Moorman. The prime, purely volcanic Seven Springs Vineyard in the Eola-Amity Hills was purchased in 2007, and farmed biodynamically since, producing top-level Chardonnay and Pinot Noir. Both are distinguished by elevation: Pinot from the lower slopes on deeper Jory soil is the fleshy, more seductive wine, while La Source, from the much shallower upper slopes on Nekia soils, is dramatically firmer, with more tension and layers. Chardonnay follows the same pattern, though confusingly, the bottling from the lower slope is called La Source, while the upper slope version is called 'Summum'. A deliciously fruity Gamay is appropriately named Celebration.

Kelley Fox Wines ★★★

2724 SW 2nd Avenue
Portland
OR 97201
kelleyfoxwines.com

Kelley Fox makes tiny amounts of outstanding wines from volcanic soils. Summed up by soaring grace and transparency, Fox approaches winemaking with an unusual degree of sensitivity. Grapes are purchased from select organically/biodynamically farmed vineyards, though she is regularly spotted working in the vines. Maresh Vineyard (pronounced 'Marsh') own-rooted, old-vine Pinot Noir is supremely delicate, Momtazi Pinot Noir more taut, edgy and intense with exotic spice. 'It's like an animal that crouches in the dark and stares at you,' Fox offers.

Phelps Creek Vineyards

1850 Country Club Road
Hood River
OR 97031
phelpscreekvineyards.com

A winery to seek out from the relatively unknown Columbia Gorge AVA. Owner Robert Morus refers to the Hood River Valley as the 'Goldilocks zone' of the AVA, between cool coastal forest and high desert. Soils are eminently volcanic, formed on highly weathered basalt flows from nearby Mt Defiance, and Morus has never needed to fertilize (although he did spread out two drums of ash gathered from the Mt St Helens eruption). Arrival of Burgundian winemaker Alexandrine Roy in 2012 heralded a new era of quality. Lynette Chardonnay, named after Morus's wife, is rendered in a restrained style, with delicate wood influence and a saline streak. Cuvée Alexandrine Pinot Noir seamlessly blends ripe new-world fruit with classic firmness, structure and savoury character.

Lange Estate Winery ★

18380 NE Buena Vista Drive
Dundee
OR 97115
langewinery.com

Singer/songwriter Don Lange got distracted by the wine business in Santa Barbara in the late 70s, eventually moving to Oregon in the early 80s to make Pinot Noir. Don's son Jesse now handles most of the day-to-day work of this sizable operation. A trio of Pinots from the main soil series is intended as a lesson in terroir: Windborne, from loess over basalt bedrock in the Chehalem Mountains, is a fine and complete wine; Ancient Sea Beds, from Willakenzie, is dark, brooding and chewy, while Magma Opus, from Jory soils in the Dundee Hills, is red-fruit dominated with the most refined tannins. All-estate Redside vineyard likewise offers the classic floral expression of Jory Pinot.

Rex Hill

30835 North Hwy 99W
Newberg
OR 97132
rexhill.com

Rex Hill has undergone a serious makeover since it was purchased by A to Z Wineworks in 2006, shifting from large, commercial operation to premium label, and quality from biodynamically-farmed vineyards is now uniformly impressive. The house style is more power than finesse; 'Agebility is important,' says co-owner Sam Tannahill. Sims Pinot Noir is more lean and structured, while La Colina is fleshier, both from vineyards in the volcanic Dundee Hills. His own label, Francis Tannahill, includes forceful and grippy The Hermit Pinot Noir, also Dundee Hills, distinctively stony and salty.

Scott Paul Wines ★★

128 South Pine Street
Carlton
OR 97111
scottpaul.com

A former music industry executive, Scott Paul launched his own label in 1999, focusing on small lots of Pinot Noir from several vineyards, including his own biodynamically farmed Azana estate. Texturally-beguiling Audrey Pinot Noir is the top of the range, named after Audrey Hepburn ('a wine that will seduce you'), from the biodynamic Maresh vineyard. In 2014, Paul sold the winery to long-time friend Cameron Healy and Ian Burch took the place of former winemaker Kelley Fox (see separate entry), so the future remains to be seen..

Soter Vineyards

10880 NE Mineral Springs Rd
Carlton
OR 97111
sotervineyards.com

Tony Soter made his name in the Napa Valley before settling in Oregon in 1997, later expanding with partners to form North Valley Vineyards and Planet Oregon, all produced under the Soter Vineyards umbrella. AVA-specific Pinots highlight regional variations, of which Eola-Amity Hills cuvée is the most distinctive and powerful made from a blend of the shallow volcanic Nekia soils of the Roserock vineyard and the mixed Jory-Nekia of the Zena Crown vineyard.

St. Innocent Winery ★★

5657 Zena Road NW
Salem
OR 97304

stinnocentwine.com

St. Innocent winemaker and founding partner Mark Vlossak has been refining his interpretation of the Willamette Valley over three decades, moving towards more transparency. He crafts sinewy and delicate wines without sacrificing structure and age-worthiness. Vineyard-designated Pinot Noirs include fine-grained but firm, beautifully-perfumed Temperance Hill, one of the Willamette's best-known vineyards in the Eola-Amity Hills AVA. Vlossak's parcel was planted in 1982 on own roots in Nekia (shallow volcanic) soil. The biodynamically grown Momtazi vineyard in the McMinville AVA experiences one of the biggest day to night temperature shifts in the Willamette, and Vlossak's rendition of Pinot offers exotic perfume that he likens to yellow curry spice. The 'Villages Cuvée' Pinot Noir, made from a blend of vineyards and soil types, is a valley benchmark.

Stoller Family Estate ★

16161 NE McDougall Road
Dayton
OR 97114

www.stollerfamilyestate.com

In 1993, on the eve the commercial family farm (in operation since the 40s with turkeys and other crops) was to be sold, Bill Stoller, a successful entrepreneur, stepped in to rescue it. His new plan was grapes, taking advantage of the property's prime Jory soils and south-facing slopes, and experience gained as a partner in the Chehalem Winery. Leadership in Energy and Environmental Design (LEED) gold-certified Stoller Family Estate is now the largest contiguous vineyard in the AVA, with much of the harvest purchased by other wineries. Stoller Estate wines range from a charming and accessible entry-level Pinot Noir full of crunchy red fruit, to the Reserve, a structured wine from selected parcels, and the top Legacy tier, a trio of Pinot Noirs, of which Cathy (named for Stoller's late wife) is the finest.

The Eyrie Vineyards ★★★

935 NE 10th Ave
McMinnville
OR 97128

eyrievineyards.com

Founder David Lett was the first to plant Pinot Noir in Oregon in 1965 and mentored countless people who went on to play prominent roles in the Oregon wine industry, so it would be hard to overplay the estate's importance. Jason Lett took on winemaking responsibilities in 2005 and, like his father, crafts fine and delicate wines, purposely stripped down to their essence with no appetite for unnecessary embellishment. Lett has an almost maniacle devotion to paleness and purity, ethereal texture and lacy delicacy, yet these Pinots have an uncanny ability to age, which can only be attributed to genuine depth. The estate's own-rooted organic vines are spread across four vineyards at varying elevations on south-facing hillsides in the Dundee Hills. The range includes rarities such as a wood-aged Melon de Bourgogne and a singular Original Vine Gris from the first plantings at the Eyrie Vineyard, full of quince and tangerine, orange peel and bay leaf. Original Vine Pinot Noir Reserve, aged for two years in old wood and unfined/unfiltered, is pale and translucent, with deceptive intensity and astonishing length.

Trisaetum ★

18401 Ribbon Ridge Road
Newberg
OR 97132-6566

trisaetum.com

Trisaetum is a family affair run by James Frey and wife Andrea making pure and precise Pinot Noir and Riesling, which accurately represent the soil types on the estate's three properties: Ribbon Ridge surrounding the winery on classic, Willakenzie sedimentary soils offers depth and muscle; Wichmann in the Dundee Hills on classic Jory volcanics favours tension and finesse, and the mixed sedimentary-marine basalts in Coast Range in the Yamhill-Carlton AVA splits the difference.

Volcano Ridge Vineyard (Heart Catcher Wines)

heartcatcherwines.com

A new joint project to watch between geologist Alan Busacca and winemaker Lonnie Wright. Planting began in 2008. Busacca wasn't in search of a volcanic terroir specifically, but quickly realized after digging pits that this hillside might well be perfect: high-elevation, steep and windy, on well-drained shallow soils derived from volcanic mudflows with low organic matter and thus naturally low vigour. It sounds like a recipe for quality wine. At time of publishing, no wines had yet been released.

Westry Wine Company ★

1065 NE Alpine Avenue McMinnville
OR 97128

westrey.com

Winemaking husband and wife team David Autrey and Amy Wesselman launched Westry in 1993. The operation has remained small, with emphasis clearly on what's in the bottle; the winery is a purely functional building in a McMinnville industrial park. New wood is used sparingly and wines show the fine tension, florality and bright red fruit of typical volcanic Oregon Pinot, shaped around site nuances. The Dundee Hills's Abbey Ridge, for example, is lighter, more lacy and filigree, while the Oracle Vineyard offers more marked salinity.

NORTHERN CALIFORNIA

THE GREAT VALLEY SEQUENCE, FRANCISCAN FORMATION, SONOMA VOLCANICS & THE CLEAR LAKE VOLCANIC FIELD

Northern California, like the Pacific Northwest, falls along the Pacific Ring of Fire, the world's most extensive 40,000-km (c.25,000-mile) arc of volcanoes and earthquake zones that circles from Patagonia to New Zealand around the Pacific Ocean Basin. California may no longer be famous for volcanoes, though the last 160 million years – since the Farallon Plate floating under the Pacific slammed into the North American Plate, like a Volkswagen hitting an 18-wheeler – have witnessed a spectacular progression of volcanic activity up and down the coast. The amazingly varied and complex soils of California wine country, too, are the result of being in a zone of highly active geology.

The subduction of the Farallon Plate gave rise to an arc of volcanism throughout the mighty Sierra Nevada Mountains. Subsequent erosion of the range, which accumulated debris to a depth of over 15 km (9 miles) in California's Great Valley, formed the **Great Valley Sequence** of sedimentary rocks. During this period, the leading edge of North America was also scraping material off the Farallon Plate, extending the western edge of the continent. This complex mélange of basaltic ocean crust, marine sediments and sediments from the neighbouring continental mass is what geologists call the **Franciscan Formation**. Although neither the Franciscan Formation nor the Great Valley Sequence is considered volcanic (even if they contain plenty of remnants of volcanic rocks), they form a large part of the underpinnings of California wine country, explaining in part the tremendous diversity of soil types.

The complex story of volcanism that directly affected Northern California picks up some 25 million years ago, when the North American and Farallon Plates were met by the north-drifting Pacific Plate somewhere near San Diego. At this point subduction of the Farallon Plate – the central part of which has been completely consumed within the earth's mantle, leaving remnants called today the Juan de Fuca Plate – was partially replaced with translation, one plate sliding laterally past another, giving rise to more volcanism and a series of unstable faults that still haunt California to this day. The San Andreas Fault is the most famous, and this triple junction – the convergence of three tectonic plates – is responsible for its notable instability, and spectacular damage potential. The junction reached Northern California some seven million years ago.

The volcanic activity in Northern California must have been apocalyptic during this era, if the remnants of diverse volcanic ashes, tuffs, pyroclastic material, lahars and abundant

OPPOSITE *Morning balloon ride over the Napa Valley, in the world capital of wine tourism.*

lavas have been properly read. Wave after wave of effusive and explosive eruptions from multiple elongated fissures threw up huge curtains of basalt lavas, andesite breccias and rhyolite tuffs, and added thick strata of powdery white volcanic ash to the landscape. Collectively, these rocks and ash make up the **Sonoma Volcanics**, the official name for the geological formation that forms the underpinning of a good part of the eastern half of Sonoma wine country and many parts of Napa. But although it's tempting see Mt Veeder in the Mayacamas Mountains, or the perfectly shaped, truncated cone of St Helena at the northern end of the Napa Valley as classic stratovolcanoes, neither was built up over successive eruptions. In fact, neither ever 'erupted' in the proper sense (Veeder is built on Franciscan Formation and St Helena is simply eroded volcanic bedrock that happens to resemble a volcano, although it's certainly linked to a subterranean volcanic system.)

The mountains and hills of North Coast wine country are instead the result of upthrusts (crinkles in the earth's crust). A slight change in the direction of the Pacific Plate about three million years ago began compressing the San Andreas Fault with enough pressure to buckle the earth – first the Vaca Mountain Range, then the Mayacamas and the rest of the coastal hills were crumpled up. Additional volcanic activity accompanied the mountain building; 3.4 million years ago a massive eruption covered the area once again with volcanic debris, if the carbon dating of the trees in Sonoma's Petrified Forest is accurate.

But although the entire region was once covered with volcanic rock, subsequent uplifting and depression, sheering, slicing and erosion have exposed different strata of underlying bedrock in a near-random pattern, like a pack of wild children digging their fingers into a layer cake. It's geology-defying to generalize, but the Vaca Range on the eastern edge of the

ABOVE *Obsidian Ridge vineyards under Mt Konocti in the Red Hills AVA, Lake County*

OPPOSITE *Terraces carved from andesite rock at Barnett Vineyards on top of Spring Mountain, Napa Valley.*

Napa Valley is predominantly volcanic in the upper elevations, from the Coombsville caldera all the way north to Howell Mountain. The top ridge of the Mayacamas Mountains that separate Napa and Sonoma is largely marine sediments of the Franciscan Formation on the Napa side, and more volcanic on the Sonoma side in the vicinity of Mt Veeder. But the Mayacamas become more uniformly volcanic as you move north to Spring Mountain, Diamond Mountain and Calistoga, and into the upper Knights Valley and Alexander Valley. To the east across Sonoma Valley, Sonoma Mountain is also largely volcanic. The lower elevations in all of these areas offer a mixed cocktail of soils, shaken and stirred by alluvial (river-washed) and colluvial (gravity-borne) sediment from the surrounding hills. But soil generalizations grind to a halt there. After that, it goes on a vineyard-by-vineyard, or even parcel-by-parcel basis. Drawing borders around specific soil series is no piece of cake.

Lake County, on the other hand, is more uniformly volcanic thanks to more recent volcanism. The county is named for Clear Lake, a volcanic caldera lake centred on the **Clear Lake Volcanic Field**, with some of the youngest volcanic soils in California. Two volcanoes dominate the landscape: the 1440-metre-high (4724-feet) Cobb Mountain, and 1306-metre (4285-feet) Mt Konocti (Koh-nock-tie), both of which are home to vineyards. But in reality, the entire area sits on a massive volcanic complex, which on the surface consists of multiple lava domes and cinder cones. Its powerful underlying magma chamber powers the world's largest geothermal power plant, producing enough energy to supply nearly a million homes. The 300,000-year-old Mt Konocti last erupted just 11,000 years ago, covering the region in a new rain of ash and pyroclastic outflow. Vineyards are littered with the remnants, including the black volcanic glass called obsidian ranging from tiny stones to pieces the size of a small car. Konocti is officially listed as dormant, although sporadic volcanic-type earthquakes occur, and the numerous hot springs and volcanic gas seeps are clear indications of its potential to erupt again. The volcano hazards programme of the US Geological Survey list Clear Lake as a 'high' threat potential.

NAPA VALLEY

Strolling down Main Street in St Helena, the scent of prosperity, and wine, is everywhere. I see fashionable boutiques and quaint antique shops, bakeries, cafés, restaurants, gourmet food shops, a speciality chocolate shop, a fancy olive oil dispensary, in short, all of the unusual amenities and luxuries of a small affluent community. Less usual, however, are the bottles of wine on display in virtually every shop: sought-after labels prominently dress windows, hooking you to buy truffles or olive tapenade or a new handbag. It's as though everything in the Napa Valley, from the business of sustaining life to the business of enjoying it, centres on wine. And it does.

It's virtually impossible to go anywhere within this relatively small, roughly 50x8-km (30x5-mile) valley without bumping into someone who's somehow involved in the business of producing or selling wine, or selling the wine country lifestyle. One grand winery after another lines Highway 29, and further east, the parallel and slightly more bucolic Silverado Trail – each a marvel of some form of classic architecture from French château to Persian palace, as varied as the immigrants who settled California. It's clichéd, but if Walt Disney had dreamed up the Magic Wine Kingdom, it would surely have resembled the Napa Valley. As far as wine tourism goes, this is the place to be; nobody does it better. While other regions in California can rightfully claim a longer wine-growing history, the Napa Valley has become the epicentre of luxury California wine and the wine country experience. And it's hard not to get swept away by the grandeur of it all.

SEARCHING FOR NAPA

Stepping back in time, the directions to Diamond Creek Vineyards couldn't be less 21st century. I'm instructed to, 'drive up the hill, turn right at the large silver mailbox, cross the small stone bridge,

fork slightly left and follow the rustic road...' The iconic winery has no sign, and even the almighty GPS is apparently unable to lead folks there reliably. But I dutifully follow the landmarks, motivated by the opportunity to taste Diamond Creek's legendary wine called Volcanic Hill and brimming with anticipation. I'm not disappointed. I even relive the development of the Napa Valley, a history foreshadowed by Diamond Creek's own.

Although Napa was already greatly admired as a wine region in the 19th century – there were over 140 wineries operating by 1889 – the 1960s witnessed the birth of the modern era. Several of today's most celebrated wineries were established then, the likes of Heitz Wine Cellars, Robert Mondavi Winery and Stag's Leap Wine Cellars, along with Diamond Creek, established in 1968 by Al Brounstein and his wife Boots. When Brounstein found his future property up on Diamond Mountain it was nothing but rocks, shrubs and redwood forest. At the time, most vineyards were on the flats of the valley floor or on the slightly elevated benches of Rutherford and Oakville. Plantings up in the hills were scarce, discouraged by the sheer difficulty of working the poor, rocky ground and the distance from water sources. Yet it would be on such ground (in many places volcanic) that many of Napa's great wines would eventually grow.

Brounstein set about clearing his new property, and discovered he had three dramatically different soil types. On the narrowly pinched flatter land between hills by the Diamond Creek itself were deep gravel soils, while directly under the future winery offices was a steep slope of amazingly red-tinged soil (andesite) that from a distance looked like a sloping terra cotta roof. Across the valley on the opposite hillside the soil was entirely different yet again, in this case blinding white, composed of volcanic ash that drifted south from the last great eruption of Mt Konocti in Lake County (see p.82). From the first plantings of Cabernet Sauvignon, Brounstein kept the wines produced from the three soils separate, following the European

---

OPPOSITE (LEFT TO RIGHT) *Diamond Creek Vineyards; Ovid; Napa Valley morning; Diamond Creek; St Helena; Arkenstone Vineyards, Howell Mountain* *(twice); Mayacamas Vineyards; Arkenstone Vineyards, Howell Mountain; Ovid; Diamond Creek Vineyards; view north from the Coombsville caldera.*

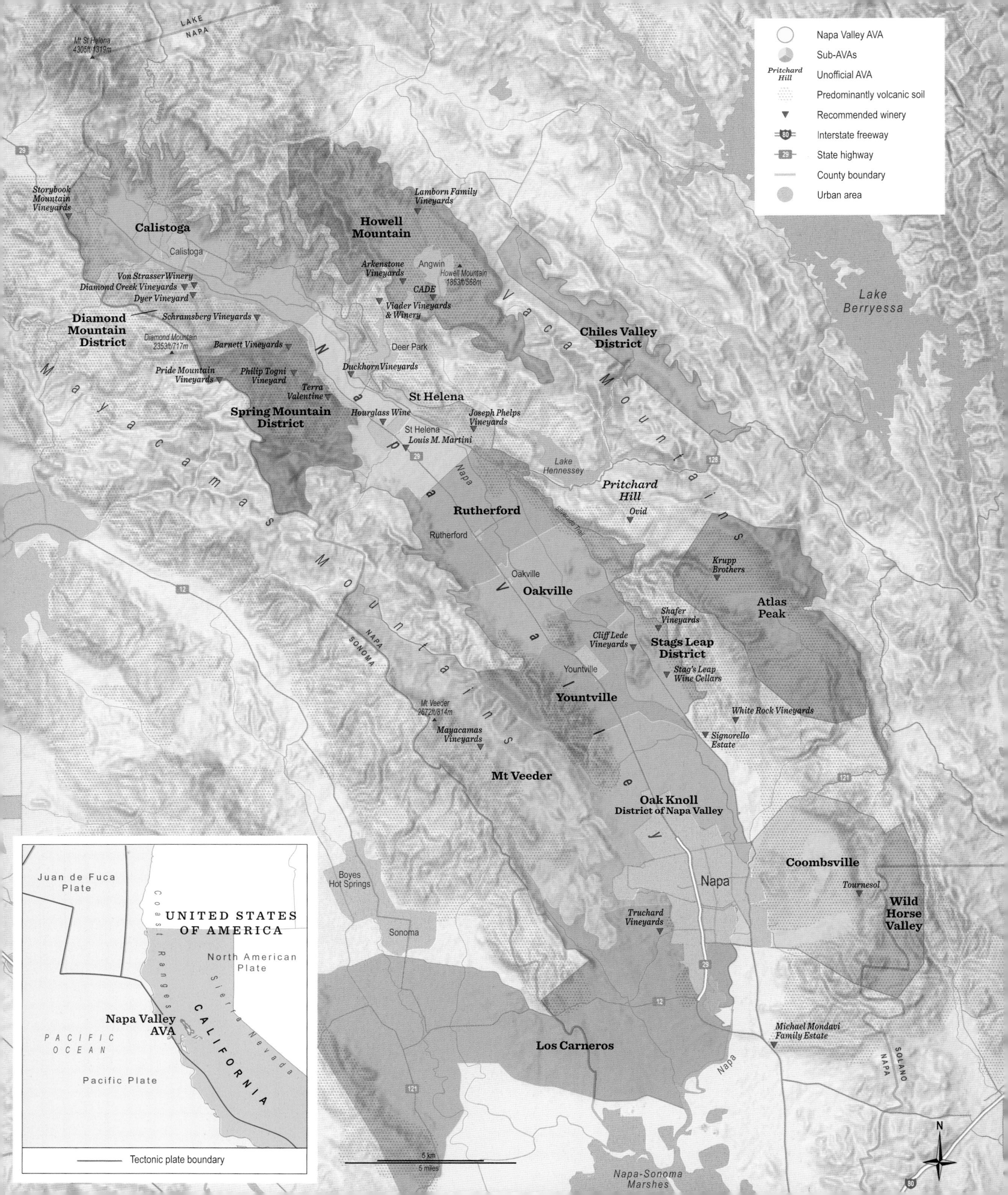

Napa Valley AVA
Sub-AVAs
Pritchard Hill
Unofficial AVA
Predominantly volcanic soil
Recommended winery
80
Interstate freeway
29
State highway
County boundary
Urban area
LAKE
NAPA
Mt St Helena 4305ft/1319m
Storybook Mountain Vineyards
Calistoga
Calistoga
Howell Mountain
Lamborn Family Vineyards
Arkenstone Vineyards
Angwin
Howell Mountain 1863ft/568m
CADE
Viader Vineyards & Winery
Von Strasser Winery
Diamond Creek Vineyards
Dyer Vineyard
Schramsberg Vineyards
Diamond Mountain District
Diamond Mountain 2353ft/717m
Barnett Vineyards
Deer Park
Pride Mountain Vineyards
Philip Togni Vineyard
Terra Valentine
Duckhorn Vineyards
Spring Mountain District
Hourglass Wine
St Helena
Joseph Phelps Vineyards
St Helena
Louis M. Martini
Napa
Lake Hennessey
Pritchard Hill
Ovid
Lake Berryessa
Chiles Valley District
Vaca Mountains
Mayacamas Mountains
Napa Valley
Rutherford
Rutherford
Silverado Trail
Oakville
Oakville
Krupp Brothers
Atlas Peak
Shafer Vineyards
Cliff Lede Vineyards
Stags Leap District
Stag's Leap Wine Cellars
Yountville
Yountville
NAPA
SONOMA
Mt Veeder 2672ft/814m
Mayacamas Vineyards
Mt Veeder
White Rock Vineyards
Signorello Estate
Oak Knoll District of Napa Valley
Boyes Hot Springs
Sonoma
Napa
Coombsville
Tournesol
Wild Horse Valley
Truchard Vineyards
Los Carneros
Michael Mondavi Family Estate
Napa
NAPA
SOLANO
Napa-Sonoma Marshes
5 km
5 miles
N
12
121
128
Juan de Fuca Plate
UNITED STATES OF AMERICA
Coast Ranges
North American Plate
Sierra Nevada
Napa Valley AVA
CALIFORNIA
PACIFIC OCEAN
Pacific Plate
Tectonic plate boundary

model of site-specific bottlings. The vineyards were appropriately named Gravelly Meadow, Red Rock Terrace and Volcanic Hill.

Brounstein was ahead of his time not only for planting in the hills, but also for recognizing that dirt makes a difference. At the time, the prevailing belief in Napa, and much of California, was that soil was simply a malleable medium in which to anchor vines. Terroir was just a pretentious French word and largely irrelevant, as great wine could be made using just good ole' American hard work and ingenuity. Soil wasn't going to get in the way of great wine.

Time would of course bear out Brounstein's beliefs. Today in the Napa Valley it's much clearer where the best wines originate. And many more have gone prospecting in the last 20 to 30 years for great sites such as Brounstein stumbled upon. There's more talk of soil than ever before, and Napa, as it turns out, has a wealth of great volcanic terroirs to offer the world.

Napa's Main Grapes & Wine Styles

When someone says 'Cabernet' in the Napa Valley, there's no confusion. Cabernet Sauvignon is, of course, the grape variety *par excellence* of the Napa Valley. It's the icon, the emblem, nuanced

enough when properly treated to reflect variations in terroir. Yet it's rarely ever solo. Most wines, even those labelled Cabernet Sauvignon, often contain ten to 15 per cent or more of other grapes, usually some combination of other Bordeaux varieties: Merlot, Cabernet Franc, Petit Verdot and Malbec. Even in small percentages, these grapes provide individuality to Napa cuvées, delivering the extra floral or spicy note or softer structure desired by each producer. Chardonnay is the principal white grape, here heady and ripe, but balanced from the best volcanic hillside sites. Beyond that, there are dozens of grapes planted in small quantities to round out each producer's portfolio.

Mountain vs. Valley Wines

Wine professionals and savvy consumers spend a great deal of time discussing the differences between Napa's 'mountain' wines and 'valley' wines, the former logically grown in the hills of the Vaca and Mayacamas Ranges, off the valley floor. And there's good reason: they taste different. Genuine mountain wines are born from stony, low-fertility, free-draining hillsides. They're denser, darker, quite often more tannic, yet more evenly ripe at lower alcohol, and they

ABOVE *Looking east across the valley to the craggy volcanic peaks of the Vaca Range.*

age magnificently. The vines themselves grow more slowly, they struggle and naturally yield less fruit per hectare. For a vine it's probably hell. For a winemaker, and wine drinkers, it's much closer to heaven. As things go, virtually all of the volcanic wines in Napa are also mountain wines, even if not all mountain wines are volcanic. The difference between those is a nuanced matter of site.

Napa's Volcanic AVAs

There are 16 sub-AVAs with the Napa Valley AVA, though few are purely volcanic. As outlined in the introduction, it's near impossible to draw precise lines around Napa's volcanic terroirs, given the overwhelmingly complex geological history. The fully detailed soil map of the Napa Valley looks like a haphazard mashing of every colour in the play-dough kit smeared onto a tabletop. Some 33 major soils series, and 100 more finely detailed sub-categories

of soils are catalogued in the valley. Geologist Jonathan Swinchatt, co-author of *The Winemaker's Dance*, a study on the geology of the Napa Valley, concedes that, 'in examining both the generalized and detailed soil maps, we can identify little or no correlation between the distribution of soil types and other specifically characterizable features of the Napa Valley AVA.' This of course contributes to the amazing diversity of wines from the Napa Valley, but it renders the discussion of volcanic wines more challenging. And so, take the generalizations below with a pinch of sediment.

Starting in the south, the **Coombsville AVA** lies in an ancient caldera east of Napa, where variations on compacted volcanic ash alternate with solid basalt bedrock, as can be clearly seen at Caldwell Vineyard. 'Shit, all we did for the first ten years was haul solid rock out of here,' John Caldwell recalls of the tribulations of planting vines, a common refrain from other hillside pioneers. Just west

---

ABOVE *Terra Valentine's Wurtele vineyard at 300 metres (1000 feet) on Spring Mountain.*

OPPOSITE ABOVE *Shafer Vineyards under the volcanic palisades of the Stags Leap District.*

OPPOSITE BELOW *Phil Steinschriber, winemaker; Boots Brounstein, owner, Diamond Creek Vineyards. at the heart of the property.*

of the property is an active basalt quarry. When it came time to carve an underground cellar out of the hill, he was sure the construction company he hired, 'was going to have a hell of a time digging it out'. They quoted him by the foot rather than by the day, which, he thought, was idiotic idea on their part. 'But turns out they knew more than I did. The whole mountainside here was pure compacted volcanic ash, easy to dig. They made good money off of me,' he smiles. Wines vary: the basalts more compact and tight, the ash wines more finessed. But the relatively cool climate of Coombsville, with breezes from nearby San Pablo Bay corralled by the crescent-shaped caldera, generally favours elegance over sheer power.

North of Coombsville, it's easy to recognize the **Stags Leap District AVA** with its highly visible palisades, towering cliffs of columnar basalt rising above the vineyards like organ pipes. Vines planted higher up in these foothills of the Vaca Mountain Range dig right into weathered basalt. Vineyards lower down pry into a mix of weathered volcanics, but also alluvial fans and other sedimentary materials. This is one of the warmest AVAs, basking in hot afternoon sun. Cabernet is invariably broad-shouldered, dark and sumptuous.

Further east above Stags Leap at the top of the Vaca Range is **Atlas Peak AVA**, where some of the highest and most rugged Napa vineyards are planted, at up to over 800 metres (2600 feet). There are only two access roads to this noticeably cooler and isolated area in the mountains where red-tinged basalt soils nurture less than

a third of a per cent of total acreage in the Napa Valley. But reputation is disproportionate to size; Atlas Peak is home to the Krupp Brother's Stagecoach Vineyards, for example, one of Napa's most celebrated, which supplies coveted grapes to many wineries. These are bold and rugged Cabernets in the mountain style.

North of Atlas Peak in the Vaca Range, eminently volcanic **Pritchard Hill** is an unofficial AVA above the Silverado Trail with a collection of revered wineries. At the very top of the hill there's virtually no topsoil and the bedrock breaks through the surface like a volcanic island arc in a shallow sea. Echoing John Caldwell, Ovid winemaker Austin Peterson recalls the difficulty in planting their vineyard, where the topsoil is measured in inches not feet, and, 'hundreds of tons of volcanic rock had to be removed just to get vines in the ground, and allow tractors to plow without constantly breaking down'. A collection of Napa's most sought-after Cabernets grows here, aligning density with finesse.

The **Howell Mountain AVA** just north of Pritchard Hill is likewise a difficult place to access, rising up to 700 metres (2300 feet) above the valley. That's high enough to be above the inversion layer (cooler days, warmer nights), ensuring a long, slow even ripening period. Soils are split between tuffs and weathered rusty basalt. Although Howell Mountain sees twice as much rain as the valley, these soils, like all volcanic hillsides, are incapable of holding much water, ensuring that vines struggle and that wine-growers can micro

manage irrigation to obtain small, concentrated berries. Howell is known for its sturdy and savoury Cabernet, capable of long ageing.

On the west side of the valley towards the northern end, **Spring Mountain District AVA** is another source of top-flight volcanic wines. The Mayacamas side of the valley is noticeably cooler and greener – with moss-covered redwoods and pines rather than the desert shrubs opposite – thanks to its eastern-facing flanks that welcome the gentler rays of the morning sun. It's named for several natural springs that provided water for the residents of St Helena in the 19th and early 20th centuries. Undulating hills or terraced slopes are carved out of andesite, but not all of the mostly small, family-run vineyards are on volcanic soils. Spring Mountain also has areas of uplifted Franciscan Formation (see p.54). Spring Mountain Cabernet is notably finessed and fine-grained.

Diamond Mountain District AVA north of Spring Mountain gets its name from the bits of volcanic crystals mixed in with red lava-derived soils and white volcanic ash, as seen in Diamond Creek's Red Rock Terrace and Volcanic Hill vineyards. Neighbouring

Dyer Vineyard's tiny site sits on rhyolitic tuff. 'When I brought my property 25 years ago, nobody wanted Diamond Mountain Cabernet,' recalls Rudy von Strasser of von Strasser Winery. 'They had a reputation for being too tannic.' Now, although techniques have evolved and tannins have softened, the wines of Diamond Mountain are still celebrated for their dense, tannic, age-worthy structure.

The **Calistoga AVA** sits on volcanic bedrock with, as in other parts of the valley, the lower slopes covered by alluvial soils and the upper slopes more purely volcanic. Magnesium and calcium-rich geothermal hot springs in the area reflect past, and continuing, volcanic activity. Calistoga is considered the warmest AVA in Napa, and while the valley's hottest spot is indeed near Bale Lane at the southern boundary of the AVA, in reality, Stags Leap, for example, is a warmer growing region overall. A gentle gap here in the Mayacamas allows cooler marine-influenced air from the Russian River to funnel in, dropping afternoon/evening temperatures to acidity-retaining levels, meaning styles range from ripe and bold to firm and fine, depending, naturally, on site.

OPPOSITE *The fog clears late morning at Philip Togni Vineyard, Spring Mountain District.*

ABOVE *Looking north from the Coombsville caldera; the truncated cone of Mt St Helena in the distance looks like a volcano, but it isn't.*

OVERLEAF *Duckhorn Vineyards' Candelstick vineyard on Howell Mountain.*

Arkenstone Vineyards ★

335 West Lane
Angwin
CA 94508

arkenstone.com

Susan and Ron Krausz stumbled upon a stunning piece of virgin land high on the western shoulder of Howell Mountain during a day trip to Napa in the late 80s; 20 years later their dream winery was completed. Bordeaux grapes are farmed organically in a mix of poor rocky tuff and Aiken loam with some parcels on up to 50 degree slopes. Obsidian is the top Cabernet blend, a classy wine with measured barrel spice, fine, tightly knit tannins and balanced acids, built to age.

Barnett Vineyards

4070 Spring Mountain Rd
St Helena
CA 94574

barnettvineyards.com

The property of Hal and Fiona Barnett commands a mesmerizing view from the top of Spring Mountain across the Napa Valley. Contoured terraced vineyards are dedicated mostly to hand-farmed Cabernet Sauvignon, planted in andesitic red soils peppered with obsidian. Estate Cabernet is approachable, soft, and fruity enough to drink on release. Flagship Rattlesnake Cabernet is a significant step up (named for the abundance of rattlesnakes found on the property when it was cleared in 1983). The same blocks tend to surface annually in the final blend: older vines on the most stressed parcels, delivering a complete package of power and balance.

CADE

360 Howell Mountain Road South
Angwin
CA 94508

cadewinery.com

Owners of Plumpjack Winery in Oakville, Gavin Newsom, (current) Lieutenant Governor of California, and philanthropist Gordon Getty bought vineyards on Howell Mountain in 2005 and renamed the estate CADE. Both winery names are Shakespeare references, the former after character Sir John 'PlumpJack' Falstaff, the latter a reference to 'cades', or casks used to ship wine in the Elizabethan era. CADE's organically-farmed vineyards on pure weathered volcanic rock are planted to Cabernet, Malbec and Petit Verdot, and wines are made in a LEED gold-certified winery completed in 2007. The aim is for, 'dense, rich and age-worthy, but not rustic or tannic [wines],' according to estate manager John Conover. Estate Howell Mountain Cabernet Sauvignon has typical formidable tannic structure, polished by toasty oak and gentle handling. Reserve Cabernet from a barrel selection of the estate's top lots is treated to 100 per cent new wood, richly textured, generously proportioned, both savoury and fruity.

Cliff Lede Vineyards ★★★

1473 Yountville Cross Road
Yountville
CA 94599

cliffledevineyards.com

Canadian Cliff Lede realized his Napa dream in 2002, sparing no expense, hiring top names like vineyard architect David Abreu, and creating a showpiece winery for art, architecture, and music, as well as wine. Bordeaux varieties are planted at the northernmost end of the Stags Leap District in fractured rhyolite. Flagship Poetry Cabernet Sauvignon (with a splash of others), from the steepest, terraced hillside section is exemplary, crafted with meticulous care, ripe with massive structure yet suave tannins – a dense and age-worthy wine.

Diamond Creek Vineyards ★★★

1500 Diamond Mountain Road
Calistoga
CA 94515

diamondcreekvineyards.com

Diamond Creek (see also p.65) makes some of Napa's finest Cabernet, wines of monumental depth and structure. There's nothing magical about the process; yields are low but not extreme, and standard (premium) winemaking techniques are applied. Yet results are anything but standard, an incontrovertible testament to great terroir. Three single-vineyard Cabernets are bottled (occasionally also a fourth, Lake Vineyard): Gravelly Meadow, from gravelly soils deposited by Diamond Creek, is the prettiest and most revealing early on, perfumed and elegant with blue fruit; Red Rock Terrace, in contrast, from stony, iron-rich red soils is the most unyielding, dusty and tannic, with fruit in the red spectrum; Volcanic Hill, grown on white volcanic ash, is always last in the tasting, magnificently concentrated, expansive, visceral, dark and smoky, the most age-worthy of the trio. As founder Al Brounstein used to say, 'I guarantee my wine will age 100 years. If it doesn't I'll give you your money back.'

Duckhorn Vineyards ★

1000 Lodi Lane
St Helena
CA 94574
duckhorn.com

A Napa household name, Duckhorn has contributed to Napa's volcanic range since 1989 with Cabernet sourced from Howell Mountain. Subsequent purchase of spectacular Candlestick Ridge and Stout Ranch vineyards underscores the Duckhorns' appreciation of the AVA, revered for its 'powerful, age-worthy wines,' according to winemaker Renee Ary. Stout Vineyard Merlot is appealingly plum-scented with fine tension; Howell Mountain Cabernet Sauvignon is aged for an extra year before release to allow typically compact tannins time to relax and unwind, gathering complexity along the way.

Dyer Straits Wine Co – Dyer Vineyard ★

1501 Diamond Mountain Road
Calistoga
CA 94515
dyerwine.com

The formidable couple of Bill Dyer, former winemaker at Sterling Vineyards, and wife Dawnine, former winemaker at Chandon, bought a small property on Diamond Mountain and made their first wine in 1996. Unusually for Napa, only one wine is made in most vintages, a Cabernet-based blend with Cabernet Franc and Petit Verdot grown on rhyolite tuff rocks with heavier iron-rich clays in the lower section of the property, harvested and fermented together. Typical floral notes and dark fruit character – black cherry, plum, blueberry – rests on intimidating scaffolding: 'Diamond Mountain has a unique tannic structure,' says Dyer. 'Berries aren't just smaller, they're more tannic.' An attractive sinewy leanness and gravelly character runs from start to long finish.

Hourglass Wine – Blueline Estate ★

1104 Adams Street
Suite 103-104
St Helena
CA 94574
hourglasswines.com

In 1992, when Dean of Viticulture at UC Davis Dr. Kliewer discovered prized Hambright soils on the Smith family property on a basalt outcropping of the Mayacamas (at the pinch of the hourglass-shaped valley), Jeff Smith set about planting Cabernet. Smith later acquired the Blueline Estate off Silverado Trail, drawn by its mounds of rocks washed down by two 'blue line' streams (constant flow streams marked on topographic maps with a solid blue line) from the Vaca Mountain Range, and planted additional Bordeaux varieties. Blueline Estate Cabernet highlights the pleasantly rustic but well-knit character of the site; Hourglass Estate Cabernet delivers a fuller, denser, darker expression with sanguine character and vibrant natural acids.

Joseph Phelps Vineyards

200 Taplin Road
St Helena
CA 94574
josephphelps.com

Although most famous for the proprietary blend Insignia, Phelps's contribution to volcanic wines comes from the Backus vineyard on the east side of the Oakville AVA, on well-drained Boomer soils (weathered metavolcanic rock) over a toe of rhyolitic bedrock sloughed off from the Vaca Mountain Range. Cabernet is rendered in a more refined and accessible expression, well-rounded with polished tannins.

Krupp Brothers

3267 Soda Canyon Road
Napa
CA 94558
kruppbrothers.com

It took a warehouse of dynamite to remove a million tons of andesitic rock, and the aid of a water witch, for Jan and Bart Krupp to get the Stagecoach vineyard planted and growing in the mid-90s. Straddling Pritchard Hill and Atlas Peak, its red-tinged soils furnish some of the most sought-after fruit in Napa. The Krupps keep a small amount for their own production, the best of which is Veraison, a plush and velvety Cabernet with more polish than is typically found in Napa mountain wines, though hardly light in structure.

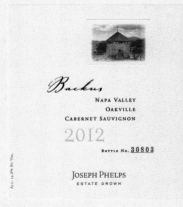

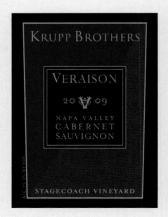

Lamborn Family Vineyards ★

1984 Summit Lake Drive
Angwin
CA 94508
lamborn.com

A small estate winery on a north-facing ridgeline at 670 metres (2200 feet) on Howell Mountain, planted to Cabernet Sauvignon and Zinfandel on weathered red andesite in the late 70s. Celebrated winemaker Heidi Barrett crafts the wines; Cabernet is rendered in a big but savoury style, with distinctly metallic, iron-like character and finely woven acid-tannin balance.

Mayacamas Vineyards ★★★

1155 Lokoya Rd
Napa
CA 94558
mayacamas.com

One of the great historic Napa wineries, Mayacamas Vineyards traces its roots back to 1889. For decades, this property, at close to 700 metres (2300 feet) near the top of Mt Veeder, has been producing uncompromising wines in a fashion-impervious style, never bending to market whims. Although soils are not uniformly volcanic (volcanic tuff mixed with cobbly red soils among many variations) the wines are uniformly excellent, some of the most age-worthy in California. Chardonnay is tuned to a tension-filled high-wire, with a terrific twang of acids (no malolactic fermentation) and genuine depth; Cabernet is upright and understated, untainted by obvious oak, rarely over 13% ABV, not released until five years after vintage when savoury herbs and fruity flavours start to co-mingle comfortably.

Michael Mondavi Family Estate ★★★

1907 North Kelly Road
Napa
CA 94558
michaelmondavifamilyestate.com

Michael, son of Napa icon Robert Mondavi, purchased a piece of land with uniformly rocky volcanic soil, tinged red by streaks of iron, atop Atlas Peak in 1999. Upon surveying the site, daughter Dina remarked that the place had animo, or 'spirit', a name that eventually stuck. Animo Vineyard Cabernet (with Petit Verdot) stretches into the very ripe end of the spectrum yet retains tightly knit tannins. Flaghship M by Michael Mondavi is even denser and more tannic Cabernet from Animo's highest blocks, with abundant scorched-earth-like flavours, built to last.

Ovid ★★★

255 Long Ranch Road
St Helena
CA 94574
ovidvineyards.com

Founding partners Mark Nelson and Dana Johnsson removed hundreds of tons of rock to plant vineyards in 2000 on the top of Pritchard Hill on the valley's east side, one of Napa's most spectacularly volcanic areas. Quality was aimed at the highest level from the start; vines are tended one-by-one, and renowned consultant Michel Rolland was engaged to speed up the curve to stardom. An unusually high percentage of Cabernet Franc (25 per cent) gives Ovid's flagship red blend unusual grace and elegance, sailing on a lovely streak of acids in a superb balancing act of power and refinement. A gentleman's Napa red.

Philip Togni Vineyard ★★★

3780 Spring Mountain Road
St Helena
CA 94574
philiptognivineyard.com

An oenology graduate from the University of Bordeaux (and student of Émile Peynaud), and inaugural winemaker at Chapellet on the top of Pritchard Hill (late 60s), Togni has retained a philosophy of proportion and equilibrium throughout his long winemaking career. Only two estate Bordeaux-style reds are produced from vineyards on well-drained volcanic soils at the top of Spring Mountain at 600 metres (2000 feet) above the fog line. Young vines Tanbark Hill is more approachable but still structured and elegant; Estate Cabernet Sauvignon (blended) is one of Spring Mountain's refined best, pure and silky, close in style to Togni's Margaux reference (he spent the 1956 vintage at Château Lascombes).

Schramsberg Vineyards – J. Davies Vineyards ★

1400 Schramsberg Road
Calistoga
CA 94515

schramsberg.com

German immigrant Jacob Schram acquired this hillside piece of land at the southern end of Diamond Mountain in 1862. Nearly 100 years and multiple proprietors later, Jack and Jamie Davies took over the property in 1965 and revived the Schram wine legacy. Schramsberg is best known for traditional method sparkling (now grown elsewhere); estate plantings of Bordeaux varieties begun in 1994 gave rise to the sister Davies Vineyard wines. Top of the line J. Davies Cabernet Sauvignon, given a floral lift by a dash of Malbec, is consistently finessed and classy, concentrated with dark fruit and grippy texture.

Shafer Vineyards

6154 Silverado Trail
Napa
CA 94558

shafervineyards.com

Doug Shafer makes no bones about his preference for maximum impact, and his mostly west- and south-facing estate vineyards, on thin, rock-saturated soils over volcanic bedrock, conveniently favour the production of large scale wines. Struggling vines and tiny berries are easily imagined in signature Hillside Select Cabernet Sauvignon, often tipping in at over 15% ABV, with massive tannic extract and ultra-ripe fruit. Cellaring is recommended.

Signorello Estate

4500 Silverado Trail
Napa
CA 94558

signorelloestate.com

The upper and eastern sections of Ray Signorello's hillside vineyards, east of the Silverado Trail in the foothills of the Vaca Mountain Range, are entirely volcanic Hambright weathered basalts. These originate the estate's top-end Padrone Cabernet blend, a massive wine with huge tannic structure and bone-warming alcohol.

Stag's Leap Wine Cellars

5766 Silverado Trail
Napa
CA 94558

cask23.com

Founder Warren Winiarski made headlines in 1976 when his 1973 Stag's Leap Vineyard (SLV) Cabernet, just the second release, finished first in a blind tasting of top Bordeaux and California wines dubbed the 'Judgement of Paris'. Today, the austere, rocky-volcanic soils of the original SLV continue to yield impressive Cabernet with big tannic structure, raw power and stony character. Added adjacent FAY vineyard is markedly different, with volcanic-alluvial-clay soils delivering more immediately appealing Cabernet, supple and engagingly perfumed; Cask 23 is the flagship barrel selection of the two vineyards.

Storybook Mountain Vineyards ★★★

3835 CA-128
Calistoga
CA 94515

storybookwines.com

Dr. Jerry Seps is arguably Napa's greatest Zinfandel producer, making uncommonly classy examples since 1983 from his organic-certified estate above Calistoga. Wines age in a century-old cave carved out of rhyolitic bedrock. Elegant Mayacamas Range Zinfandel highlights the variety's generous, spicy, brambly fruit. Even better, paradigm-shifting Eastern Exposures Zinfandel from cooler, east-facing vineyards offers marvellous perfume and silky texture, suffused with minerality and freshness. Also memorable Seps Estate Reserve Cabernet Sauvignon from a north-facing hillside, complex and fragrant, fully ripe at under 14% ABV. All are age-worthy.

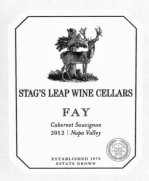

Terra Valentine

264 Crystal Springs Road
St Helena
CA 94574
terravalentine.com

Terra Valentine's Wurtele vineyard sits on a knoll at 300 metres (1000 feet) on Spring Mountain, benefitting from full 360 degree sun exposure. Cabernet planted in dark-red volcanic-clay soils produces an authentic expression of mountain wine, tightly tannic with natural saliva-inducing acidity.

Tournesol

PO Box 5307
Napa
CA 94581
tournesolwine.com

Estate vineyards in the cool Coombsville AVA lie on a gently-sloping bench above the valley floor, on the edge of the eight-million-year-old Coombsville caldera and its rock and ash soils. Cabernet-based Proprietor's Red Blend is charmingly savoury, floral and gritty, in the lighter, edgier spectrum; Napa Valley Cabernet from a special, gently-rising, north-facing slope is more muscular, powerful and concentrated, though still as finessed as the terroir dictates.

Truchard Vineyards

3234 Old Sonoma Road
Napa
CA 94559
truchardvineyards.com

Truchard's vineyards straddle the toes of Mt Veeder, and a fault line that slices through the property marks the dividing line between classic Carneros clay to the south and the Mayacamas volcanic soils roughly to the north. Clays favour Pinot Noir, Chardonnay and Merlot, while volcanics are better suited to Zinfandel, Roussanne and (especially) Syrah, here revealing solid architecture and an appealing range of blue-fruit character, comfortably between smoky Northern Rhône and riper, fruitier New World styles.

Viader Vineyards & Winery ★★

1120 Deer Park Road
Deer Park
CA 94576
viader.com

Argentina-born Delia Viader planted vineyards in an enviable eastern position near the top of Howell Mountain in 1986 in especially poor, well-drained red soils formed from weathered rhyolitic tuff (the Forward-Aiken series). Estate reds are the sole focus of this family affair, and Viader Proprietary Red Blend, dubbed 'Liquid Cashmere', is the signature – a magnificently floral blend of mostly Cabernet with Cabernet Franc packed with fresh black fruit, contained by elegant but ample, dusty-chalky tannins and succulent acids.

Von Strasser Winery ★★

1510 Diamond Mountain Rd
Calistoga
CA 94515
vonstrasser.com

Rudy von Strasser's estate vineyards occupy the mid-elevation of Diamond Mountain, between 200 and 400 metres (650 to 1300 feet). Similarly, he sits comfortably in the balanced middle-of-the-style spectrum, seeking neither exaggerated over- nor under-ripeness. Parcels with differing exposures, soil depth and vine age are harvested separately to produce three tiers – ranging from the soft, fruit-forward Cartel Red through a handful of parcel-specific Cabernet Sauvignons to the top Estate Vineyard Cabernet, a mountain wine through and through, well constructed on a solid base of dense, dark fruit and capable of long slumber in the cellar. An Estate Reserve is bottled in certain vintages from top blocks. Austrian Grüner Veltliner nods to the von Strassers' heritage.

White Rock Vineyards ★★

1115 Loma Vista Drive
Napa
CA 94558
whiterockvineyards.com

A storied property in the Vaca Mountain Range at the southern end of Stags Leap, north of the Coombsville caldera. Dr. J Pettingill planted the first vines here in the 1860s and carved the original cellar by hand out of the white volcanic ash hillside. He trademarked White Rock Vineyards. The Vandendriessche family, current owners, carried on digging, by machine. Estate Chardonnay is a highlight, particularly intense and mineral, on the leaner and more chiselled end of the Napa spectrum, barrel fermented but with minimal new oak.

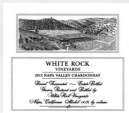

ABOVE (LEFT TO RIGHT) *Alexander Valley; Lancaster Estate; Repris Wines, Moon Mountain (three); Louis M.Martini's Monte Rosso vineyard; Lancaster Estate; Richard Dinner Vineyard; Laurel Glen Winery; Sonoma Coast; Louis M.Martini; view southwest from Moon Mountain.*

SONOMA COUNTY

Glen Ellen is a quaint, quiet town that captures the rural, country spirit of Sonoma County nicely, in sharp contrast with the more showy settlements over the hills in Napa County. There's a supermarket (grocery store), a modest village market and a western saloon. Mud-speckled pick-up trucks rumble down the main street in succession. A makeshift wine bar abuts a dentist's office in a weather-beaten, one-storey, wooden building. There's no glitz, no double magnums of expensive wines in storefronts to lure well-heeled travellers, no Walt Disney version of the magic wine kingdom. This is Sonoma County, real and earthly.

It's a bit of a stretch to think that Sonoma was once the epicentre of North Coast wine-growing, with a longer history than Napa's. The first Russian *émigrés* who arrived in the early 19th century planted grapes out at Fort Ross on the Sonoma Coast a quarter century before George Yount planted grapes in the Napa Valley.

Sonoma is also the birthplace of modern California wine, thanks in no small measure to the heroics of another immigrant, this one of Hungarian descent. Count Agoston Haraszthy, a rebellious dynamo with a flair for accomplishment, founder of a small town in Wisconsin, sheriff of San Diego and creator of Sonoma's Buena Vista Winery, was also the ultimate suitcase

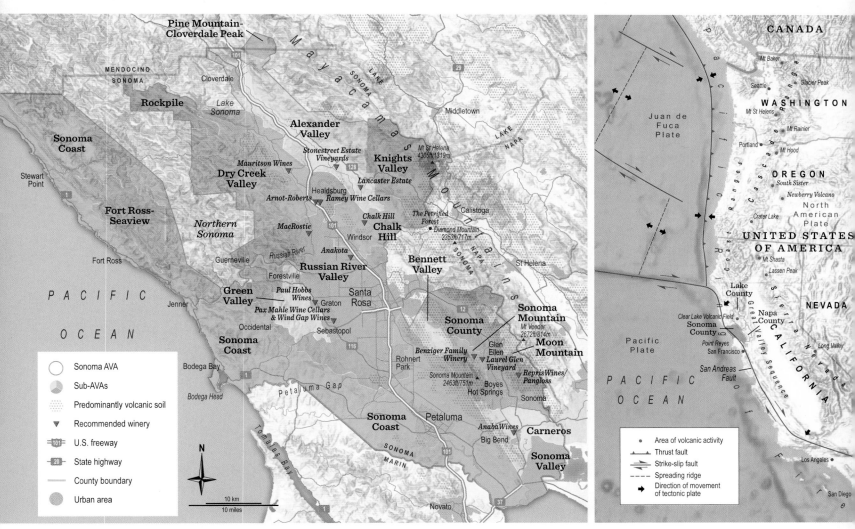

clone supplier. After persuading the governor of California to sponsor him, Haraszthy embarked on an extensive wine research trip to Europe in 1861, returning with cuttings of nearly 500 grape varieties. Vineyards proliferated and quality rose apace.

Haraszthy lost most of his plantings to phylloxera in the late 1800s, and most of his fortune along with them, at around the same time that Sonoma's sun was setting and Napa's star was rising over the California wine industry. But his legacy in Sonoma's winelands was already history. That Haraszthy's days reportedly came to an end in the jaws of a Nicaraguan crocodile seems appropriately fitting for this new world adventurer.

Over a century later, Sonoma is firmly re-established as one of California's, and the Americas', pre-eminent wine regions. Yet despite the impressive rebirth and growth of the industry over the last couple of decades, Sonoma has held on to its rural charm, where a 19th-century pioneer would feel right at home.

SONOMA COUNTY TO A FAULT

The most agreeable way to reach Sonoma wine country from San Francisco is to head north by car on the 101, across the iconic Golden Gate Bridge. Then, just past Sausalito, take a short geological detour west on Highway 1 towards the Pacific, and stay parallel to the coast northwest towards Point Reyes and Tomales Bay. You'll be driving up a valley several hundred metres (feet) deep, and may notice that the valley floor is curiously accidented, criss-crossed by low ridges breaking many dozens of metres (feet), disrupting stream beds, and sending their waters in opposite directions. There seems to be no logic to the landscape, no reason for ponds to be sitting halfway up hillsides.

But then again this is no ordinary valley; you're driving along the San Andreas Fault, where the Pacific and North American Plates scrape against one another with the force of passing continental freight trains. Every few decades or so as the tension between plates builds beyond what frictional resistance can hold, a correction to release the pressure occurs. The earth heaves and shudders like a rumbling giant rudely awoken from peaceful slumber, cracking its back to get comfortable before laying back to rest. In the San Francisco earthquake of 1906, the fault slipped nearly five metres (16 feet), virtually destroying the entire city.

Closer in time, the parallel, minor West Napa Fault slipped in August of 2014 around the city of Napa causing a 6.0 magnitude earthquake. Wineries from Napa to Sonoma shook and swayed with the vibrating earth, many suffering damage: broken tanks, and crashing barrels and bottles. It was another unsubtle reminder of the region's violent geologic past, and present, and of yet another uncontrollable aspect to add to the wine-grower's list of daily concerns in an earthquake-prone, volcanic zone.

Tracing Sonoma Volcanics: AVAs, Grapes & Wine Styles

Sonoma is the most diverse wine-growing county in California. From extremes of cold on the far Sonoma Coast, to extravagant warmth in the upper Alexander and Knights Valleys, virtually every grape variety (some 60 different grapes are planted) can find a little climate oasis in which to thrive, and the range of wine styles is unparalleled.

Currently 16 AVAs fall within the general Sonoma County AVA, which in turn lies within the larger North Coast AVA (along with Napa Valley, Mendocino and Lake County AVAs). As outlined in the introduction to this chapter, the geology of California's north coast is staggeringly complex, and finding pure volcanics is like finding the proverbial needle in the haystack. But some rough lines can be traced around the 11 most volcanic AVAs.

West of the San Andreas Fault the bedrock is mostly ancient granites; there's not too much grape-growing out there – it's too cold. East of the fault, on the other hand, is a generous geological smorgasbord of sedimentary, metamorphic and igneous rocks (see Glossary, p.248). West-central Sonoma rests largely on marine sandstones, formed when the area around Sebastopol was submerged under the Wilson-Grove Sea around three million years ago. The sandy-loamy soil it weathers into – Goldridge – is the Russian River Valley's most coveted dirt for Pinot Noir and Chardonnay. Some isolated, upthrust rocky outcrops and veins of ash and pumice from more violent volcanic episodes account for the occasional volcanic vineyard in the **Russian River Valley** and **Sonoma Coast AVAs**, but they're infrequent. Similarly, slices of volcanic soil are found in higher elevations of the **Carneros AVA**, in the last gasps of the Mayacamas Range before it gives way to the clay-rich rolling hills of southern Carneros.

The greatest concentration of volcanic soils and associated AVAs lie further inland, east of the solidified Wilson-Grove Sea. During the same period when the future sandstones were accumulating, an impressive series of gaping fissures was violently voiding the bowels of the earth in an area now roughly defined by

Mt St Helena south to Carneros, and Sonoma Mountain east to the Vaca Mountain Range in Napa.

The recent (2013) <u>Moon Mountain AVA</u> is Sonoma's most volcanic; indeed the petition to gain the appellation hinged on the distinction that the soils and bedrock are entirely volcanic, specifically three-million-year-old lava flows of andesite, basalt and rhyolite mixed with ash. The drive up leaves the Sonoma Valley floor far behind to where the first vineyards root on the rocky ridges of the western Mayacamas, up to nearly 700 metres (2300 feet) above sea level on the Sonoma side of Mt Veeder. The red andesites and basalts are most visually obvious in Louis M. Martini's historically significant Monte Rosso (Red Mountain) vineyard, where reportedly the oldest Cabernet Sauvignon in the USA still grows, planted in the 19th century; though outcroppings of reddish volcanic rocks break through the meagre topsoil everywhere. In other pockets, veins of white volcanic ash and rhyolite can be clearly seen.

Erich Bradley of Repris describes the difference in Cabernet Sauvignon grown on the two different soils, 'the Cabs grown on rhyolite have both higher pH and higher acidity consistently, and more sour-red-cherry and carob flavours. The Cabernets from basalts have darker and riper fruit character.' More generally, most vineyards are above the inversion level, which means that they stay warm all night – in the metabolism sweet spot – ready to jump into photosynthesis at first light while vines below are shrouded in morning fog. West-facing slopes also capture the hot afternoon sun, so the net result is ultra-ripe grapes with ultra-thick skins, while high potassium soils (especially rhyolites) drive the pH even higher. Cabernet Sauvignon and Zinfandel, the two emblematic varieties of the mountain, are wines of striking power and structure.

Directly west across the valley watching over sleepy Glen Ellen is the <u>Sonoma Mountain AVA</u>, where similar volcanic geology unfolded. Aspect is a major difference, however; Sonoma Mountain vineyards face east and thus awaken to the gentle morning sun, resting in cool, late afternoon shadows while vines across the valley are still fending off strong post meridian rays. Cabernet Sauvignon has uncommon tension and spring, needing time to relax and unwind in the bottle. Even cooler microclimates harboured in the irregular folds and crevices of the mountainside are repairs for white grapes such as Chardonnay, Sauvignon Blanc and Semillon.

Within the large Russian River Valley AVA, <u>Chalk Hill AVA</u> is sufficiently distinguished by its soil, climate and elevation to merit its own appellation. The name is not a geologic reference – there's no limestone here – but rather a textural description of the hill's chalky volcanic white ash soils. White varieties from Chalk Hill are particularly admired, especially Sauvignon Blanc and Chardonnay. Yet it's not for the coolness that usually comes with elevation – the AVA's vineyards sit mainly above the fog line and thus experience more sunlight and warmth than those on the valley floor, and ripeness is rarely an issue. But these well-drained soils nonetheless imbue wines with a balancing measure of acidity and finesse, and encourage a slow build of intense varietal character.

Bordering Chalk Hill to the northeast, <u>Knights Valley AVA</u> lies in the morning shadow of Mt St Helena. This remote valley is essentially a northern extension of the Napa Valley, separated from it only by a low gap in the Mayacamas. Carry on northwest over another set of low lying hills and you'll descend into the <u>Alexander Valley AVA</u>, Sonoma County's most planted, which runs alongside the Russian River. As in Napa, valley floor vineyards in both appellations root in mixed-alluvial-sedimentary soil, save for some irregular volcanic mounds that rise off the floor, as at Lancaster Estate. But those that creep up into the western hillsides of the Mayacamas, trade fertile topsoil for spartan rocky volcanic terroir. The Knights Valley's protected bowl shape, and the Alexander Valley's distance from the cooling Pacific explain the relative warmth of these regions; fog does not penetrate this far and summer temperatures regularly soar into the 30s (90s Fahrenheit) and beyond. This is mainly Cabernet and Zinfandel country, with a few exceptions in the southern (slightly cooler) end of the Alexander Valley, where well-endowed Chardonnay and barrel-aged Sauvignon Blanc perform well.

Even more extreme in terms of elevation and rockiness, <u>Pine Mountain-Cloverdale Peak AVA</u> spills into Mendocino County from the northeast corner of the Alexander Valley. Once famous for its mineral-heavy spring water, this is high, remote country where Cabernet is king. Vineyards start at 500 metres (1640 feet) and top out at over 900 metres (3000 feet), hammered out of the volcanic rocks of the Mayacamas. Closer to the coast and bordering Mendocino, the northwest corner of the <u>Dry Creek Valley AVA</u> where it overlaps with the <u>Rockpile AVA</u> offers similarly extreme terroirs. Vines on ridges above the fog line plunge desperately into meagre, red-pebbly soils formed from iron-rich igneous rocks in search of sustenance. Although Lake Sonoma and proximity to the Pacific moderate the climate significantly, this is still bold red wine country.

OPPOSITE ABOVE *Harvest at Repris Wines, Moon Mountain.*

OPPOSITE BELOW *Impressive cellars at Repris: bored and blasted from volcanic hillside on Moon Mountain.*

SONOMA COUNTY – THE WINES & THE PEOPLE

Anaba Wines

60 Bonneau Rd
Sonoma
CA 95476
anabawines.com

John Sweazey turned his passion into a business with Anaba Wines. His focus is Pinot Noir and Chardonnay from Sonoma's cooler pockets, and Rhône varieties from warmer areas, including radical Bismark vineyard in the Moon Mountain AVA, one of the highest in the Mayacamas where even cover crops are tough to grow in the poor, rocky rhyolite soils and strong winds regularly shut down vine growth. Bismark Syrah is all black fruit with fully ripened tannins.

Anakota ★★

421 Aviation Blvd
Santa Rosa
CA 95403
anakota.com

Established by Frenchman Pierre Seillan at the turn of the millennium, Anakota is now one of the ultra-premium properties within the Jackson Family Wines portfolio, producing pure Cabernet from two single vineyards on the rugged volcanic slopes of the Mayacamas in the upper Knights Valley. Vines struggle more in the Helena Montana vineyard near 300 metres (950 feet) on a 30 degree slope, yielding a robustly tannic wine, more grippy and edgy, with detailed acid etching and dense dark fruit. Helena Dakota, just 60 metres (200 feet) lower, produces the richer, more opulent Cabernet, filled with masses of dark fruit and cherry liqueur, and velvety tannins. Both are excellent.

Arnot-Roberts ★★

33 Healdsburg Ave
Healdsburg
CA 95448
arnotroberts.com

Childhood friends Duncan Arnot Meyers and Nathan Lee Roberts united their destinies in 2001 to focus on small-lot, single-vineyard wines from contract vineyards that have since attracted a legion of fans for their counter-culture, minimalist, natural styling. A cult-favourite, pale and saline, delicate and transparent Trousseau, formerly entirely from the volcanic cobble of the Luchsinger Vineyard in Clear Lake AVA, is now blended with two other North Coast vineyards as of 2015. Poor volcanic soil, along with old, dry-farmed Cabernet, was the attraction to the Montecillo Vineyard, scratched out of a ridge atop the Mayacamas, eeking out exceptionally flavour-saturated Cabernet Sauvignon from naturally low yielding vines.

Benziger Family Winery

1883 London Ranch Rd
Glen Ellen
CA 95442
benziger.com

Mike and Bruno Benziger bought a ranch on Sonoma Mountain in 1980; by 2000 estate vineyards were certified biodynamic. Of the considerable, well-respected range sourced from throughout Sonoma (all wines are at least certified sustainable or organic) top volcanic contribution Obsidian Point Cabernet grows on an estate block over an ancient lava flow flecked with obsidian at the cooler southern end of Sonoma Valley, a slender, neatly-drawn example, unashamed of pleasant leafiness in cooler vintages, properly restrained.

Chalk Hill ★

10300 Chalk Hill Rd
Healdsburg
CA 95448
chalkhill.com

Bill Foley's stunning property on a natural amphitheatre carved into the hills of eastern Sonoma has a baker's dozen of different soil types in which volcanics play a large role, especially the white 'chalky' ash from which the AVA takes its name. Chardonnay is a consistent performer, crafted in a rich but balanced, satisfying and savoury style. Cabernet-based Estate Red is rendered in a full and bold style, pushing ripeness to the limits without tipping over.

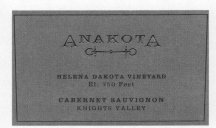

Lancaster Estate ★★

15001 Chalk Hill Rd
Healdsburg
CA 95448

lancaster-estate.com

One of Bill Foley's collection of premium estates, Lancaster's hillside vineyards lie at the southeast end of the Alexander Valley AVA, near the border with the Chalk Hill on mixed volcanic soils. Limited organic matter, 'allows you to dial in vine vigour, which is a huge advantage,' says winemaker Jesse Katz. Several dozen small blocks are harvested and vinified separately, the top lots of which go into signature Lancaster Estate Cabernet Sauvignon (with other Bordeaux grapes), a consistently cedary-spicy wine with opulent power tempered by appealingly gritty texture, and minimal oak influence. Samantha's Sauvignon Blanc, unusually without malolactic and bottled unfiltered, is one of Sonoma's most intriguing, a textural wine with fine richness and creamy texture tightened by bright acids.

Laurel Glen Vineyard ★★

969 Carquinez Avenue
Glen Ellen
CA 95442

laurelglen.com

Former Napa Valley Vintners Marketing Director Bettina Sichel bought the historic (1880s) Laurel Glen winery on Sonoma Mountain in 2011, the ultimate show of faith in Sonoma's volcanic terroir. Organically-farmed, shallow, well-drained, rocky andesite and basalt over old marine sediments are planted mainly to Cabernet, in particular the unique Laurel Glen clone originally planted on the property in 1968, later propagated for newer plantings (some 19th-century vines still exist). Pre-Sichel, Laurel Glen wines were notorious for needing a decade to soften, but she and winemaker Randall Watkins are aiming for a less intractable style, dropping yields and increasing ripeness and body along the way, a transition evident from 2012 forward. Yet the site naturally favours age-worthy wines, with high flavour at relatively low alcohol levels, firm but finessed. Counterpoint Cabernet Sauvignon is the earlier maturing 'second wine'; Crazy Old Vine Rosé from a remaining 1880s mixed row of vines is worth seeking.

Louis M. Martini ★

254 St Helena Hwy
St Helena
CA 94574   (*shown on Napa map*)

louismartini.com

Italian immigrant Louis Martini started a winery in the Napa Valley shortly after Prohibition was repealed. Nearly 70 years later, it attracted the financial might of E&J Gallo, who left third-generation vintner Mike Martini at the helm, doing things pretty much as he wants, 'but with more money'. Monte Rosso is the company's marquee vineyard purchased in 1938, a spectacular site (Mike was married there) above the fog line in the Mayacamas in the Moon Mountain AVA. Originally planted in the 1850s, a few 120-year-old+ mixed vines are still producing from its deep-red, iron-oxide-rich weathered volcanic soils, including some of the world's oldest, gnarly Cabernet Sauvignon. Monte Rosso Cabernet Sauvignon is full-scaled, bold and thoroughly ripe yet balanced in a modern style.

MacRostie

4605 Westside Rd
Healdsburg
CA 95448

macrostiewinery.com

Actively engaged in wine-growing since 1974, and under his own label since 1987, Steve MacRostie sources Pinot Noir and Chardonnay from a varied collection of celebrated vineyards in the Russian River Valley, Carneros, and especially Sonoma Coast AVAs. But some of his most-prized bottlings are produced from grapes he personally planted in the Wildcat Mountain vineyard in 1998, a cool, foggy, coastal, windswept volcanic terroir near the Petaluma Gap (Sonoma Coast AVA). Naturally low-yielding Wildcat Mountain Chardonnay bridges generous California fruit with the nervy, steely, minerally character of this edgy site, notably saline on the finish.

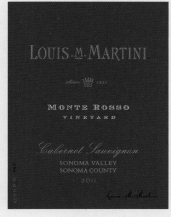
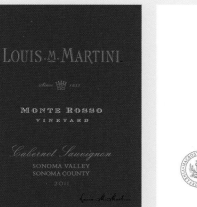

Mauritson Wines

2859 Dry Creek Rd
Healdsburg
CA 95448

mauritsonwines.com

With a grape-growing history stretching back to 1868, the Mauritson family finally got around to making wine in 1998. Pritchett Peaks Zinfandel is their fine volcanic offering from a vineyard in the Rockpile AVA on the eastern border of Lake Sonoma (bordering the original Mauritson homestead). Near the Healdsburg and Rodgers Creek Faults at the top of the Rockpile ridgeline, the vineyard differs from the rest of the family's holdings with its free-draining and windy eastern exposure and dramatic 30-degree rocky slope; Zinfandel is full-bodied, rich and fruity, with an underlying tannic backbone and a range of savoury flavours.

Paul Hobbs Wines ★★

3355 Gravenstein Hwy N
Sebastopol
CA 95472

paulhobbs.com

It's a wonder how Paul Hobbs manages it all: a successful international consulting business, a winery in Argentina (Viña Cobos) and two in California (Paul Hobbs Wines and Crossbarn), plus a wine importing business, among other projects. But everything is done at the highest level; no corners are cut and vineyards are given their maximum expression. With wines from Atlas Peak and Coombsville in Napa as well as Sonoma Mountain, he has much to offer the world of volcanic wines. The latter's north-facing Richard Dinner Vineyard Chardonnay on layers of volcanic tuff has been in the portfolio since the winery's founding in 1991. Harvested at sensible ripeness, wild fermented in barrel and bottled unfined and unfiltered, it's beguiling, rich and concentrated, full-bodied but balanced, the sort of wine you can cosy up to on a cold winter's night.

Pax Mahle Wine Cellars & Wind Gap Wines ★★★

6780 McKinley Street
Suite 170
Sebastopol
CA 95472

paxwine.com

windgapwines.com

Wine-buyer-turned-winemaker Pax Mahle was inspired enough by the wines he was sourcing for Dean & DeLuca to launch his own label in 2000. A risky initial focus on bold Syrah paid off, and he quickly developed a cult-like following. But seeing other possibilities, Mahle began experimenting on the side with cooler sites, earlier harvesting and non-mainstream grapes – wines for which he eventually created the Wind Gap label. The range now includes the fruit of several vineyards, 'influenced by one wind gap or another,' geological breaks in the coastal hills that allow cold Pacific wind to funnel inland. Very steep and stony Gap's Crown Vineyard Pinot Noir on the west side of Sonoma Mountain is Wind Gap's volcanic contribution, cooled by the Petaluma wind gap, yielding a wine of evidently muscular fruit tightly contained in a straitjacket of acids and tannins, deeply textured. The original Pax Mahle range has grown to cover Rhône varieties, from Paso Robles to Mendocino, the most volcanic of which is Southern Rhône-inspired The Vicar North Coast Red, Grenache-led with Mourvèdre and Syrah from the Mountain Terraces vineyard in the purely volcanic Moon Mountain AVA (on rhyolite), a hugely sweet-savoury, herbal red that manages impossible freshness at well over 15% ABV, suffused with salty rocks.

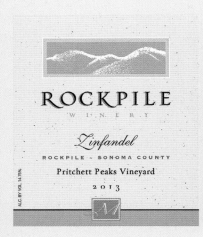

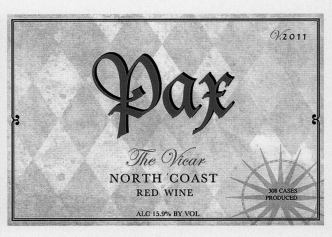

Pride Mountain Vineyards

Spring Mountain Rd
St Helena
CA 94574   *(shown on Napa map)*
pridewines.com

The historic Summit Ranch (planted in 1869) now owned by Jim and Carolyn Pride straddles Napa and Sonoma Counties atop Spring Mountain – the crush pad is bisected by a brick inlay that defines the county line – and so several of the all-estate grown wines carry a two-county designation. Goulding and Aiken soils dominate (formed from metavolcanic rock and basalts respectively) and high elevation brings both cooler average temperatures than the valleys on either side, and more sunshine above the fog line. Multiple lots for a dozen (mostly red wine) labels age in a cave dug out of the mountainside. Maximum impact is the aim: high ripeness, full-body, toasty oak and black fruit, as in creamy Napa Valley Cabernet and sweet-fruited Sonoma Valley Cabernet Franc.

Ramey Wine Cellars ★★★

25 Healdsburg Ave
Healdsburg
CA 95448
rameywine.com

David Ramey is among California's most admired winemakers, with a long past trajectory through top Napa and Sonoma wineries. Through it all he has championed a hands-off, artisanal approach, radically different than the UC Davis directives of the era. His eponymous operation was set up in the mid-90s (he still consults for several north coast clients), with a focus on top-end single-vineyard wines from both sides of the county line. Cole Creek is Ramey's source of Sonoma's volcanics, a vineyard tucked in a small valley

on the eastern edge of the Russian River Valley AVA with mixed gravels of volcanic origin, where Syrah ripens past the smoky/peppery phase into deeper, dark fruit while remaining taut and energetic. Pedregal vineyard ('rocky place' in Spanish), on the eastern slopes of Oakville AVA above the Napa floor and its iron-rich, red-basalt soils yields monumental dense and sumptuous Cabernet Sauvignon framed by graphite and scorched earth.

Repris Wines / Pangloss ★★

1700 Moon Mountain Rd
Sonoma
CA 95476
repriswines.com

The Moon Mountain AVA owes much to Repris winemaker Erich Bradley, who has been farming these rugged slopes of the western Mayacamas since 1999 and was instrumental in assembling the AVA petition. The spectacular property, a former hippie commune now owned by Jim Momtazee, has been organically farmed since 1996, and rises on undulating slopes to over 600 metres (2000 feet) above the Sonoma Valley on layers of iron-rich basalt and volcanic ash. The cellar is no less impressive, 5500 square metres (18,000 square feet) bored and blasted from the hillside on which the winery perches. Although Repris wines are sold exclusively at the winery (and to club members), they're worth the spine-tingling drive up; Cabernet Franc performs marvellously, reaching elegant floral heights. Merlot-based Right Bank blend offers velvety, inviting texture, plush but compact, while Cabernet is also at the highest level, especially Jennifer's Block, focused on firm elegance. Also fine Rhône varieties. Sister label Pangloss is for more immediately approachable wines, made from declassified lots and purchased (organic) mountain vineyard fruit.

Stonestreet Estate Vineyards ★★

7111 CA-128
Healdsburg
CA 95448
stonestreetwines.com

Another jewel in the Jackson Family Wines portfolio, the extensive vineyards and untouched natural terrain of Stonestreet's Alexander Mountain Estate cling to the high western ridge of the Mayacamas, overlooking the Alexander Valley. The Clear Lake Volcanic Field just eight km (five miles) away blanketed the area in rhyolite and tuff, layered over the older volcanic bedrock that underpins the mountains. Of the excellent range of vineyard-designated wines, Broken Road Chardonnay, from a tectonically active vineyard (the road up to it needs constant repair) has the most definitive volcanic sapidity, 'typically our most savoury, acid-driven wine,' says Jackson Family Wines Education Director Gilian Handelman. Steep Rockfall Vineyard Cabernet grows on the youngest, least-developed soils, composed of fractured basalts from an outcrop above that fell into place, with the evident density and gravitas conferred by struggling vines: savage and resinous, authoritative without being dictatorial. 'Extremely well-structured tannins and a savoury element separate it from our other Cabernet vineyards,' explains Handelman.

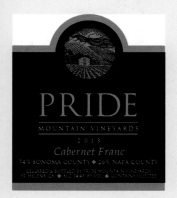
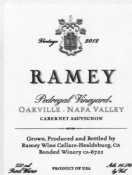

LAKE COUNTY

Standing on the top of Mt St Helena at the northern end of Napa Valley, looking north on a clear day you can see the volcanic cone of Cobb Mountain some ten km (six miles) to the northwest, the highest peak in the Mayacamas Mountains. Beyond it about the same distance lies Mt Konocti, the dormant volcano that looms ominously over the shores of Clear Lake, with Kelseyville in its morning shadow. These and other peaks, referred to locally as the Mountains of the North Coast, are where Lake County's best vines grow.

Yet there's a good chance you haven't heard much about Lake County wines. That's likely to change. There was once more grapevine acreage here than in either Napa or Sonoma, before Prohibition. And now, after a quiet period in the 20th century, interest in Lake County is once again on the rise, helped by both quality potential and more down-to-earth land prices than in the renowned counties to the south. If you're after authentic and age-worthy wines from California that aren't priced though the stratosphere, Lake County is a good place to start searching.

TRUE MOUNTAIN WINES

Not just volcanic soils, but also topography define Lake County's volcanic wines. These are 'mountain wines' in the truest sense, grown in some of the highest vineyards in California. Most of the county's vines are planted above 500 metres (1150 feet), and

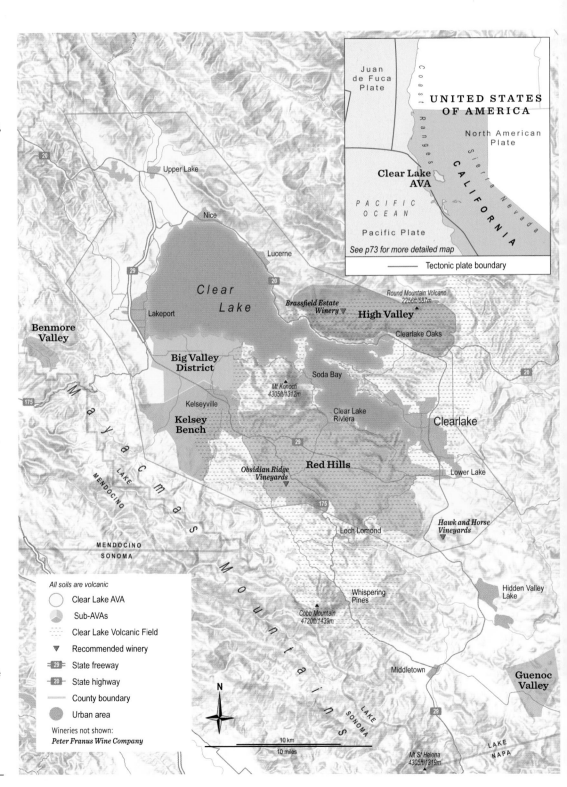

ABOVE (LEFT TO RIGHT) *Obsidian, Lake County; Obsidian Ridge Vineyards; Brassfield Estate Winery vineyards under Round Mountain volcano; obsidian;* *Brassfield Estate Winery; obsidian at Obsidian Ridge Vineyards; red volcanic soils, Hawk and Horse Vineyards; Obsidian Ridge Vineyards aerial view;* *Lake County diamonds; Hawk and Horse Vineyards; now what do we do... planting at Obsidian Ridge Vineyards; Obsidian Ridge Vineyards, Mt Konocti.*

some up to twice that. High elevation means drier and cooler, tempering the otherwise scorching temperatures for which Lake County is known. Cooling fog, so much a part of wine-growing elsewhere in California, is not a factor here, although cooler air masses occasionally drift in from the coast, keeping air moving and stripping out the worst of summer heat. Temperatures swing dramatically between day and night, hitting highs well over 35°C (95°F) before dropping off quickly to around 10°C (50°F) after the sun sets in the middle of the growing season.

Climate extremes mean that disease pressure is low. Cold winters knock back the population of troublesome pests, and humidity is also very low – typically around 20 per cent – so moulds and mildews are likewise reduced. As a result, Lake County uses fewer pesticides per acre than anywhere else in California. Some 15 per cent of vineyards are organic, and over 75 per cent of the 170-odd growers in the county are members of the California Sustainable Winegrowing Alliance.

Perhaps the greatest challenge for wine-growers is that the growing season is so compact – vines bud later and ripen earlier than in Napa or Sonoma. 'We're always hoping that the acids will relax and the tannins will fully ripen before the fall frosts,' Peter Molnar tells me (Obsidian Ridge Vineyards, and chair of the Lake County Winegrape Commission). Tannins also accumulate in abundance thanks to being so high up, where UV light is around ten per cent higher than what's measured at sea level. As the vine works to protect its seeds from intense sunlight, skins thicken and fill out with phenols – tannins and colour pigments – making the red wines of Lake County especially deeply coloured and firmly structured.

Lake County Grapes

Cabernet Sauvignon is the signature and most planted grape. Berries tend to be very small and concentrated, with high skin-to-juice ratio, which further reduces yields. A ton of Red Hills AVA Cabernet, for example, will net only about 500 litres (26 US gallons) of juice after pressing, which is about 100 litres (132 US gallons) less juice than an average ton of Cabernet from elsewhere in California, even from premium low-yielding Napa Valley vineyards. Factor in the especially thin and stony, extremely free-draining volcanic soils, high-diurnal swings that retain acids, and Lake County wines, especially the reds, can be downright burly and muscular. Like the mountain wines of Napa and Sonoma, these are rarely soft

and velvety wines, but rather built for ageing. Other red varieties planted include Petite Sirah, Merlot, Malbec, Mourvèdre, Grenache, Syrah, Cabernet Franc, Zinfandel and Tempranillo.

Sauvignon Blanc is Lake County's signature white grape, frequently rendered in a ripe, tropical fruit-inflected style; Chardonnay and Riesling are also grown.

Lake County Volcanic AVAs

Lake County lies within the North Coast AVA (which also includes Mendocino and Napa and Sonoma Counties), and has seven AVAs: Lake County AVA itself is the largest and encompasses the smaller Red Hills, High Valley, Big Valley District and Kelsey Bench, all around Clear Lake. Guenoc Valley and Benmore Valley lie isolated to the south and west respectively. Although the soils across the county are mainly volcanic, two AVAs (Red Hills and High Valley) stand out for their dominant volcanic character.

The vineyards of the **Red Hills-Lake County AVA** lie on the slopes of Mt Konocti where the particularly iron-oxide-rich, deep-red coloured variations on weathered basalts ('Aiken' soils) and obsidian ('Arrowhead' soils) was the inspiration for the AVA name. Molnar and other growers speculate that the highly available iron contributes to the firm character of Red Hills wine. Clear, semi-precious quartz crystals (Lake County Diamonds to locals) are also a unique feature of the region, found only scattered in the soils around Mt Konocti.

The name of the **High Valley AVA** on the north side of the lake opposite Mt Konocti is rather appropriate; even the valley floor lies at nearly 600 metres (2000 feet) above sea level, the same elevation as Howell Mountain. Round Mountain Volcano, a satellite cinder cone of Mt Konocti in the eastern end of the valley, erupted and filled the valley with volcanic debris to a level over 130 metres (425 feet) above Clear Lake. The Valley's east-west orientation, one of the few in California, combined with elevation makes it one of the cooler regions in the county. Like the Red Hills AVA, volcanic soils here are very well drained, deep red and are composed mainly of medium-grade basalts, andesites and gravel-like scoria particularly rich in calcium, iron and magnesium. Though not all the vines are planted on volcanics; the western part of the appellation lies on uplifted shales from the Franciscan Formation (see p.54). The red wines of High Valley show a slightly more genteel nature, less angular in youth than those from the Red Hills, judging by current examples.

OVERLEAF *Obsidian Ridge Vineyards, under Mt Konocti.*

OPPOSITE *Brassfield Estate Winery's Volcano Ridge vineyard in the High Valley AVA, under Round Mountain Volcano.*

LAKE COUNTY – THE WINES & THE PEOPLE

Brassfield Estate Winery

10915 High Valley Rd
Clearlake Oaks
CA 95423

brassfieldestate.com

Jerry Brassfield purchased land in High Valley for a cattle ranch and wildlife reserve in 1973, eventually planting vineyards in 2001. About half is on purely volcanic soils, according to winemaker Jason Moulton, including 40 ha in the Volcano Ridge Vineyard on Round Mountain. 'There's a noticeable difference,' says Moulton. 'Volcanic wines can age better than anything else grown on this property. There's a perception of minerality. It's not a taste, but more of a density, a feeling, a dusty-earthy, structural element,' he finishes. Eruption is the fine entry into the volcanic range, a zesty, balanced blend of Syrah, Malbec, Mourvèdre and Petite Sirah. Volcano Ridge Vineyard Malbec highlights the grape's floral-violet character, with appealingly soft tannins that still lend enough grip – arguably the best performer in the vineyard.

Hawk and Horse Vineyards ★

13048 CA-29
Lower Lake
CA 95457

hawkandhorsevineyards.com

A Demeter-certified, organic/biodynamic ranch on the upper slopes of Mt Konocti run by Tracey and Mitch Hawkins. Vines planted in 2001 are irrigated with spring water and cover crops grow between rows to add much-needed organic matter to thin, rocky soils. Yields are low and wines

highly concentrated, slow to evolve. Flaghsip Cabernet Sauvignon, one of Lake County's best, has class and elegance, with fruit corralled by a streak of iron and distinctively dusty Red Hills tannins. Port-style Cabernet Sauvignon is a curiosity, fortified with artisanal pot still brandy, firm and unyielding, surely long-lived.

Obsidian Ridge Vineyards (Tricycle Wine Partners) ★★

23568 Arnold Drive
Sonoma
CA 95476

tricyclewine.com

A Lake County leader with 40 ha planted high up on Mt Konocti in 1999 and 2000, on an abandoned walnut orchard with volcanic soils littered with obsidian – over 250 tons, some pieces up to 20 or 30 kg (45 to 65 lb), were removed for planting. Brothers Peter and Arpad Molnar partnered with winemaker Michael Terrien in 2003 to form Tricycle Wine Partners, incorporating the Molnar family's Poseidon Vineyard in Carneros with Obsidian Ridge. Half is bottled, the remaining grapes are sold. Molnar recalls the steep learning curve, 'in the early years we did three-week soaks on Cabernet, the standard recipe in California. But tannins were off the charts.' The wines include dense and brooding Estate Cabernet Sauvignon and The Slope Cabernet Sauvignon, more finely etched and intricately woven, from the steepest, highest elevation parcels. Top cuvée Half Mile Proprietary Blend (Cabernet Sauvignon/Petit Verdot) is made in suitable vintages from top blocks yielding what could almost be called elegant and refined. Syrah is also noteworthy.

Peter Franus Wine Company ★

PO Box 10575 Napa
CA 94581

peterfranus.com

Peter Franus is surely better known for his excellent wines from Napa Valley, but his Lake County foray is superb. He started working with Red Hills fruit in 2007, 'one of my best growers had taken a gamble and purchased a spectacular property on top of Cobb Mountain,' Franus recounts. 'Soils are thin and drain instantly. Elevation places vines well above scorching summer heat, and exposes them to cool Pacific breezes, with a dramatic temperature drop at night. Grapes develop intense flavour and colour. The quality of fruit is special, and that's thirty years of experience talking!' Franus makes a single, excellent Syrah/Grenache/Mourvèdre blend, succulent, ripe but fresh – genuinely complex and deep. Pure Mourvèdre is planned.

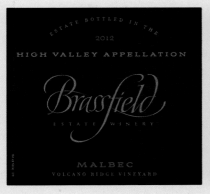

CHILE
THE ANDEAN VOLCANIC BELT

The Cordillera de los Andes is the Earth's longest, still-growing mountain chain that stretches 7000 km (4300 miles) from Venezuela to Tierra del Fuego along the western edge of South America. Within the range is a staggering number of volcanoes, collectively part of the Andean Volcanic Belt. Chile alone is home to some 500 volcanoes including the world's highest, the active Ojos del Salado near the Atacama Desert at 6893 metres (22,615 feet). Both the mountains and the volcanoes within them arise from the same phenomenon: subduction of the oceanic Nazca and Antarctica Plates under the continental South American Plate, converging at a sprightly eight cm (three inches) per year. As elsewhere along the Pacific Ring of Fire, tectonic pressure has crumpled the continental margin, thrusting up the majestic Andes and the more modest Coastal Range, while the sinking and melting crust has also supplied monstrous magma chambers with the necessary fuel to find issue and burst forth on the earth's surface.

The simply named 'Southern Volcanic Zone' (SVZ) is the most active segment of the Andean Belt in Chile, running from Santiago (33°S) to Patagonia (46°S) and thus looms over the vast majority of Chile's considerable vineyard acreage. At least 123 volcanoes are considered active, having erupted at least once in the last 10,000 years. Chile's last major volcanic event was in 2015, when the energetic stratovolcano Villarica 750 km (460 miles) south of Santiago erupted in mildly explosive fashion. Slipping faults along plate frontiers likewise give rise to frequent earthquakes, like the one that rocked southern Chile on February 27, 2010 – the sixth largest ever recorded at magnitude 8.8, centred near the city of Concepción. With an average of one eruption per year in the SVZ, Chile is surely a safe bet among the countries chronicled in this book to make the next headlines for volcanic or seismic activity.

OPPOSITE *Viña Koyle's biodynamic vineyards in the Andean foothills of the Alto Cachapoal Valley.*

Itata | Wine region
Andes zone
Entre Cordilleras zone
Costa zone
Predominantly volcanic soil
▼ Recommended winery
5 Highway
160 Main road
Country border
Regional boundary

Wine companies not shown:
Bodegas Volcanoes de Chile
Cono Sur
Luis Felipe Edwards
Santa Carolina
Viña Koyle

— Tectonic plate boundary

PACIFIC OCEAN
Nazca Plate
South American Plate
Antarctica Plate
CHILE
Atacama Desert
Ojos del Salado 22 549ft/6873m
Southern Volcanic Zone
Andean Volcanic Belt
Patagonia
Pacific Ring of Fire

100 km
100 miles

Map labels:

Aconcagua
Viña von Siebenthal ▼
San Felipe
Aconcagua 22 837ft/6961m
Los Andes
Viña del Mar
Valparaiso
Casablanca
Algarrobo
SANTIAGO
San Antonio
San Antonio
Volcán San José 19 127ft/5830m
Leyda **Maipo**
Rancagua
Altair ▼
Rapel Alto Cachapoal
MontGras ▼ *Casa Silva* ▼
San Fernando
Colchagua
Viu Manent ▼
Volcán Tinguiririca 14 041ft/4280m
Curicó
Curicó
Constitución
Volcán Peteroa 13 418ft/4090m
Talca
Laberinto Wines ▼
Linares
Cauquenes
Maule
Campanario 12 929ft/3941m
CHILE
ARGENTINA
Itata
Chillán
Talcahuano
Concepción
Clos des Fous ▼
Cacique Maravilla ▼
Cabrero
Punta Lavapié
Volcán Chillán 10 538ft/3212m
Chos Malal
Bío-Bío
Los Angeles
Volcán Antuco 9773ft/2979m
Lebu
Malleco
Victoria
Isla Mocha
Volcán Longuimay 9399ft/2865m
Temuco
Zapala
Pitrufquén
Cautin
Lake Villarica
Volcán Villarica 9340ft/2847m
Lanco
Región Austral de los Andes
Lake District
Valdivia
Punta Galera
Volcán Mocho-Choshuenco 7946ft/2422m
Lake Ranco
Volcán Puyehue-Cordón Caulle 7335ft/2236m
Osorno
N
ANDES
PACIFIC OCEAN

CHILE – AN EXPLOSIVE FUTURE

With its suave Mediterranean climate and fertile soils, Chile has been a wine-growing paradise since Spanish conquistadores first arrived with grapevines in the mid-16th century. It's also the most volcanically active wine-producing country in the world, a volcanologist's utopia. But oddly, at least as far as this book is concerned, this fact has so far largely escaped Chilean wine-growers. Many of Chile's great volcanic terroirs have yet to be exploited. So consider this chapter as just the tip of the volcano – the real story has yet to be written. But when it is eventually penned – and the wine industry is evolving very rapidly in this most conservative of South American countries – it will be a modern epic.

Searching for Chile's Volcanics

When I meet Pedro Parra in Talca, about halfway between Santiago and his home in Concepción, he greets me with a quizzical look. 'But why volcanic soils?' he asks with genuine bewilderment. 'In Chile they are some of the worst for grapes.' Parra is a self-described 'terroirist', a vineyard consultant who has dug pits, analyzed soils and made recommendations to dozens of clients internationally as well as a who's who of Chilean companies, in addition to a couple of wine projects of his own, so he knows what he's talking about. 'Always the worst cuvées are the volcanic ones; I avoid volcanic clays,' Parra finishes. But he's referring mostly to the past and current state of volcanic affairs, not the future.

Despite Chile's alarmingly active and widespread volcanism, and abundance of volcanic soils, most of the country's vineyards are concentrated in the fertile Central Valley between the Andes and the Coastal Range, south of Santiago and north of Concepción, away from the direct

ABOVE (LEFT TO RIGHT) *Vineyards on the Colchagua Valley floor; Manuel Moraga, Cacique Maravilla; LFE 900 Project vineyards; Santa Carolina's Piedras Pizzaras vineyard; Laberinto Wines, Alto Maule; Cono Sur Rulos del Alto vineyard, Bío-Bío Valley; Cristobal Undurraga, Viña Koyle; Laberinto Wines, Alto Maule; MontGras Ninquén estate; organic Matetic vineyard, San Antonio Valley; Cacique Maravilla's 200-year-old+ País vines; MontGras Ninquén estate.*

influence of volcanic rocks and ash. The soils of the Central Valley are largely alluvial – mixed eroded material carried by rivers into the depression from the surrounding hills, and colluvial (rocks and dirt transported by landslides and earthquakes). There is volcanic influence, but it's heavily 'contaminated' with widely varying geologies and especially the wrong type of heavy clays, with poor drainage and low available minerals. Add in overabundant sunshine, and overirrigation and fertilization, and the result is unbalanced wine, at once jammy and green, excessively soft and alcoholic, with no mineral *élan*. These are the 'bad' volcanics.

But the 'good' volcanics lie in the hills and in the deep south. 'In stony volcanic soils, quality goes up 100 per cent,' Parra tells me. 'Basalt, andesite, tuff... it doesn't matter, you go immediately to other level, you get more depth, tension and the kind of minerality I really like.' But only a few of these sites have been exploited in the past. The future is another story.

Chile's Wine Regions

Much recent investment has gone into planting vineyards in the Andean foothills, from the Aconcagua to Maule Valleys, where soils are far rockier, frequently of volcanic origin, with all of the attendant benefits like free-draining, fast-warming and low fertility/organic matter, as well as the coolness and lower humidity that comes at higher elevations. Look for the recent complementary mention 'Andes' or 'Alto' attached to the name of a valley in the Denominación de Origen (DO), Chile's appellation system, as in **Alto Cachapoal DO**, for the wines most likely to be volcanic. The odd lateral extension of the Andes Volcanic Belt into transversal valleys, as in the **Colchagua Valley**, also offers both elevation and stony, volcanic soils, some of which are already under vine, and although the Coastal Range is mostly built on granite, the eastern flanks facing the Central Valley are covered in the 86-million-year-old lavas, tuffs, ash and breccias of the Lo Valle Formation. Given Chile's dry, Medeterranean climate, these ancient volcanic rocks are barely weathered.

ABOVE *Volcanic rocks in Luis Felipe Edward's LFE 900 project vineyards, overlooking Colchagua Valley.*

OPPOSITE *Santa Carolina's exceedingly rocky and steep Piedras Pizzaras vineyard in Totihue, Alto Cachapoal.*

The deep south is equally exciting, for both climate and soils. For Parra, where we are in Talca is roughly the dividing line between the sunny, warm north and the cool, cloudy south, where he believes some of Chile's best terroirs have yet to be planted. Less sunshine means less vine stress, and irrigation is not necessary. And, 'south of Maule is where the real basalts, "good volcanics", start,' he states.

So far, only Sebastian and Marco De Martino and their trail-blazing winemaker Marcelo Retamal have planted vineyards in these rocky basalts. The site, in Chile's Lake District 800 km (500 miles) south of Santiago in the pre-Andes hills near volcanic crater Lake Villarica and the hyperactive volcano of the same name, has experimental plots of Pinot Noir, Chardonnay and Riesling. The first wines are imminent – and where De Martino leads, others will follow.

Volcanic ash from the Antuco and Lonquimay volcanoes, among others, has also rained heavily in southern Chile, giving rise to a specialized soil type called locally *trumao*, especially abundant in southern **Maule, Bío-Bío, Itata, Malleco**, and even further south in the **Región Austral**, 900 km (560 miles) from Santiago, where Casa Silva's lonely Lago Ranco vineyard lies in the shadow of the active Mocho-Choshuenco and Puyehue-Cordón Caulle Volcanic Complexes. New and rediscovered old vineyards in these regions are already yielding exciting wines. It's a challenge to get anyone to live and work that far from the capital, but enough enlightened companies have taken the first important steps, and the future looks indeed bright in the cloudy, volcanic south.

Chile's Grapes

Cabernet Sauvignon is Chile's most planted red by a wide margin, even if Carmenère is considered a signature. Merlot, Syrah, Malbec, Pinot Noir, and Cabernet Franc round out the headliners by acreage, though interest in Mediterranean varieties like Carignan, Mourvèdre and Grenache is (logically) growing. Once-derided País (the Canaries' Listán Prieto) was the first grape planted in Chile, and is enjoying a fashionable renaissance. Chardonnay is the most planted white, followed closely by Sauvignon Blanc, often excellent value. Newcomer Viognier shows promise, and I'd also expect to see other Mediterranean white grapes emerge in the future, such as Grenache Blanc, Marsanne, Roussanne and Picpoul, already being experimented with and so naturally well suited to Chile's climate. Interest in Riesling has been revived thanks to the shift to cooler areas, especially in the south.

CHILE – THE WINES & THE PEOPLE

Altaïr (Viña San Pedro) ★

Fundo Totihue
Camino Pimpinela s/n
Requínoa
Cachapoal
altairwines.com

Chilean giant Viña San Pedro's icon estate
and wine of the same name Altaïr is a mix
of volcanic soils in the Alto Cachapoal Valley.
Up to 80 parcel vinifications are made each year
from soil variations before the final assemblage.
Winemaker Marco Puyo's preferred soil profile
is composed of alluvial gravel deposits from the
Andes over volcanic-andesitic bedrock, with a
mix of flint, mica-schists and calcium carbonate,
the grapes from which are used for Altaïr, a wine
of immense power and dark fruit, cinched by
suave tannins. Less performing parcels (heavier
clays), wind up in the second wine, Sideral.

Bodegas Volcanes de Chile

volcanesdechile.com

The 'boutique' winery within the Grupos
de Vinos del Pacifico (also owners of Viña
Undurraga), created in 2009 to produce wines
from soils of volcanic origin. Winemaker María
del Pilar Díaz describes her whites as having
'firm natural acidity, gun-powder scents and
minerality'. Reds have, 'great structure, lots
of tannin and graphite.' Summit Reserva is the
entry range; Tectonia represents the 'truest
volcanic expressions', as in tight and grainy
Tectonia Pinot Noir from sandy basalt in Bío-
Bío. Robust Parinacota Syrah/Carignan is the
top of the range, named after the volcano in the
extreme north of Chile, but grown in the south.

Cacique Maravilla

Viña 33
Yumbel
Bío-Bío
caciquemaravilla.cl

Manuel Moraga Gutierrez's vineyards in Bío-Bío
on deep *trumao* soils host País vines believed to
be over 250 years old, brought by his ancestors
from the Canary Islands. Viticultural is beyond
organic; only sulphur is dusted sparingly, and
winemaking follows ultra-natural principles.
Unfined, unfiltered, unwooded, wild fermented
País Pipeño is pure and infinitely drinkable.
País-based Capricci (with Cabernet Sauvignon
and Malbec), fermented in ancient 7000-litre
(1850-US gallon) Rauli vats, is excellent.

Casa Silva ★

Hijuelas Norte s/n
PO Box 97
San Fernando
casasilva.cl

Colchagua-based, family-run Casa Silva has
blazed the southern-most trail in Chile with
their Lago Ranco vineyard in the Región Austral
near the town of Futrono, planted in 2006. The
region's high rainfall is managed thanks to the
sloping site and free-draining *trumao* soils
mixed with pyroclastic rocks. Sauvignon Blanc
is lean, more saline than fruity, distinct from
examples grown further north. Pinot Noir,
Chardonnay and Riesling are due next.

Clos des Fous ★★

2 Norte 385 Lonco Oriente
Chiguayante
Concepción

Vineyard consultant Pedro Parra puts his money
where his mouth is with this personal project,
in league with three equally crazy ('*fou*') partners.
Only extreme terroirs – high-altitude, outer-
coastal, or deep-southern – at the margins of
ripening are sought to produce distinctive wines,
successfully. Traiguén vineyard in the Malleco
Valley, 700 km (430 miles) south of Santiago,
is the source of Pinot Noir Latuffa, a challenging,
resinous, dried-spice and smoke-tinged wine
with typical firmness and succulence, and iron-
like minerality from volcanic tuff. Grillos
Cantores vineyard in the Alto Cachapoal on
alluvial volcanics laced with limestone offers
pure and fresh (no malo) Chardonnay Locura 1.

Cono Sur ★

conosur.com

A large company admired for its sustainable/
organic, and, in some parcels, biodynamic
vineyards, Cono Sur's Single Vineyard range
includes two volcanic wines: dry-farmed Block
Nº23 Rulos del Alto in the cool Bío-Bío has
the oldest Riesling in the valley (1983) planted
in red clay *trumao* soils, yielding high-intensity
jasmine and fresh-stone-fruit flavours, made
essentially dry. Merlot Block Nº14 Suelo Blanco,
grown on stark white *pumacita* soils (tiny
pumice stones) in coastal Colchagua, is
unusually lithe and light-footed.

Laberinto Wines ★★

Campo lindo
Rivera Sur
Lago Colbún Km 14
Maule
laberintowines.cl

Early volcanic grower Rafael Tirado started planting this small, premium estate in 1993, driven by the goal of making 'wines with extreme personality'. The cooler climate and rocky *trumao* soils of the Alto Maule were deciding factors in selecting this unproven region on the sloping shores of Lake Colbún in the Andean foothills. Sauvignon Blanc is among Chile's best, firmly built on naturally high acids, infinitely more stony than fruity. Also fine Pinot Noir and age-worthy Cabernet-based red blend.

Luis Felipe Edwards ★★

lfewines.com

Luis Felipe Edwards Sr pioneered Chile's highest vineyards under the 'LFE 900 project', with vines up to 900 metres (2950 feet) above the Colchagua Valley on an extension of the Andean Volcanic Belt now yielding some of Chile's best grapes. Freshness and natural balance are promoted by a longer maturation cycle, while stony volcanic soils encourage low yields and dense structure. Mediterranean grapes thrive, evinced by the flagship LFE 900 Single Vineyard red blend (Syrah, with Petit Sirah, Monastrell, Grenache and Tempranillo), a marvellously savoury wine.

MontGras

Camino Isla de Yáquil s/n
Palmilla
O'Higgins Region
Colchagua
montgras.cl

Ninquén is MontGras's volcanic 'island mountain' vineyard in the Colchagua Valley, part of the eastern Coastal Range volcanic sequence with tuffs, lavas and volcanic breccias. The best parcels have the shallowest topsoil where yields are barely half those on the valley floor, and the wines tighter and naturally balanced. Antu Syrah is lively, refined and floral; Ninquén red blend (Cabernet Sauvignon with one-third Syrah) is elegant and attractively herbal.

Santa Carolina

santacarolina.cl

Santa Carolina purchased the volcanic and schist Piedras Pizarras vineyard in Totihue, Alto Cachapoal, in 2012 for its Specialties range from unexplored terroirs. The very steep, rocky, relatively cool hillside has a mix of notably acidic soils, 'three to four times more expensive to farm than the valley floor,' reveals chief winemaker Andres Caballero. The inaugural, as yet unreleased, Cabernet Sauvignon shows tremendous elegance, floral perfume, and consummate natural balance, a wine to anticipate.

Viña Koyle

koyle.cl

The Undurraga family farms their volcanic-andesitic vineyard in Los Lingues (Colchagua-Andes DO) biodynamically, and interfere minimally in the winery. Wines are ripe and intense. Royale is the top range, and dark-fruited, plush yet structured Syrah the most impressive, from the thinnest and stoniest upper terraces.

Viña von Siebenthal ★

Calle O'Higgins s/n
Panquehue
Aconcagua
vinavonsiebenthal.com

One of the few truly volcanic projects north of Santiago, founded by former Swiss lawyer Mauro von Sibenthal in 1998. Wines are extreme, aimed at the top level. Half of the estate's soils are classified as andisols (of volcanic origin), including the Parcela 7 block yielding an intensely flavoured Cabernet Sauvignon based blend, plus top Carmenère Tatay de Cristóbal, a dense, hyperconcentrated but balanced wine.

Viu Manent ★

Carretera del Vino Km 37
Cunaco
Colchagua
VI Región
viumanent.cl

A rare east-west extension of the Andean Volcanic Belt in the Colchagua Valley gave rise to the prized El Olivar vineyard, clinging to the steep, rocky hillside. Andesite underlies red clays, thinning at higher elevations to almost pure rock in winemaker Patricio Celedon's favourite parcels. Syrah El Olivar shows uncommon freshness and refined structure. Malbec Secreto highlights the grape's floral character in a lighter and highly drinkable style.

MACARONESIA
THE FORTUNATE ISLANDS

Early Greek geographers described the mid-Atlantic volcanic landmasses west of the Straits of Gibraltar as *makaron nesoi*, 'the islands of the fortunate'. Today, Macaronesia refers to the archipelagos of the Azores and Madeira (Portugal), the Canary Islands (Spain) and the island nation of Cape Verde. All were important staging posts on maritime trading routes that developed from the 15th century onwards, for merchants heading to the East Indies and westward to the newly discovered Americas. The earliest European settlers brought grapevines, and all, save Cape Verde, became famed wine producers; a fresh supply of wine was part of the islands' allure. Many singular wines styles, especially fortified wines, originated on these islands, arising from the combination of their unique volcanic terroirs, the great distances between ports of call and the extreme ageing conditions of wine-filled barrels in the gently swaying, warm, humid cargo holds of ancient sailing vessels plying the Seven Seas.

ABOVE *Arriving at Pico Island, Azores, with unmissable volcanic peak, Pico Mountain, rising above the clouds.*

OPPOSITE Currais *in Lajido da Criançāo Velha zone, Pico Island: UNESCO-designated world heritage site.*

THE AZORES (OR AÇORES)

There's a massive rift zone in the mid-Atlantic that stretches from north of Iceland to south of Capetown. The sea floor along this fault line is being ripped apart as the Americas slowly drift away from Europe and Africa at the blistering pace of 2.5 cm (1 inch) per year. The resulting deep cracks in the earth's crust have allowed mass quantities of magma to seep out onto the sea floor from profound depths, and over time a submarine mountain range as grand as the Rockies has been built up. The Mid-Atlantic Ridge is now the longest submarine mountain chain in the world.

In a few remote places, the growing mounds of lava have reached the surface of the sea to form islands. Iceland, Ascension, Saint Helena and Tristan de Cunha, along with the Azores, are among the nascent archipelagos raised along the Mid-Atlantic Ridge.

The Azores is an autonomous region of Portugal consisting of a nine-island archipelago between 37° and 39°N latitude, about the same as Lisbon and Atlantic City, New Jersey. Depending on the island, it's about 1500 km (900 miles) to the European continent and nearly 4000 km (2500 miles) to the closest point of North America, but the spread between the islands is sizable:

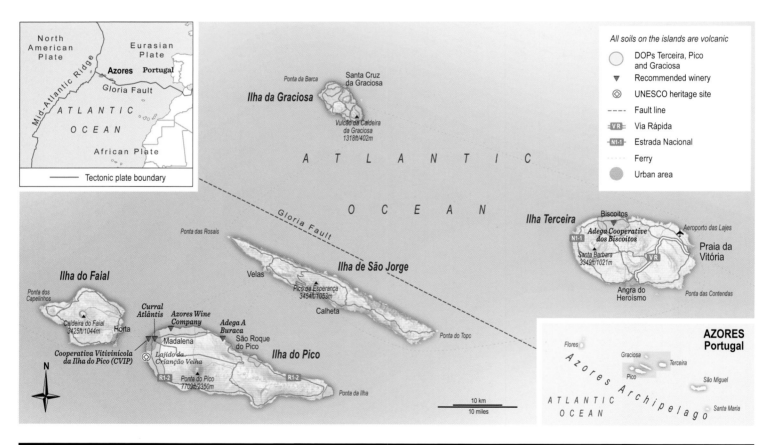

OPPOSITE (LEFT TO RIGHT) *Angra do Heroísmo, Terceira; crossroads on Terceira; layers of lava on Terceira; Biscoitos vineyards, Terceira;*

Pico Island from the air; vineyards on Pico (twice); Paulo Mendonça props up a Verdelho vine in Biscoitos; Pico Island 'port' for loading wine to ship to Faial for

export; Pico vineyards from the air; Biscoitos Co-op, Terceira; Angra do Heroísmo, Terceira.

600 km (370 miles) separate Santa Maria in the east from Flores in the west. And the distance between islands in increasing. Flores and Corvo sit on the eastward drifting North American Plate, while the rest sit in the rift zone between the Eurasian and African Plates, along the so-called Gloria Fault. The latter is floating southwest while the former moves northeast.

In addition to being a highly active zone of volcanism, this complex triple junction of moving tectonic plates and associated rifts is also one of the most seismically energetic places on earth. Virtually everyday there is a minor earthquake somewhere around the islands, and more occasionally a major one. Statistically there has been a volcanic eruption in the Azores every 50 years, and since the last one occurred in 1957 on Faial, the archipelago is scheduled for another volcanic outburst any time.

STRADDLING THE MID-ATLANTIC RIDGE

Of all the wine regions chronicled in this book, the Azores have the longest road ahead to notoriety. Despite 500 years of wine production, and international renown up to the early part of the 19th century, the current generation knows little about the volcanic wines of this Portuguese archipelago. First there were downy and powdery mildew, two devastating fungal diseases from the Americas, and then phylloxera. By the 1860s, quality wine had been all but wiped out. Sensitive *vitis vinifera* grapes were replaced with hardy North American varieties and hybrids, and the wine they produce, called *vinho de cheiro*, is a dark legacy for all but nostalgic émigrés. Today, production is tiny and the wines are far from uniformly impressive. But their fascinating story is worth including in this journey.

Moreover, the region is not static. Aside from being volcanically active, the spark of wine renaissance, and in some cases just plain naissance, is growing in intensity. The raw materials are present in the form of three original varieties, Verdelho, Arinto dos Açores and Terrantez do Pico, and a supremely volcanic terroir. Prominent wine-growers from outside the Azores have already taken notice of the quality potential hidden under barren basaltic stones. The EU's mission to safeguard and develop important heritage has not forgotten the Azorean wine industry, nor has the protective fold of UNESCO overlooked its patrimony-worthy vineyards. New plantings are in the ground and old ones have been rehabilitated. In time, the surely distinctive wines of the Azores will find their champions.

Azores' Grapes & Wines

Among dozens of planted grapes, three traditional white varieties stand out. Arinto dos Açores, the most widely planted (but different from the Arinto of the mainland), is a jolt of acid and citrus flavour. Verdelho is marvellously aromatic, botanical and fruity, while Terrantez do Pico, the rarest (and not the same as the Terrantez of Madeira), fuses herbal, floral and green citrus notes with mineral salts and seaweed. All three are used to make both dry and sweet wines, alone or in blends. Rare reds and rosés are made from unlikely grapes like Cabernet Sauvignon and Merlot for the local market, though interest in Saborinho (aka Tinta Negra Moll) for lively, characterful reds is growing.

Out in the middle of the Atlantic, the ocean shows all its unmitigated mightiness, and the cool, wet and windy climate wields the most influence over wine style. Regardless of variety, when rendered in dry, fresh versions, young Azorean whites are tangy and electric, variations on sweet green herbs soaked in brine with citrus in myriad shades liberally sprinkled with sea salt. They have a charm and beauty of their own. But the traditional-style *vinhos licorosos* are the most original. Made in dry (*seco*) and sweet (*doce*) versions, occasionally fortified, (the *licoroso* category doesn't mean sweet necessarily; the official designation goes by alcohol and texture), these generously alcoholic, wood-burnished, salted-caramel-flavoured wines belong in museums along with other 16th-century volcanic relics like Madeira or Tokaji Szamorodni to protect a drinking experience that is in danger of extinction.

Wine Regions of the Azores

Though small quantities of wine are produced on almost all of the islands, only three, Terceira, Pico and Graciosa, have DOP wine regions. However wine production on Graciosa (under the DOP Graciosa) is anecdotal, and the wines rarely, if ever, make it off the island. PGI Açores covers wine produced anywhere in the archipelago.

Terceira (literally 'third') is the third largest island in size, and is home to **DOP Biscoitos** one of the Azores' three DOP wine regions. From the air the island looks like a deep green sponge rimmed by black – the basalt rock edges forming low cliffs down to the sea. Like all relatively young volcanic islands (c. 2.5 million years), there are virtually no beaches. The west end of the island is dominated by the large volcanic crater of Santa Barbara, the

highest point on the island at a modest 1023 metres (3356 feet). The volcano's last eruption was 1761, though submarine vents just off shore were active as recently as 2000.

When I arrive on the island I'm met by Paulo Mendonça, the president of the cooperative winery of Biscoitos, the island's largest and only really export-equipped winery, and the winemaker Nuno Costa. During the short drive to the village, I see no vines. Mendonça, noticing my disappointment, admits that grape-growing is not a priority on Terceira. 'But just wait,' he says. And when we reach Biscoitos, I catch a first glimpse of some of the strangest vineyards I've ever seen.

It's only a small area, but one of the most singular vineyard landscapes on the planet. On the gently rolling hills beneath the village is the most amazingly geometric, chessboard-like pattern of squared-off, dry stonewalls fashioned out of lumpy basalt rocks, each surrounding a few wild-looking, bushy vines. 'These are the *curraletas,*' Mendonça announces, without disguising his pride. Literally 'little corrals' these enclosures protect the vines from the buffeting winds and salty sea spray of the Atlantic, with the added advantage of absorbing and radiating heat back to the vines, a necessary ripening aid in this rather cool maritime climate. 'The size of the *curraletas* is determined by the quality of the ground,' Mendonça continues. 'The poorer the ground, the smaller the *curraleta.*'

The land around Biscoitos is desperately poor. Indeed, there's virtually no soil, just crushed rock. How do vines survive, I wonder. It's like growing a plant in a jar of pebbles. Even when it rains, there's nothing to hold the water. The answer lies beneath, in the deep root system of the vines and in the volcanic geology of the island. Successive lava flows created laminate-like strata of rock between which water runs. The hills above Biscoitos are covered with sponge-like sphagnum moss that absorbs up to ten times its weight in water, which is then released slowly into the ground, trickling down and then flowing between the sheets of lava, eventually reaching the vineyards where deeply rooted vines have plunged their roots in desperate search of moisture. It's like natural underground irrigation. Later I see miniature streams of water emerging from the rock faces down by the coast, as though the walls were weeping. This 'mineralized' water also carries enough dissolved mineral nutrients to sustain the vines.

The wine of Terceira has never commanded much attention. But Mendonça, unsurprisingly, has an explanation for their past reputation of mediocrity. 'The vineyard area is tiny,' he says, pointing out the obvious. 'The old farmers were great viticulturalists, but with so few grapes, they wanted to squeeze out every last drop to stretch production. They were terrible winemakers working with great grapes.'

Nuno Costa and a small handful of other winemakers on Terceira, however, are good winemakers. And from such an extraordinary place, authentic and original wine can be made.

Pico is the youngest island in the Azores, just 300,000 years above the sea, and the one with the most area under vine covered by the **DOP Pico**. The formation of the island along a roughly east to west fault line is clear: there's a remarkably evenly spaced string of volcanic cones that punctuate the land east of Pico Mountain in a near straight line. From above, it looks like a freshly made belt with holes poked through the leather at regular intervals. Pico Mountain on the far west end of the island is the last, and by far the largest, hole in the belt.

Western Pico has the youngest volcanic soils on the island, and some of the youngest in the archipelago. Soil has not even had time to form on the most recent lava flows. As is often the case, vines were planted in this inhospitable area called Lajido da Criação Velha where nothing else would grow; arable land elsewhere was reserved for food.

The first grape-growers used iron bars and mason's mallets to deepen and widen natural crevices in the rock. Soil had to be brought from the neighbouring island of Faial and poured into the cracks to support vines. As on Terceira, the stones pried out of the ground were piled up to form protective walls. But the scale here is vaster, over ten times the vineyard size of Biscoitos, some 250 hectares. The larger enclosures, here called simply *currais* (corrals), also have different architecture, though serve the same purpose.

It is this remarkable cultural landscape, itself corralled between the sea and the imposing peak of Pico, that was inscribed into UNESCO's World Heritage list in 2004. It's the recognition of a totally unique lanscape, and of the sheer will, or necessity, of humans to eke something out of inhospitable volcanic rock in a hostile climate. The wines produced here, too, are worth protecting.

OPPOSITE ABOVE Currais *of the Lajido da Criação Velha on Pico Island: walls are offset in a zigzag pattern so there is no direct cross-flow of wind.*

OPPOSITE BELOW LEFT *Steady, mild temperatures and humidity encourage funghi and sprays are a* sine qua non. *Everything is done by hand.*

OPPOSITE BELOW RIGHT *Pillow lava formations where lava flows met seawater on Pico Island.*

THE AZORES – THE WINES & THE PEOPLE

Adega A Buraca

Estrada Regional 35
9940-232 Santo António
São Roque do Pico
Açores
adegaaburaca.com

Leonardo Ávila Silva, a radiologist by profession, runs this small family business. Only two wines are made: the 100 per cent Arinto Curraleta white IGP is a dry, old-school, oxidative, honeyed white, compellingly savoury. The Vino Licoroso Seco DOP from Verdelho and Arinto dos Açores, weighing in at 17% ABV, is a true relic, triangulated between amontillado Sherry, Marsala and Madeira. Although dry it gives an impression of sweetness, with lovely burnished-wood and salted-caramel flavours – a style worth preserving.

Adega Cooperative dos Biscoitos

Canada Santo António
9760-051 Biscoitos
Açores

The largest winery on Terceira, with 50 members, is still tiny by any measure. Magma is the company's top brand, a perfectly crisp, crunchy, citrus-salty blend of Verdelho plus 15 per cent Terrantez. A one-off project in 2011 with Anselmo Mendes, respected winemaker from the Minho region in northern Portugal, yielded perhaps Terceira's best wine in modern times. Muros de Magma (Walls of Magma), a pure Verdelho fermented in wood, has an attractive creamy, sharp, tangy texture and signature saltiness.

Azores Wine Company ★★

Rua Dos Biscoitos 3
São Mateus
Madalena
Pico
Açores
azoreswinecompany.com

Established in 2014, Antonio Maçanita is the winemaker and dynamic force here (also owner of Fita Preta in the Alentejo and consultant in Portugal). This is the Azores' best hope for export success. Both the Arinto dos Açores DOP Pico and the Verdelho 'O Original' PGI Açores under the Rare Grapes Collection show the fine tuning of an experienced but not overbearing hand. There is also a project to resurrect the near extinct Terrantez do Pico variety; the highly promising experimental wines made so far on San Miguel island by Maçanita show an engaging mix of herbal, floral, green citrus and salty flavours.

Cooperativa Vitivinícola da Ilha do Pico (CVIP)

Avenida Padre Nunes da Rosa 29
9950-302 Madalena
Pico
Açores
picowines.net

This is the largest producer in the Azores, founded in 1949, with 236 members covering 90 per cent of the UNESCO designated vineyard area of Lajido da Criação Velha. Terras Lavas is the competent entry range (white, rosé and red), while the Frei Gigante DOP Pico Branco, made from Arinto dos Açores with a splash of Terrantez do Pico and Verdelho, is fragrant and herb-scented, named for the father of grape-growing on Pico, friar Pedro Gigante. Lajido Reserva Doce Pico DOP is a rich but well-balanced, marvellously complex wine, aged eight years in barrel to simulate the ageing conditions on ancient sailing ships.

Curral Atlântis

Travessa do Valverde
9950-365 Madalena
Pico
Açores
curraldeatlantis.pt

Marco Feria started Curral Atlântis in 1995, now one of the more serious operations on Pico. After unconvincing early trials with non-Azorean varieties, Feria replanted endemic white grapes, but continues to make Merlot and Cabernet for local interest. Colheita Selecionada, a Verdelho/Arinto dos Açores blend, is a highlight, relatively soft, with wide appeal. Néctar dos Currais DOP Pico Doce is a medium-sweet, pleasantly rustic wine with almost 19% ABV (but unfortified), aged six years in wood.

Czar de José Duarte García ★

zeduarte.com

Fortunado Duarte García, like his father José before him, makes only one wine: Czar. The brand name was chosen when García learned that Pico wine was discovered in the Winter Palace in St Petersburg after the Bolshevik revolution. It's harvested late when half the grapes – Verdelho, Arinto and Terrantês (aka Terrantez) – are raisined, then wild fermented in old wood (Garcia recounts an extreme vintage that reached an impossible 21.5% ABV without fortification), and aged five years in cask before bottling. The wine is a mind-bending play of dry toasted nuts and sweet, honeyed fruit. 'But,' says Garciá, 'there's a big inconvenience. I can't make the same wine every year. Every year is completely different.'

MADEIRA

Strategically located in the North Atlantic Ocean 1000 km (600 miles) from mainland Portugal and 500 km (300 miles) from Morocco, Madeira was once one of the world's most important ports. The multi-isle archipelago, of which Madeira itself is the largest, is made up of the southernmost tips of a vast volcanic iceberg that spans 200 leagues under the sea. The submarine ridge is the result of a presumed buckle in the African Plate, which in turn is likely caused by a hotspot of welling magma under the lithosphere.

The islands jut sharply out of the sea while the sides plummet into the marine abyss. Between Madeira and nearby Porto Santo, the only other inhabited island, the sea is over 2 km (1.25 miles) deep. This contributes to Madeira's famous diversity of fish, and frequent visits from dolphins and whales. The island's exposed rock has been eroding for over 18 million years since it first emerged from the sea, cutting steep, spectacular valleys at semi-regular intervals over the island's 57 km (35 mile) length and 22 km (14 mile) width. A near-permanent array of fluffy white clouds, and a few ominous

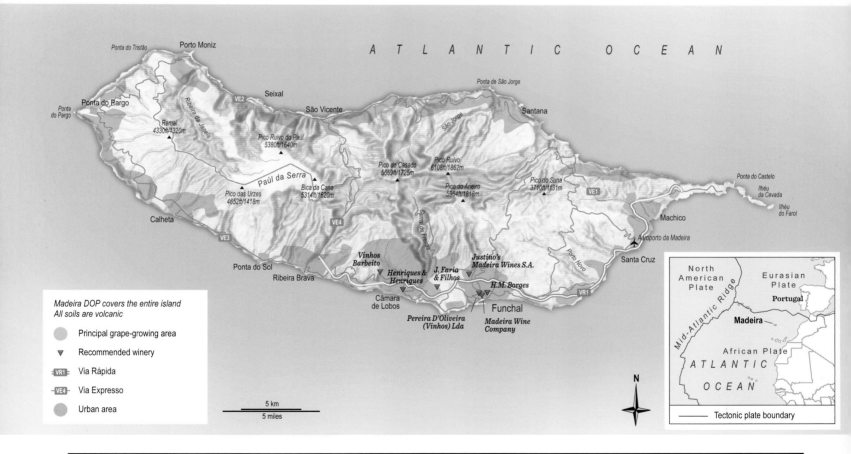

Madeira DOP covers the entire island
All soils are volcanic

- Principal grape-growing area
- ▽ Recommended winery
- VR1 Via Rápida
- VE4 Via Expresso
- Urban area

5 km
5 miles

OPPOSITE (LEFT TO RIGHT) *Vineyards on Madeira's north side; rare Bastardo Madeira, Barbeito; Blandy's Lodge bottle stash; old Madeira shipping vessel;* *Câmara de Lobos; Madeira's eastern tip; Câmara de Lobos; Humberto Jardim, Henriques & Henriques; Madeira's south side; walking Madeira's levadas;* *old Madeira tasting at IVBAM, Sercial 1862; still-operational fishing boast, Câmara de Lobos.*

dark ones, cover the craggy peaks of the interior of Madeira, as though Velcroed to the heavily forested mountainsides. Thus cooled and moistened, the climate determines a style of wine quite unlike any other, where barely ripe grapes are transformed by ingenious methods into the most long-lived wines on earth.

While driving through one of the many dozen freshly-built tunnels that perforate the island like Swiss cheese, I notice that the asphalt in places is rippled like corduroy. Why are these recent road projects as rough as country lanes? The answer, I'm told, is buckling caused by pressure from gases beneath the road. Although volcanic activity on Madeira petered out about 6,500 years ago and is believed to be extinct, engineers discovered the trapped gases while digging the tunnels. Presumably, the gases emanate from deep within the island. Perhaps Madeira is just slumbering after all.

DRINKING HISTORY

Madeira is the name given to a fortified wine made from specified grapes grown on the island of Madeira. It's aged using a peculiar heating process, unique in the world, born accidentally thanks to the island's fortunate mid-Atlantic location and the wine's original destiny as an export product. The complex production regulations are now enshrined in the **DOP Madeira**. Though there are many wines with a deep connection to history, none can claim as ready and direct a link to generations past as the grand old wines of Madeira. This 550-year-old wine recalls the great age of exploration, the Renaissance, and the beginnings of trade with the Americas and India, when sailors challenged the wild waters of the Atlantic in search of fortune. Known for its legendary longevity, casks and bottles of Madeira dating back to the late 18th century still rest in the lodges of Funchal, and in no small measure. I'd wager that the island has greater stocks of century-old wines than anywhere else on earth.

In the earliest days, Madeira was a major supplier of sugar to Europe. Sugarcane, brought originally from Sicily, was the island's most important crop and the main source of wealth earned by the first settlers in the 15th and 16th century. Cheaper exports from Brazil would later erode Madeira's European markets, inadvertently setting the island on a path to wine production. Vineyards replaced most sugarcane plantations, and the product of what remained was transformed from refined to distilled form. It would be the combination of wine and sugarcane spirit that would transform Madeira wine into the ultimate sea-worthy beverage, which in turn would carry Madeira's name to the four corners of the earth and ensure the worldwide fame of this tiny volcanic rock in the Atlantic.

Cascading down the steep ravines running out to the coast are a series of near-continuous, narrow green terraces called *poios*, punctuated by the terra cotta roofs and white walls of houses clinging to the hillsides. Each narrow strip of sloping land is held in place by dry stonewalls to prevent precious soil from washing down to the sea. Each small plot is meticulously cultivated, all by hand out of necessity. Most land remains in the hands of smallholders, and all of the island's wine producers without exception purchase grapes.

Considering the small allocation of arable land per household, it's not surprising that locals have adopted a form of vineyard trellising that maximizes land use. *Latada*, the name given to this traditional pergola-like system, is a lattice of horizontal wires supported by wooden stakes on which vines are trained, creating a roof of shoots and leaves parallel to the ground. The height of the pergola, ranging from about 1 to 2 metres (3 to 6 feet), depends on the elevation of the vineyard: the higher up, the lower the pergola to the ground. This helps to regulate ripening, as average temperatures drop as you move up hillsides, and grapes trained closer to the ground benefit from the stored and reflected heat off soil and stones. Vines planted at the very highest viable elevations nearing 800 metres (2600 feet) are grown practically on the ground, a system called *vinha do chão* (vine of the ground) to get that critical ripening nudge. Additionally, *latadas* allow airflow under the canopy to mitigate the high disease pressure of Madeira's warm, moist climate. But the real advantage for farmers is that they also allow for other crops to be planted underneath grapevines.

The heavy weathering of Madeira's basalt bedrock has yielded famously fertile soils, and farmers, for example, get three crops of potatoes per year instead of the two typical on mainland Portugal. The vigorous volcanic soil is also partly the origin of Madeira's rather prolific vineyards, with maximum permitted yields set at a staggering 150 hl/ha. This is three times the average for quality vineyards elsewhere. But, as we shall see, Madeira is just as much a wine of process as vineyard, and high yield/lower ripeness are indeed desirable.

Madeira's Grapes

At last count there were about 450 hectares of European vinifera varieties in production, a fraction of the acreage in the glory days of Madeira, but again on the rise. The main varieties include the black-skinned **Tinta Negra**, by far the most important variety. That it accounts for 85 per cent of wine production yet covers only 55 per cent of planted land, reveals its main advantage: productivity. It's also more resistant to mildews and fungi, and is stylistically versatile. Tinta Negra is the only variety that can legally be produced in all of Madeira's official sweetness categories. It accounts for nearly all of the three and five year age-indicated wines, and has historically been considered second-rate; until early 2015, the name was not even permitted on the label. But shippers such as Vinhos Barbeito, Justino's and Henriques & Henriques, believe in its potential, so expect to see fine quality, vintage-dated Tinta Negra Madeiras on the market.

White **Verdelho** is the next most planted grape, one of the historic 'noble varieties'. It's one of the easiest grapes to fully ripen, which accounts for its particularly ripe, tropical-fruit flavours, and why it's also preferred for the small but growing production of dry white table wine. Madeira Verdelho is produced exclusively in a medium-dry style. The aromatic, white-skinned **Malvasia**, the island's oldest variety, was brought from Greece (from the port of Candia in Crete) via Sicily in the 15th century. 'Malmsey', as Malvasia is also known, makes the richest, sweetest style of Madeira.

Sercial is grown mainly on the north side at high elevations, up to 700 metres (2296 feet), and is usually the last grape to be harvested. It's appreciated for its razor-sharp acidity and makes the driest style of wine produced on the island. **Boal** (aka Bual), on the other hand, is produced only in a medium-sweet style. When young, it offers a waft of fragrant pear and apple fruit, but with age it turns particularly smoky and tobacco scented, like a cedar box full of Havana cigars.

Bastardo is the only other red-skinned grape permitted for Madeira production, though plantings are anecdotal. And while the white-skinned **Terrantez** is likewise a footnote in production statistics, it lives on as one of the most legendary and sought-after grapes on the island. Bottles and casks of old Terrantez are treasured like family heirlooms. The variety's pale, thin skins make it highly susceptible to disease. One grower relates having had a vineyard full of perfect, nearly ripe Terrantez, only to return

While journeying through the interior of the island I marvel at another feat of engineering, the complex and extensive system of irrigation channels called *levadas*, from *levar*, meaning to carry. Aside from dense vegetation and mountainous terrain, water availability was another obstacle to viable farming. Although rainfall is generous overall, distribution is uneven. As on Tenerife in the Canary Islands (see p.120), the moisture-bearing prevailing winds arrive from the northeast and slam into the steep cliffs on the north side of Madeira where they drop their load, some 3000 mm (120 inches) of rain yearly. The hills on the south side receive only about half that amount, while the lower south coast where the majority of people live sees a scant 500 mm (20 inches) yearly. Water for irrigating crops and vineyards is thus redistributed from north to south through this ingenious network of over 2500 km (1500 miles) of mini-aqueduct *levadas* that criss-cross the island, dating back to the 16th century and still in use today.

Although it would be fair to assume that the grapes grown on the cooler, wetter north side of the island would be tangier and less ripe, paradoxically, the average ripeness is higher. Winemaker Juan Teixeira of Justino's explains that the typical polyculture practiced on the south side has the effect of increasing grape yields, since the land is constantly fertilized and watered throughout the year for crops other than grapes. And, as virtually everywhere else on the planet, higher yields result in lower average ripeness. Fewer inhabitants on the north side means less pressure on land use, and thus many parcels are dedicated to vines alone, and the even steeper topography also makes combined grape and vegetable farming less practical. The net result is vineyards with lower yields and higher degrees of ripeness.

ABOVE *Vines trellised on high* latadas: *allows air to flow and other crops to be planted underneath.*

OPPOSITE ABOVE *The steep cliff faces of Madeira's north side and Angel's Hair Falls.*

OPPOSITE BELOW *Seixal village with terraced* poios *above: north sees up to six times more rain than south.*

a couple of days later to harvest and find that every single bunch had rotted. But, it's one of the most beguiling of all Madeiras, traditionally (and now legally) made in medium-dry or medium-sweet styles.

Madeira's Winemaking: Influence of Volcanic Soils

In a sense, Madeira shares a lot in common with Champagne. For both, a relatively neutral, high-acid, low-alcohol wine is transformed through lengthy processing into a radically different product, so much so that the starting point becomes virtually indiscernible in the end point.

To make Madeira, grapes are harvested between the end of August and early October at no more than 9% to 11% ABV. Wait for higher ripeness and you run the risk of loosing the entire harvest to regular autumn (fall) rains. In any case, the high acidity of barely ripe grapes is one of the secrets to Madeira's ability to survive the unusual heating process to which it is subjected, and age magnificently afterwards.

Madeira wine's low pH (related to high acidity) can also be attributed in part to the chemistry of the volcanic soils, and their deficiency in acid-buffing potassium: less potassium in grape must translates to lower pH in wine. The soils themselves are also highly acidic (low pH), which 'creates a struggle for grapes to fully ripen', according to Teixeira. Although soil and wine pH are not directly connected, the absorbtion of macro and micro elements by vine roots is heavily influenced by soil pH. In the case of Madeira, the

acid soils result in slower sugar accumulation. If Madeira were a chunk of limestone, for example, the wines would be dramatically different: riper, but also less age-worthy, and less able to withstand the heating-oxidizing process, Teixeira hypothesizes. Madeira as we know it would never have existed.

Madeira is also fortified, which in turn means that the transformation of harsh malic acid into lactic acid that many other wines undergo – called malolactic fermentation – is inhibited. This further accentuates its acidic but life-preserving character. Madeira is practically indestructible, a wine that defies time. And unlike most other wines, which turn smooth and mellow with age, Madeira grows more concentrated and fiery during its long sojourn in wood.

Madeira Heating: Estufagem & Canteiro

Two critical modifications to Madeira were made during the 18th century. First, sometime around the middle of the century, it was discovered that wine was far more apt to survive long sea voyages if blended with high-proof alcohol, in this case the sugarcane spirit produced then, as now, on the island. From this point on Madeira would become a fortified wine. Shortly thereafter, it was noticed that Madeira improved considerably during these long sea voyages, rolling and sloshing in the tropical heat and humidity of the holds of sailing ships navigating across the equator and back.

Thus was born the *vinho da roda*, or round trip wine. Merchants took to shipping barrels of Madeira to India and back for the sole

---

purpose of enhancing wine quality and raising its value. But the practice was both very expensive and evidently limited in scope, and demand quickly outstripped supply. Shippers sought cheaper and scalable alternatives to replicate the conditions on board sailing ships. In 1794 Fernandez Pantaleão hit upon a method of controlled, gentle but rapid heating in a system he devised called the *estufagem,* from *estufa,* meaning stove or hothouse. Pantaleão's *estufagem* consisted of a set of coils within a large wooden ageing vat through which hot water was run to indirectly heat the wine. This is still the system in use today for less expensive Madeira, even if the technical specs have improved. Top-quality wines, on the other hand, are aged in the naturally warm upper lofts of warehouses called *canteiros,* occasionally for up to several decades.

Madeira Styles: Decoding the Label for Sweetness

The profusion of styles, ranging from virtually dry to fully sweet, bottled at various stages of ageing, from a single harvest or a blend of different vintages, with or without the name of a grape variety and a host of other 'traditional' mentions on the label, are confounding to say the least. But the Madeira Wine Institute (or more correctly IVBAM – Instituto do Vinho, do Bordado e do Artesanato da Madeira), strictly controls production from vineyards to bottle to labelling – neither a bunch of grapes nor a drop of wine moves, nor a bottle sold, without the institute's approval. The regulations are thus strictly defined.

All Madeira comes in one of the officially-regulated sweetness categories listed below. The approximate sugar levels are helpful for context (though the official measurement is in degrees Baumé). Keep in mind that Madeira's high acidity makes even the sweetest wines taste drier than other wines with the same amount of residual sugar (sugar left after fermentation, measured in g/l). It can be confusing that the name of a grape on a label also indicates a sweetness level. The reason for this anomaly is that over the course of centuries, the main grapes became closely associated with distinct styles. So when the official regulations were drawn up, authorities simply codified the traditions of the past.

Dry or Extra Dry (*Seco*): 50 to 60 g/l; Extra Dry has less than 20 g/l. All wines made with Sercial fall in this category.
Medium Dry (*Meio Seco*): 60 to 80 g/l. All wines made with Verdelho and some Terrantez fall in this category.

Medium Sweet or Medium Rich (*Meio Doce*): 80 to 100 g/l. All wines made with Boal and some Terrantez fall in this category.
Sweet or Rich or Full Rich (*Doce*): 100+ g/l. All wines made with Malvasia fall in this category.

Madeira's Age: What the Numbers Mean

Madeira can be either a blend of vintages, or from a single harvest, but all are at least three years old – the legal minimum.

Blended wines come with an age designation of 5, 10, 15, 20, 30, 40, 50 or over 50 Years. Like tawny port, the number indicates neither the actual age nor the average of the wine, but rather that the wine 'displays the characteristics of a wine that has been aged for the indicated period of time'. If it sounds confusing, that's because it is. Complexity and overall quality rise as the age indication increases.

Vintage Dated Wine is from a single harvest and can be labelled as Colheita (harvest), along with the vintage year, after it has aged at least five years in wood. In practice Colheitas are aged for much longer. Single-vintage wines that have spent at least 20 years in wood and aged exclusively in a *canteiro* are entitled to the mentions Frasqueira (literally, a place where you store wine) or Garrafeira. Both Colheitas and Frasqueiras must also mention the year of bottling on the label, an important piece of information that tells you how long it likely spent in wood, and how long it has been in bottle.

Solera is yet another mind-bending category, a sort of hybrid single-vintage blended wine. It's reserved for wines that are initially from a single harvest and aged at least five years in wood (in a *canteiro*). Then after the five-year period, a maximum of ten per cent of the volume can be removed within any calendar year (and sold theoretically as a Colheita) and replaced with a younger wine of the same variety. But the ten per cent draw from the solera can only be carried out a maximum of ten times over the course of the wine's lifetime. The bottle bears the mention 'Solera', along with the vintage of the first lot laid down.

A number of other traditional mentions can appear on the label, the legacy of centuries of unregulated wine production and common usage in various languages:

Reserva, *Velho,* Reserve, Old, *Vieux*: 5 Year age indicated Madeira.
Reserva Velha, Reserva Especial, *Muito Velho*, Old Reserve, Special Reserve, Very Old: 10 Year age indicated Madeira.

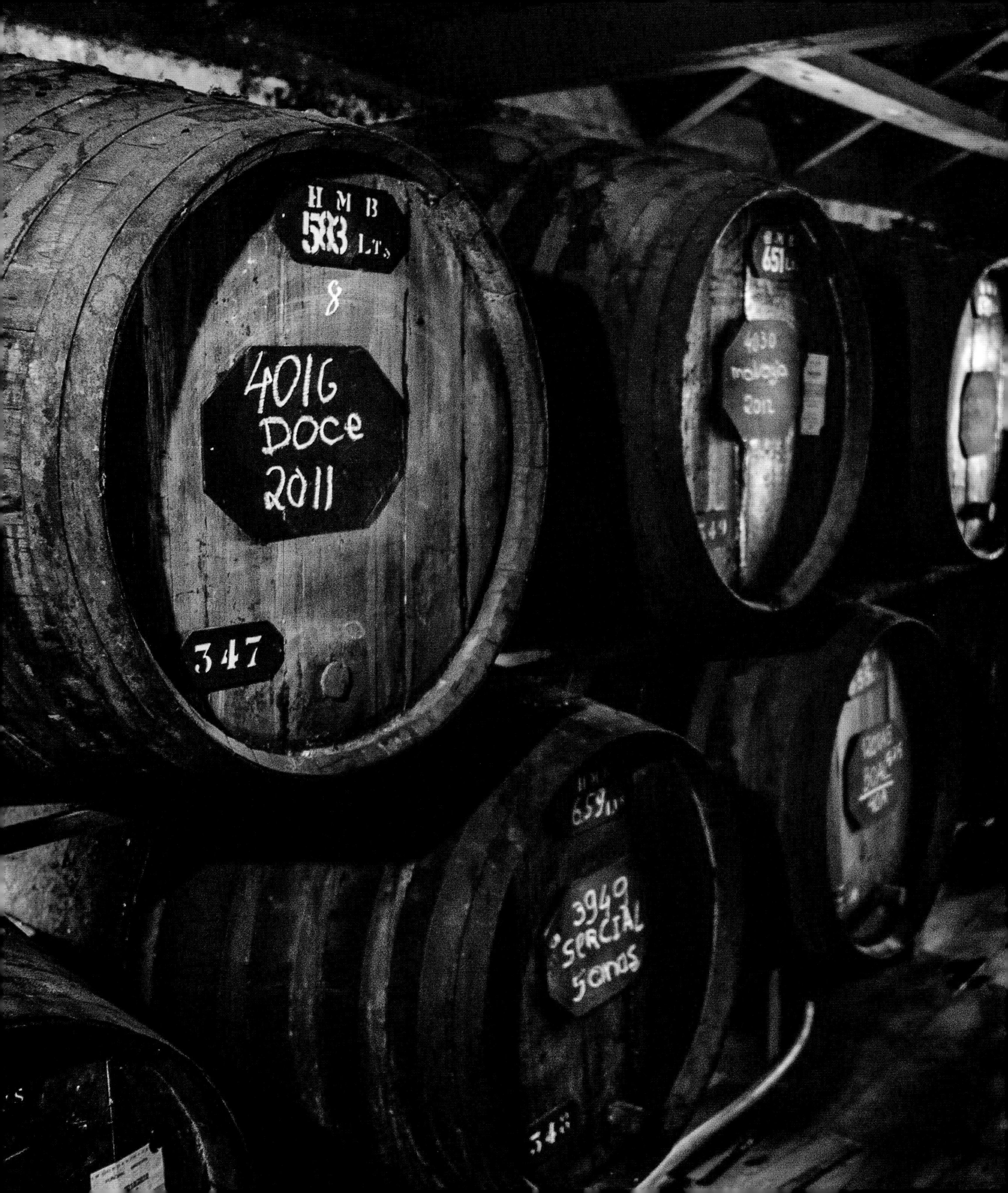
H M B
583 LTs
8
4016
Doce
2011
347
3940
SERCIAL

Reserva Extra, Extra Reserve: 15 Year age indicated Madeira. **Fine, Finest,** *Seleccionado,* **Selected, Choice**: unregulated mentions that appear alongside any of the other official ones above, such as Finest Rich Reserve for a sweet, five year age indicated Madeira. These terms are usually applied to wines deemed superior in their given age/sweetness category.

Rainwater is an historic term for a particular style of wine. According to legend, a shipment of Madeira casks headed to the USA was left on the Funchal beach to be collected. Heavy rain fell before the casks were picked up, and the wood absorbed water, diluting the wine. After initially complaining, the buyer found that the wine was well received and requested more. Today, this designation is reserved for pale or light-gold-coloured, medium-dry Madeira, with an indication of 10 Years or less.

Dry Table Wines under the DOP Madeirense and IGP Terras Madeirenses appellations for red, white and rosé (unfortified) wines are more recent (1999 and 2006 respectively). Whites are made mostly from Verdelho and reds/rosés from Tinta Negra and an unlikely handful of late-ripening grapes like Cabernet Sauvignon, Merlot and Touriga Nacional. The wines, so far at least, are of local interest only.

The Madeira Shippers

Today, there are just seven commercial producers of Madeira (an eighth, the Adega Cooperativa, is on its way), though in Madeira's heyday there were up to three dozen. Most producers make wine under several brand names – as well as producing wines for lines of buyers' own brands – which gives the illusion that there are more. Since virtually all vineyards are in the hands of growers (only Henriques & Henriques and the Madeira Wine Company own any acreage of consequence), and most grape-growers sell to several producers, everyone is working essentially from the same base material. The notable differences in style between the various shippers and their brands stem thus from the production process and ageing conditions.

ABOVE *The tasting room at Pereira D'Oliveira, housing the greatest stocks of old wines on the island.*

OPPOSITE *Funchal, the capital of Madeira on the main island's south coast in the twilight. About one million tourists visit Madeira each year.*

MADEIRA – THE WINES & THE PEOPLE

H.M. Borges ★ ★

Rua 31 de Janeiro 83
9050 Funchal
hmborges.com

Main Brands: H.M. Borges, Adega Exportadora de Vinhos da Madeira, Borges Madeira Lda., Araújo, Henriques e Ca. and J.H. Gonçalves

Isabel Borges is the fourth generation in the Borges family to run the company founded by her great grandfather, Henrique Menezes Borges, in 1877. The house style is understandably traditional, on the drier side of the spectrum, aiming for balance rather than opulent grandeur. A lower temperature *estufagem* is favoured and the wines are of very good quality across the board. The Verdelhos in 10, 15 and 20 Year age designations are particularly compelling, the latter offering silky texture, energetic acidity and tremendous length. Borges makes no table wines; Isabel finds the trend alarming since Verdelho is already in limited supply. 'In the past it was easy to buy Verdelho, but the last five years have been more difficult,' she laments. Considering the beauty of Verdelho Madeira and the modest quality of table wine, the concern is justified.

Henriques & Henriques ★

Sítio de Belém
9300-138 Câmara de Lobos
henriquesehenriques.pt

Main Brands: Henriques & Henriques, Belem's Madeira, Carmo, Veiga Franca, Casa dos Vinhos de Madeira, Antonio Eduardo Henriques, Silva, buyer's own brand for Sandeman's

Henriques & Henriques (H&H) is one of the oldest producers still operating on the island, established in 1850 by João Gonçalves Henriques, even if it was purchased in 2011 by the French group La Martiniquaise. The company has a large modern facility and owns 17 hectares of vineyards, including nearly all the Terrantez on the island. H&H has agreements with several Scotch and Irish whisky producers to 'season' barrels for them, so some Tinta Negra spends about two years in new wood. It's then used, as MD Humberto Jardim reveals, as a seasoning twist to blends. No style distinction is made between brands – only the label changes. 'As early as the 1930s several brands were needed to cover the markets – even within the same market,' Jardim explains. The price of each brand does change, however, so, go with the least expensive one you can find. H&H sits in the middle of the sweetness spectrum, in a modern, widely appealing, approachable style with relatively low acidity. The pale, extra-dry Monte Seco is an H&H invention for the apéritif category, made from Tinta Negra. Several Colheitas are made from both Tinta Negra and the white skinned varieties, and a special treat is the 20-Year-Old Terrantez, a medium-dry, single lot blended from five vintages. Solera Madeiras are also a house speciality.

J. Faria & Filhos

Travessa do Tanque 85/87
9020-258 Funchal
jfariaefilhos.pt

Latecomers to Madeira wine, J. Faria is a company specializing in rum, liqueur, brandy and fruit juices. Wine production began in the 1990s. The majority is sold on the island, and, so far at least, three and five year old entry-level wines make up the vast bulk of production.

Justino's Madeira Wines S.A. ★

Parque Industrial da Cancela
9125-042 Caniço
justinosmadeira.com

Main Brands: Justino's, Colombo (table wine and madeira), East India Madeira, buyer's own brand for Broadbent, Madère Cruz

Justino's is Madeira's largest producer and exporter, accounting for nearly half of production, with the largest stocks of Madeira wines, some two million litres (five million US gallons). Originally established in 1870, French group La Martiniquaise took a majority position in 1993. Of the company's brands, Madère Cruz is the most basic, made for the French market. Broadbent, a buyer's own brand launched by British wine critic Michael Broadbent, is at the softer and sweeter end of the spectrum for the US and UK markets. Justino's, the main brand, is light and finessed, not the most complex or dramatic wine on the island, but balanced with wide appeal. The Colheitas are a real treat, always made in a rich style and selected from the best lots of Tinta Negra.

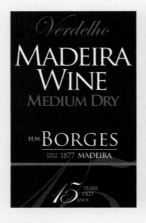

Madeira Wine Company ★

Rua Dos Ferreiros 82
9000 Funchal
madeirawinecompany.com

Main Brands: Blandy's, Cossart Gordon, Leacock's, Miles

The mid-sized Madeira Wine Company is the result of multiple mergers and acquisitions over the last century. The main driving forces behind the company were the Blandy and Leacock families, who amalgamated their interests in 1925. Today, the Blandy family is the majority shareholder, and Blandy's is the flagship brand, originally established in 1811. It occupies the premium price segment along with Cossart Gordon, which lays claim to being the oldest Madeira shipper – established in 1745. Leacock's falls between, while Miles has become the company's supermarket (grocery store) brand. The company is headquartered in the Blandy's Wine Lodge in central Funchal, built on the site of a 16th-century convent, and was the first to produce Colheita Madeiras – mainly to fill the price gap between 15-Year age-indicated and vintage-dated Frasqueiras. Alvada was another innovation, a 5-Year-Old rich blend of Malvasia and Boal launched under the Blandy's label in 2002 with radically modern packaging aiming to draw in younger consumers and to shed Madeira's stuffy image. It's a soft, sweet and seductive wine full of burnt orange, dried fruit, honey and caramel, which accurately represents the Blandy's range – the sweetest in the company's portfolio. Cossart Gordon sits at the other end, offering a more concentrated, intense, drier style, such as the deeply-coloured 10-Year-Old Verdelho.

Pereira D'Oliveira (Vinhos) Lda ★★★

Rua Dos Ferreiros 107
9000-082 Funchal
perolivinhos.pai.pt

The small, family-run house of Pereira D'Oliveira is the most extreme producer in Madeira, holding steadfastly to tradition and drawing on the largest stocks of old wines on the island. The style is immediately recognizable: very complex, deeply structured, highly concentrated and challenging, always seemingly older than the wines of other shippers in the same age categories. The business was founded by João Pereira D'Oliveira in 1850. Since then, the D'Oliveira family has purchased five other firms, the oldest dating to 1820, enabling the consolidation of rare wine stocks. The company is owned and operated today by the fifth generation (with the sixth already involved). Unique to Madeira, all blends, from dry to sweet, are made predominantly from Tinta Negra. 'It doesn't make sense to use the white grapes in the blended styles. There's not enough quantity grown on the island,' Luís D'Oliveira argues, reserving them exclusively for vintage Madeiras. The blends are on average a couple of years older than the indicated age, and are excellent across all categories, even if they are anything but easy and approachable wines. Although sugar levels are high on average, the wines seem drier thanks to concentrated acids and heavy extract, and the pleasant bitterness this brings to balance. The real show stoppers are the Frasqueiras, with wines all the way back to 1850 still available. All are bottled unfined and unfiltered. I can think of nowhere else in the world where you can taste such a vast and breathtaking range of old wines. Pereira D'Oliveira is a time machine.

Vinhos Barbeito ★★★

Estrada Ribeira Garcia, Lote 8
9300-324 Câmara de Lobos
vinhosbarbeito.com

Barbeito is a small family-run-operation based high up in the hills above Câmara de Lobos where innovation and tradition find a happy understanding. The company was founded in 1946 by Mário Barbeito Vasconcelos and today is run by his grandson Ricardo Diogo Freitas, who is also the winemaker. The Kinoshita family from Japan came on as financial partners in 1991, the year that Barbeito abandoned bulk wine production to concentrate exclusively on bottled wines. A new modern facility was built in 2008 complete with a robotic lagar. Barbeito wines are among the most distinctive and easily recognizable Madeiras, always the driest and highest acid wines in any given category, and they taste older than the age indication. 'It is the great acidity that defines Barbeito wines,' states Freitas. The small size affords an unusual flexibility to experiment, the best of which are Freitas bottles under the Signature Series, often single casks. Tinta Negra is held in particularly high esteem here, and Barbeito pays a premium for top-quality grapes, up to 20 per cent above the market average, including parcels of organically grown Tinta Negra. Even though these are not the most approachable Madeiras, they are highly complex wines that continually evolve in the glass – with a single pour revealing multiple faces.

THE CANARY ISLANDS (OR ISLAS CANARIAS OR CANARIES)

The Canary Islands form an Atlantic archipelago with seven major islands under the Spanish flag. From largest to smallest, the islands are: Tenerife, Fuerteventura, Gran Canaria, Lanzarote, La Palma, La Gomera and El Hierro. From the easternmost point of Fuerteventura, it's just 52 nautical miles (100 km/60 miles) to the southern coast of Morocco.

Like Madeira, these oceanic volcanoes are the result of continental drift over a mantle plume 'hotspot'. Their formation follows the roughly east to northeast moving African Plate on its journey towards the Moroccan coast; thus the easternmost islands – Fuerteventura and Lanzarote – are the oldest, emerging from the sea some 20 million years ago. It took close to 19 million after that

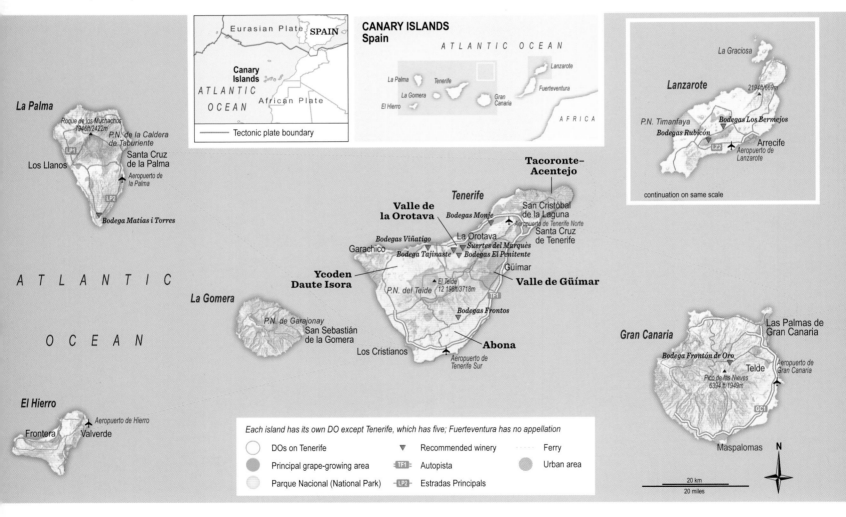

Each island has its own DO except Tenerife, which has five; Fuerteventura has no appellation

- ○ DOs on Tenerife
- ● Principal grape-growing area
- ○ Parque Nacional (National Park)
- ▽ Recommended winery
- TF1 Autopista
- LP2 Estradas Principals
- ┄┄ Ferry
- ● Urban area

OPPOSITE (LEFT TO RIGHT) *El Teide, Tenerife; sea of clouds, Tenerife; Bodegas Monje, Tenerife; a family affair, Bodega Tajinaste, Valle de la Orotava, Tenerife;* *crossroad of the spice route; trenzado vines, Valle de la Orotava, Tenerife; morning in Tenerife; walled vineyards, Lanzarote; tapas in Lanzarote; camel tours,* *Timanfaya, Lanzarote; volcanic layers, Tenerife; trenzado vines, Valle de la Orotava, Tenerife..*

120   MACARONESIA

BAR STOP

TAPAS Y VINOS
DESDE 1890

for the plate to drift 500 km (311 miles) over the fixed hotspot to where El Hierro rises up at the westernmost point, the youngest island at just over one million years. But nowhere in the archipelago is volcanism considered properly extinct. Indeed La Palma and El Hierro are still floating over the hotspot, while Lanzarote boasts the geatest concentration of 'youthful' volcanism thanks to renewed drifting and rifting.

The most majestic volcano, however, is Tenerife's El Teide. It's the biggest of all of the islands' hundreds of volcanic cones, and at 3718 metres (12,198 ft), the tallest peak not only of the Canaries, but of all Spain, and the world's third highest volcano. El Padre Teide, as Tenerife's inhabitants reverentially refer to it, also altered the history of Canary wines. On May 5, 1706, an eruptive fissure opened on its northern flank above the town of Garachico, spilling a tsunami of lava that flowed for several weeks in a spectacular display of earth force. Garachico, until then the principal port for all shipments leaving the Canaries, was all but destroyed, and the massive quantities of lava that flowed into the harbour blocked access to the port, severely hampering exports.

Although its last eruption was over 100 years ago, in 1909, El Teide is still on the list of 'Decade Volcanoes', one of 17 volcanoes identified by the International Association of Volcanology and Chemistry of the Earth's Interior (IAVCEI) as worth keeping a close eye on in light of their history of destructive eruptions and proximity to populated areas. It's a reminder that El Padre Teide is still in charge.

THE LAST WINE-GROWING COUNTRY

When the Catholic Kings Ferdinand and Isabella embarked on the conquest of the Canary Islands in the dying years of the 15th century, they engaged the help of soldiers for hire from across Europe. In exchange for their efforts, the mercenaries were granted land in the archipelago after the Spanish victory over the native Guanches population. These new immigrants from across the Iberian Peninsula and elsewhere brought grapes from their home regions and established vineyards, as any good European would. It could then be asked, should the Canary Islands be considered the last wine-growing country of the old world, or the first one from the new world?

ABOVE *Low volcanic stone walls on Lanzarote, built to protect the* hoyos *and the vines contained within from strong winds.*

OPPOSITE ABOVE *Gently sloping vineyards at Bodegas Monje, in the Tacoronte-Acentejo DO on Tenerife's north coast.*

OPPOSITE BELOW *DO Valle de Güímar's labour-intensive* parrales *allow minimally-pruned vines to share space with other crops.*

After a golden era for the wine industry in the 16th and 17th centuries, unfavourable international trade agreements, eruptions and other uncontrollable events sent Canary wines into a long decline in fortunes. Recovery wouldn't begin until the 1980s, though since the 90s, the wine industry has been restructuring from bulk to bottle and rebuilding its lost reputation. And the prospects look highly promising, as the islands have many strengths to work with. Critically, like many other volcanic regions, the Canaries were spared the scourge of phylloxera that destroyed most of Europe's vineyards in the late 19th and early 20th centuries, and remain phylloxera-free. The vineyards, left unmolested, evolved as though frozen in time, with many antique grapes still in production, while in many cases their peninsular ancestors have all but been abandoned and become extinct. The famous biodiversity of the Canaries thus extends to grapes; some 80 varieties grow in the islands today. Although the names are tongue-twistingly difficult to remember, let alone pronounce, such an embarrassment of varietal riches will surely become a great advantage in the near future.

Another fashionable plus is that the average age of these ungrafted grapevines is high, and many vineyards, with their queer growing and trellising systems, like the scooped out, walled-in bunkers of volcanic ash on Lanzarote, or the metres- (feet-) long, plaited (braided) vine tendrils of the Valle de la Orotava in Tenerife, make for a marketer's dream of points of difference to play upon. Canary wines now seem to be enjoying the status of 'the next greatest thing', as they once had almost 400 years ago. These wines are ripe for rediscovery.

The Canaries Grapes

Listán Blanco, the most planted white variety, is better known as the Palomino Fino of Sherry, a white variety of modest aromatic intensity and at best crisp and lively, with lemon-lime and green-apple flavours, made without oak for the most part. Ignacio Valdera of Los Bermejos on Lanzarote tells me it was originally planted to produce the brandy used to fortify the Malvasia wines destined for overseas markets. It produces its most meaningful wines in the cooler, high-elevation vineyards of Tenerife and Gran Canaria.

Listán Negro, the most planted red grape, is a variety of modest structure, ageability and complexity. At best it makes light, peppery, low-tannin, chill-worthy reds, sometimes using carbonic maceration, or crunchy rosé. It's as indigenous as it comes in the Canaries, believed to be a local crossing of Listán Blanco and Negramoll (Madeira's Tinta Negra), though DNA studies are inconclusive. What has been established beyond doubt by Juan Jesús Méndez Siverio (aka Dr. Grape) of Bodega Viñátigo on Tenerife, with help from the University of Tarragona, is that Listán Negro was the first widely exported grape variety to the new world. It's better known under its American synonyms: Mission in California, País in Chile and Criolla in Argentina. The current revival of interest in old País vineyards in South America may well have a positive impact on the Canaries' Listán Negro, if history is any guide.

Temptingly, but apparently unrelated Listán Prieto (*preto* means negro, or black in Portuguese) is a similarly light, wild-berry-scented red variety of unknown origins, less widely planted.

White Malvasía, which was once the most important variety for the popular sweet marmaladey fortified wines of yore, is still significantly planted. There are two distinct variations: the orange-blossom-tinged Malvasía Aromática (aka Malvasía di Candia, found throughout the Mediterranean), is widely planted in the western islands and still often

---

OPPOSITE ABOVE *Hand-excavated* hoyos *on Lanzarote: mini-craters in the ash, usually with a single vine rooted in underlying soil, with small semi-circular, protective volcanic rock walls on windward side of each crater.*

OPPOSITE BELOW *Valle de la Orotava's traditional* trenzado *vine training: braided vine tendrils were once swung out of the way off season to allow other crops to grow, after which they were replaced.*

ABOVE *French-trained winemaker Agustín Farráis at the family bodega, Tajinaste, in Tenerife's Valle de la Orotava.*

rendered in sweet, late-harvest/dried-grape and/or fortified versions. The Malvasía of Lanzarote, or Malvasía Volcánica is genetically distinct, believed to be a crossing of Malvasía Aromática and Bermejuela/Marmajuelo, the latter a variety of Portuguese origin. It makes Lanzarote's best dry and sweet, salty whites.

Less common, pure Bermejuela/Marmajuelo (the name used depends which island you're on) is one of the islands' most distinctive, full-bodied, tropical-fruit scented white varieties, as is the late-ripening, extract-rich Vijariego of Tenerife (aka Diego on Lanzarote), a grape originally from the Alpujarras Mountains in Andalucía. Confusingly, El Hierro's Vijariego is genetically distinct, with higher natural acidity.

Gual (Madeira's Boal) is possibly the most promising white variety of them all, at least according to Méndez Siverio. In the decomposing basalts of Tenerife's DO Ycoden Daute-Isora, Gual is expressed as an unusually whisky-lactone-rich variety, giving dry whites with a distinctive coconut-vanilla nuance even in stainless-steel versions (lactones are usually only found in the aromatic profile of oak-aged wines).

Among the more interesting red varieties is the abundantly spicy, tannic and pleasantly bitter Tintilla, the suave and easy-drinking Negramoll, a very promising black-skinned variant of Vijariego Negro (Catalonia's Sumol) and Baboso Negro (Portugal's Alfrocheiro), a deep-coloured, soft and fruity variety on which many growers are pinning their mostly dry, but occasionally sweet, red wine hopes.

The Canaries Wine Appellations

The **DOP Islas Canarias** covers wine produced anywhere in the archipelago (Fuerteventura is the only major island that doesn't produce any wine). But the highly changeable climate and variations on the theme of volcanic soils within the Canary Islands has led to the creation of ten separate DOs. Five of these are on the largest island of Tenerife, with one each for the islands of Lanzarote, La Palma, El Hierro, Gran Canaria and La Gomera, in decreasing order of hectares planted.

Tenerife has three appellations on the north side of the island, all directly exposed to the Alisios trade winds that bring cool, moist air from the North Atlantic. These vapour-charged winds slam into

ABOVE *The astonishing pockmarked vineyard landscape of La Geria, Lanzarote.*

the volcanic ridge that splits Tenerife roughly east to west, and discharge enough rain to keep the north side luxuriantly green. **DO Tacoronte-Acentejo** is the largest, with the oldest, most weathered, clay-rich volcanic soils, with high nutrient availability for vines, favouring red varieties like Listán Negro and Negramoll. Neighbouring **DO Valle de la Orotava** was the first region planted on Tenerife, where vineyards spill down from 800 metres (2600 feet) towards the Atlantic. The valley has relatively young, undeveloped acidic volcanic soils that have been rejuvenated from time to time by volcanic activity. Iron and aluminium-rich basalts and rhyolites contribute, at least in part it would be guessed, to the common metallic tang in the valley's vines, both white and red. Ancient, *trenzado*-trained vines, unique to Orotava, are a memorable sight.

In the **DO Ycoden Daute-Isora** vineyards climb to over 1400 metres (4600 feet) in the skirt folds of landscape-dominating El Teide. The proximity to the volcano and its recent activity means that the soils of the region are the youngest. Although young, minimally weathered volcanic soils are often rich in nutrients, the majority of soils in Ycoden Daute-Isora have the peculiarity of easily fixing phosphorous, which reduces fertility considerably. As a result the DO is best suited to white varieties, especially in the cooler upper elevations.

Few rain clouds make it to the southern side of Tenerife, where the sky is almost always clear, temperatures higher and the ground more parched. In contrast to the darker, basaltic-derived soils of the north side, the majority of vines on the south side are grown in a compact, pale, *café-con-leche*-coloured volcanic pumice that the locals call *jable*, a Spanish deformation of the French word *sable*, meaning sand. In certain areas loose *jable* was physically brought in by farmers to cover soils like mulching. In addition to limiting weed growth, *jable* acts like a sponge and retains the limited moisture deposited overnight by dew, providing the water vines need in this very dry climate. Little organic matter keeps yields naturally low.

DO Abona is the largest on the south side and boasts the highest vineyards in Europe, and some of the highest in the world, up to 1700 metres (5500 feet). The **DO Valle de Güímar** to the east is named for a volcanic depression centred around the town of Güímar. Delicate and fruity white wines are the most convincing from the sandy soils of these two appellations, especially from high-elevation sites, though producers aiming for riper international-style reds take advantage of warmer coastal conditions. Indeed in all of Tenerife's appellations, altitude is a key determining factor for ripening period and wine style, with harvest sometimes stretching out over as long as four months, from the lowest, earlier ripening sites to the highest, high-tension wine producing vineyards.

There would be no **DO Lanzarote** were it not for the prolonged eruption that lasted on this arid island from 1730 to 1736. It was

soon discovered that the tephra storm that covered over 200 square km (77 square miles) in a thick – up to two to three metres (six to ten feet) – cover of black ash and lapilli, made grape cultivation possible, surely an unexpected biblical give-and-take. Like the *jable* of Tenerife, the ash acts like a layer of mulch over older soils and bedrock. Although the dark surface is scorching under the blazing Canaries sun, dig just a few inches below and it's cool, and a few more and unexpected moisture appears in this desert environment. The ash prevents what little ground moisture there is from evaporating, while at the same time absorbing airborne humidity and the occasional raindrop for future use. Ingenious cultivation methods deal with the fierce winds that race across the low-lying island virtually unimpeded, and find ways to anchor vines in the much more ancient, life-giving soils underlying, since the unweathered ash itself has no nutrient availability.

Of the other four wine producing islands in the archipelago, **DO La Palma** on the far west side of the archipelago covers the entire island, but like Tenerife, its microclimates vary dramatically. The three distinct sub-zones are Fuencaliente-Las Manchas in the south, Hoya de Mazo in the west and Norte de Palma in the north. Malvasía Aromática is the most planted grape, used mostly to produce the classic sweet wines that are perhaps the closest to the Canary Sack of Shakespeare's time.

DO Gran Canaria with its terraces of bush vines and *parrales* was the most recently granted appellation in the archipelago. Uniquely for the Canaries, red wine production exceeds white, led by Listán Negro along with Negramoll and Tintilla. Listán Blanco is the most planted white, even if other varieties like Albillo and Vijariego seem to give more interesting results. Soils vary widely from sandy at the lower elevations, to volcanic ash and heavier weathered clays, making style or quality generalizations of limited value. Production is small, though some have found export success.

DOs El Hierro and **La Gomera** wines are little known outside the archipelago due to anecdotal production, at least for now.

OPPOSITE ABOVE *The apocalyptic beauty of Lanzarote's National Park, Timanfaya, epicentre of volcanic activity 1730 to 1736, and ongoing.*

OPPOSITE BELOW *Lanzarote's* chabucos: *areas where lava flows split and cracked open as they cooled, leaving gaping crevices that reach down to the original soil and bedrock underneath the vines.*

ABOVE *Vines planted by pick-axe struggle in the fresh basalt lavas of Fuencaliente-Las-Manchas, La Palma. Teneguía volcano was the last to erupt in the Canary Islands in 1971.*

THE CANARY ISLANDS – THE WINES & THE PEOPLE

Bodegas El Penitente

Camino de la Habanera 286
38300 La Orotava
Santa Cruz de Tenerife
bodegaselpenitente.es

Américo García Núñez has an enviable collection of vines grown using the ancient *trenzado* system in the Valle de la Orotava, and has produced wine since 1999. The most authentic and enjoyable wines are the entry-level bottlings under the Arautava brand, from a transparent, green-apple-tinged Listán Blanco, to the lively, strawberry-leaf-scented Rosado and the pleasantly twiggy and tart-berry-flavoured Kryos made from carbonically macerated Listán Negro.

Bodega Frontón de Oro

Finca el Frontón s/n
35329 Vega de San Mateo
Gran Canaria
frontondeoro.com

One of the main exporting bodegas from Gran Canaria, Frontón de Oro focuses exclusively on Canary varieties in a style that's neither fully rustic nor polished and modern. Among whites, the pure Albillo Seco takes the variety into uncommon later-harvest territory, an unusually full-bodied and dried apple, pear and pineapple flavoured wine. Malpaís, a blend of 70/30 Listán Prieto/Listán Negro and Tintilla, is the most convincing, with firm, cherry and liquorice (licorice) flavours, vaguely reminiscent of light Nebbiolo, given four months in American oak.

Bodegas Frontos

Lomo Grande 1 – Los Blanquitos
38600 Carretera General del Sur
Granadilla de Abona
Tenerife
frontos.es

A small estate in southern Tenerife planted on *jable,* producing simple, crisp, modern wines. Notable is the delicate, organically-certified Blanco Seco Ecológico, a Listán Blanco grown at up to 1700 metres (5577 feet) in the rocky soils of Spain's, and possibly Europe's, highest vineyard. The Blanco Clásico (Albillo/Verdello/Marmajuelo) uses each variety for its pre-destined purpose (acid, aromatics, tropical fruit, respectively) to yield a balanced and complete wine.

Bodegas Los Bermejos ★

Camino a Los Bermejos 7
35550 La Florida
San Bartolomé de Lanzarote
Gran Canaria
losbermejos.com

Winemaker Ignacio Valdera and his partner Carmelo Gonzalez operate this leading Lanzarote bodega established in 2001. Only traditional grapes are vinified for over a dozen labels, including Lanzarote's first organically certified wines. The wines are clean and articulate, delicate and precisely crafted, made for drinking rather than wine competitions. An intriguing Diego Seco gains from, and indeed needs, a few years in bottle to show its best, with chewy, palpable extract. Malvasía Fermentado in Barrica, fermented and aged for three months in wood, is also a revelation, with textural harmony and crisp, salty flavour. NV solera-style Malvasía Naturalmente Dulce is outstanding.

Bodega Matías i Torres ★★

Calle Ciudad Real s/n
38740 Fuencalliente
La Palma
Santa Cruz de Tenerife
matiasitorres.com

Juan Matías Torres Pérez produces tiny quantities in an old family bodega dating back to 1885, from the Fuencaliente sub-region of La Palma. The approach is simple: limited production, minimal vineyard treatments (copper and sulphur only) and minimal winemaking intervention (no processing aids, wild yeast fermentations). 'Ours is a traditional family bodega. Inherited knowledge and intuition are our guides,' says Torres. The Listán Blanco Las Machuqueras, a single parcel of 40 to 100 year old vines, is among the finest examples of the variety in the Canaries; also excellent are Albillo Criollo and red Negramoll, both aged in large pine vats and old oak casks.

Bodegas Monje

Camino Cruz Leandro 36
38359 El Sauzal
Tenerife
wbodegasmonje.com

Bodegas Monje is arguably as well-known for its legendary Wine & Sex events (not exactly what you're thinking, but eroticism is the theme) as for its wines. The Monje family traces its winemaking roots back to 1750, though the company was offically established in 1956. In Tenerife's Tacoronte-Acentejo appellation, Felipe Monje is the winemaker, producing a range of variations on Listán Blanco and Negro, Negramoll, Tintilla and Vijariego Negro. Tinto Monje is a pure Listán Negro made using both carbonic maceration and traditional vinification ('designed for tourists'), with an earthy volcanic signature enlivened by flashy fruit. Vino Padre Listán Negro Dulce 'Miguel Monje', a sweet fortified wine with four years in barrel and bottle each before release, is a cascade of chocolate, coffee, fig and Christmas cake.

Bodegas Rubicón

Carretera Teguise-Yyaiza 2
La Geria 2 codigo postal
35570 Yasia
Lanzarote
bodegasrubicon.com

Rubicón is set in the heart of La Geria, the most dramatic vineyard area on Lanzarote overlooking the National Park of Timanfaya. Don Germán López Figueras acquired the 17th country house and winery in 1979 to devote himself to winemaking. Records found in the old house reveal the history of extensive cultivation of cereal crops in the area of La Geria, before the prolonged eruption of 1730 to 1736 covered it in volcanic ash and destroyed one of the richest meadows of Lanzarote. Amalia is the top selection of pure Malvasía Volcánica, made with ancient vines from La Geria (which the bodega claims are nearly 300 years old), a subtle, stony, oak-free wine that takes patience to tease out its delicate nuances.

Bodega Tajinaste ★★

C/El Ratiño 5
38315 La Perdoma
La Orotava
Santa Cruz de Tenerife
tajinaste.net

Winemaker/owner Agustín García Farráis, following French schooling and training, took the reins here in the late 90s and has managed the difficult transition of modernizing. The oldest vines on the estate, Listán Blanco and Negro, were planted in 1914, and are still farmed in the traditional *trenzado* system. The full range is finely crafted, including an especially memorable 50/50 blend of Malvasía Aromática from the Abona DO and Marmajuelo from the estate in the Valle de la Orotava called Paisaje de las Islas. Barrel-aged red 'CAN' (Listán Negro/Vijariego Negro) is complex and richly aromatic.

Bodegas Viñátigo ★★

Travesía Juandana s/n
38441 La Guancha
Santa Cruz de Tenerife
vinatigo.com

Juan Jesús Méndez Siverio, (aka Dr. Grape) established Viñátigo in 1990 as much as a research centre for forgotten varieties as a commercial winery. There are 17 different labels, and tasting here is a lesson in Canaries grapes – from crisp and clean, green-apple and citrus-scented Listán Blanco to brilliantly mineral, crisp yet weighty Gual and tropical, orange-blossom, and passion-fruit flavoured Marmajuelo. Wood-aged Vijariego Blanco has more than enough depth to remain balanced with a pinch of salt. Tintilla red is an intellectual experience – twiggy, herbal and spicy. Plummy Vijariego Negro and raspberry-jam flavoured Baboso Negro are more immediately appealing.

Suertes del Marqués ★★★

Tomás Zerolo 15
La Orotava
Santa Cruz de Tenerife
suertesdelmarques.com

The El Esquilón estate, in the area known as Las Suertes in the Valle de la Orotava, is sub-divided into 21 parcels from 350 to 700 metres (1150 to 2300 feet), with each farmed according to soil composition, elevation and orientation. Jonatan Garcia Lima vinifies each parcel separately. Their most treasured plots contain centenary, *trenzado*-trained Listán Blanco and Negro vines in the highest elevations where, according to Garcia Lima, soils are poorer, with less clay, and give 'more complexity and minerality to the wines'. Since its launch in 2006, Suertes del Marqués has become the model to follow: maximum respect for terroir, applying organic and biodynamic practices (but not certified) and natural, minimal-intervention winemaking. The range is consistently excellent, from entry-level 7 Fuentes to Vidonia, a marvellously flinty reference for Listán Blanco from centenary vines. La Solana red, a woodsy single-parcel Listán Negro from 80 to 100 year-old-vines has archtypical volcanic savoury tension.

ALSACE & GERMANY
THE UPPER RHINE GRABEN & EIFEL VOLCANIC FIELD

Unless you're a serious volcanophile, it's unlikely you associate the lumbering Rhine River and its tributaries, the surrounding pastoral fields, fertile plains and dense forests with violent volcanism. Yet beginning some 400,000 million years ago in the epoch known as the Devonian, this corner of southwestern Germany and northeastern France was the site of fierce tearing and crumpling of the earth's crust, and the inevitable volcanic activity that accompanies it. While most of the volcanism ceased long ago, some small pockets are still clearly active.

The inheritance of this geological commotion is some of northern Europe's most prized vineyard land. Yet here one must sift carefully through the complex geology to find the volcanic spots. Alsace and Germany offer a mind-bendingly intricate patchwork of soils, and only a few vineyards are considered volcanic, often small islands in a sea of other geologies. But praises for the wines they yield have been sung for a thousand years.

OPPOSITE *Terraced vineyards in the Kaiserstuhl;*
Weingut Franz Keller blends perfectly into the hillside.

ABOVE *The Nahe flows beneath the porphyry Rotenfels*
near the town of Traisen and its superb vineyards.

ALSACE & THE RANGEN DE THANN GRAND CRU

For geologists, Alsace is an entire textbook sandwiched into a single region. Rocks from multiple ages are dispersed like a handmade chequerboard, with short distances separating millions of years of geological formations. Like Germany's Pfalz region to the north, the winelands of Alsace lie along the western margin of the Oberrheingraben (the Upper Rhine Graben) – a fault system on the grandest scale. The trench through which the Rhine River flows northward out to the North Sea has sunk several kilometres (miles) into the earth's crust as rifting tore apart the once-united Voges and Black Forest Mountains, the latter now some 50 km (30 miles) across the valley in Germany. The lowlands are ideal for pasture, but the finest grapes grow on the foothills on either side of the valley.

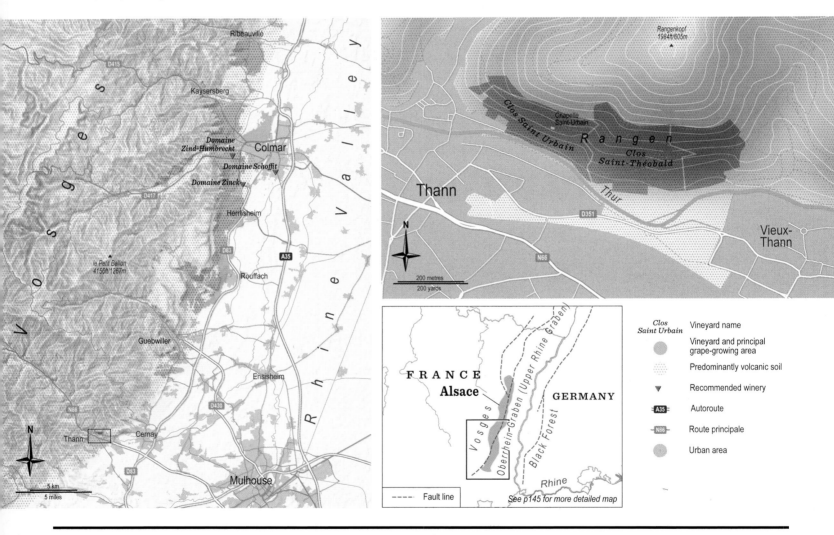

Legend

Clos Saint Urbain — Vineyard name

Vineyard and principal grape-growing area

Predominantly volcanic soil

▼ Recommended winery

A35 Autoroute

N66 Route principale

Urban area

- - - Fault line

See p145 for more detailed map

OPPOSITE (LEFT TO RIGHT) *Daunting harvest on the Rangen; Rangen mid-summer; hand harvesting; Lower Rangen, with exposed volcanic rock and the River Thur; Domaine Zind-Humbrecht; Saint Urbain Chapel; Clos Saint Urbain under the 'Witches Eye'; Olivier Humbrecht MW; village of Thann and the River Thur; plowing in the Rangen by wench (three times).*

Volcanism began several hundred million years ago underwater, and appears to have accompanied the Upper Rhine Graben formation more or less continuously from pre-rifting times (70 million years ago) until as recently as seven million years ago, around the edges of the rift zone. Isolated volcanic cones formed at several spots along fissures, spewing out ash and lavas of various compositions over a complex mélange of sandstones, granites, limestones, marls and more. Vestiges are scattered here and there, as at the Muenchberg Grand Cru vineyard in Nothalten where a dusting of volcanic sand and ash lend those wines palpable saltiness. But the clearest evidence of volcanism can be seen above the town of Thann in southern Alsace, where a single celebrated vineyard has reigned supreme for a thousand years: the Rangen de Thann Grand Cru.

ALSACE AT THE CROSSROADS

Alsace sits at the crossroads of Europe, a frontier land wedged between the religious, linguistic and philosophical influence of two of continental Europe's dominant cultures, Latin and Germanic. Here, Cartesian reason clashes with Goethean romanticism, French Catholicism with German Protestantism. There is hardly a tribe that hasn't passed through the area at one point or another to either trade or make war, and politically, Alsace has changed hands multiple times, most recently falling again under French control after World War I. This eternal tug-of-war and oscillation of ideologies has moulded the complex and ever-changing landscape of Alsatian wine.

Yet through it all, the majestic vineyard known as Rangen has stood unchallenged. From the first known writings of the 12th century, its wine has been considered among the most extraordinary in all of France. 'Rangen is unique and cannot be compared to other *grand crus* from Alsace. It flies in another dimension,' says Philippe Zinck of Domaine Zinck, who makes a tiny amount of Rangen Grand Cru. 'The signature of the terroir is so strong and so unusual, with its smoky flint and dark earth flavour, it can really catch people off-guard if they are not prepared.'

The Soils of Rangen Grand Cru

The eminent Rangenkopf rises nearly 600 metres (1950 feet) above the Thur River Valley at the southernmost point of the Alsace appellation, squarely above the principal Vosges Fault Line. The top of the hill commands a breathtaking view: west, deep into the heart of the Vosges Mountains, and east across the Rhine Valley to the Black Forest and Switzerland in the distance. Below lie the communities of Thann and Vieux Thann, which have slowly encroached on vineyard land; in the Middle Ages there were 500 hectares planted on the hillside and down into the valley. Today, due in part to extraordinarily steep slopes (60 to 70 per cent on average) and the effort and expense to farm them, only a fraction of Rangen (whose name means 'slope' in old German) remains planted. But it's the choicest piece, fully south-facing, between 350 and 450 metres (1100 to 1500 feet): the highest in Alsace.

Rangen is the only truly volcanic terroir in Alsace, with a unique composition of friable, extrusive volcanoclastic rocks, tuffs and andesites, mixed with volcanic sediments over hard greywacke. Like many volcanic terroirs, it's shallow, just 40 to 60 cm (1.5 to two feet) to the fractured bedrock, very poor in organic matter and clay, free draining and rich in potassium and magnesium. The dark grey-brown-black colour aids ripening via absorbed and radiated heat. Yields are naturally very low, in the order of 30 hl/ha, and often under 20; sweet Vendange Tardive and botrytis-affected Sélection de Grains Nobles yield considerably less. Despite the southerly aspect and 'warm' soils, high elevation makes Rangen a windy, slow-ripening site, one of the coolest and latest terroirs in Alsace with an extremely long maturation cycle.

The Wines of Rangen Grand Cru

These characteristics make Rangen a cru *par excellence* for Riesling and Pinot Gris, among the most flamboyantly mineral and opulent in the region, though fine Gewurztraminer is grown in the slightly warmer and less windy lower elevations. In 1993, the growers of Rangen chose to adopt a strict charter imposing lower yields than permitted under AC regulations, higher planting density and banning pesticides, chaptalization and acid adjustment, among other aspects of production aimed at protecting and raising quality of the entire cru. But aside from Zinck, only Zind-Humbrecht, Schoffit and Wolfberger produce commercial quantities of Rangen Grand Cru.

The widely respected Olivier Humbrecht of Domaine Zind-Humbrecht, commissioned studies to get a better understanding of the various terroirs he farms, with fascinating results. The reports, prepared as final theses by two students of France's Diplome National d'Oenologue, compared four vineyards of different geological origin as directly as possible: planted around the same time with the same Riesling clone on identical rootstock and trellising and farmed biodynamically since 1989. Various parameters of grape composition, must and wine (vinified identically) were analyzed over two vintages. The students found that volcanic Rangen wines consistently had the highest level of ash, that is, sugar-free dry extract – a measurement of the mineral content of wine (which includes potassium, calcium, magnesium, organic acids and mineral salts) – more than 20 per cent higher than the next highest site.

In sensory analysis, Riesling from Rangen was also consistently judged as the 'most mineral' with notable salinity, and having the greatest weight and concentration. Humbrecht has also observed over time that Rangen wines have consistently higher pH (related to soil potassium levels, as well as the late-harvest nature of the vineyard), deeper colour – amber-tinged even in youth – and 'acid perception that is more saline and less "green" or vegetal'. Descriptive terms such as gunflint, roasted and smoky are frequently applied.

These studies lend some scientific credence to what has been known for a thousand years: the wines of the singular terroir of Rangen are indeed unique, due, in no small measure, to the volcanic origins of its soils. These are wines for those seeking something assertive and original.

ALSACE – THE WINES & THE PEOPLE

Domaine Schoffit ★★

68 Nonnenholz Weg
68000 Colmar

An excellent family domaine run by Bernard Schoffit and son Alexandre, making wines of purity and precision from their Rangen monopole Clos Saint-Théobald, named after the monks of the Collégiale Saint-Théobald who farmed it from the 13th century. Bernard painstakenly reconstructed the vineyard in the 1980s. Pinot Gris gives a rich and weighty, smoke-tinged, often botrytis-affected expression in the lower slopes, firmer and tighter in the upper parcels. Riesling planted in the 1970s in the mid-slope is drier, forceful but balanced between steely freshness and intensity with marked salinity. A small parcel of old Gewurztraminer from the lower slope's deep soils is characteristically ripe, opulent, billowing with exotic fruit.

Domaine Zinck ★

18 Rue des Trois Châteaux
68420 Eguisheim

zinck.fr

Philippe Zinck couldn't believe his luck when a grower in his village with a hectare in the Rangen asked if he would like to buy some grapes in 2001. 'I thought he was joking... who could refuse buying grapes from Rangen? It is an honour,' relates Zinck. Production is minuscule, just a few hundred bottles, and not every vintage (the grower keeps some grapes for himself), but Zinck's interpretation is accurate and representative of the cru: late-harvested, smoky, flinty, incomparably structured, rising in richness from Riesling through Pinot Gris to Gewurztraminer.

Domaine Zind-Humbrecht ★★★

4 Route de Colmar,
68230 Turckheim

zindhumbrecht.fr

Among the most admired producers in France, making an unforgettable range with unparalleled concentration, density, balance and vineyard expression, from ten terroirs, certified biodynamic (Biodyvin) since 1998. Humbrecht's Clos Saint Urbain monopole in the Rangen is named for Thann's patron saint of wine-growers, and boasts a chapel erected in his honour. According to Olivier Humbrecht MW, 'the top sector is later ripening and cooler. The soils have a greater percentage of rocks, less topsoil and tend to be more acidic (natural drainage results in soil pH between 5.5 at the top and 7 at the bottom). The lower slope produces richer, robust, more powerful wines.' Pinot Gris and Riesling are blended from various elevations; Gewurztraminer is planted at the bottom near the Thur River where more heat, reflected sunlight and higher clay favour its maximum expression. All wines, from dry to the rare Sélection de Grains Nobles, are top level.

GERMANY

***German wine dates from the first Roman garrison in Trier. Today interest in winemaking studies is exploding, attracting more than just the next generation from traditional wine-growing families. Wine is in fashion, and sales, domestic and international, are strong. Prices have not quite yet returned to 19th century highs when a bottle of German Riesling sold for more than cru classé Bordeaux, but the wine scene is erupting. And Germany has much to offer to the world of fine volcanic wines. The Verband Deutscher Prädikats-und Qualitätsweingüter (VDP), a respected association of over 200 of Germany's top wineries with its own vineyard classification, recognizes dozens of volcanic vineyards as Erste Lage or Grosses Gewächs (GG), the German equivalent of* grand cru.**

CLASSIFYING WINES BY BEDROCK

Germany's geological diversity and the dominance of Riesling (nearly 60 per cent of the world's acreage, planted in all 13 official regions), make it an ideal place to study the influence of bedrock on wine profile. And perhaps no one in the world has looked at this more closely than Dr. Ulrich Fischer, Head of Viticulture and Oenology and Sensory Evaluation at the DLR-Rheinpfalz in Neustadt. Dr. Fischer has studied the sensory and chemical impact on Riesling from a number of bedrock and soil types, and across consecutive vintages. His findings were conclusive. In scientific parlance, 'variance and discriminant analysis showed a clear impact of terroir on the sensory properties of German Riesling, despite vintage and winemaking influences. Sensory patterns could be seen, and they varied depending on the geological substrate the wines originated from.'

In short, Dr. Fischer found that Riesling grown on the same soil type showed greater similarities, even when separated by large distances, than Riesling grown in nearby vineyards on different soils. In just one example, Dr. Fischer studied the aroma, flavour and taste profile of Riesling from the Kieselberg vineyard in Deidesheim and its sandstone-derived soils, and the Pechstein vineyard in Forst and its dark volcanic basalt soils just 2 km (1.25 miles) away, both produced by the same estate (Weingut Bassermann-Jordan). 'The two types of bedrock had a highly significant impact on nine odour and four taste attributes,' Fischer concluded. The wines from basalt were perceived as, 'markedly fruity-aromatic, with high intensities in "cantaloupe", "peach/apricot", "mango/passion fruit", "lemon/grapefruit" and "smoky,"' (related to higher thiol content, a class of aromatic organic compounds). Sandstone 'produced a Riesling with lower fruit intensities, more vegetative aromas and a stronger acidity, which was perceived as being harsher and which led to a hard mouthfeel.' Sensory evaluations were confirmed by analysis of aroma compounds and other measurable parameters, 'with meaningful correlations,' and the study was repeated over several vintages and with bottle age, showing similar results. Dr. Fischer also found aroma/flavour/taste correlations between the Rieslings of the distant Ürziger Würztgarten vineyard in the Mosel and its iron-rich, red rhyolite volcanic tuff, and those grown on the similar red

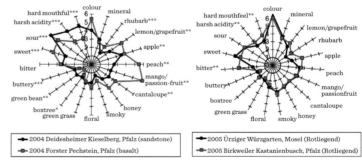

Figure 1: Sensory profiles of the bedrock types of sandstone (Kieselberg) and basalt (Pechstein), both vinified at the Bassermann-Jordan estate (n = 20 jdgs. x 3 rep.).

Figure 2: Sensory profiles of the Riesling from two Rotliegend terroirs, vinified at the experimental cellar (n = 13 jdgs. x 3 rep.).

OPPOSITE (LEFT TO RIGHT) *Scenic, volcanic stretch of Nahe River; Würzgarten vineyard, Mosel; hiking signposts, Kaiserstuhl; Kuperfergrube GG, Nahe; Weingut Salwey; Kaiserstuhl panorama, with volcanic cones; top Nahe vineyard, Hermannshölhe; old basalt quarry on Pechsteinkopf, Pfalz; Pechstein vineyard, Pfalz; Weingut Franz Keller; Würzgarten vineyard with Mosel River below; Weingut Armin Göring, Kaiserstuhl.*

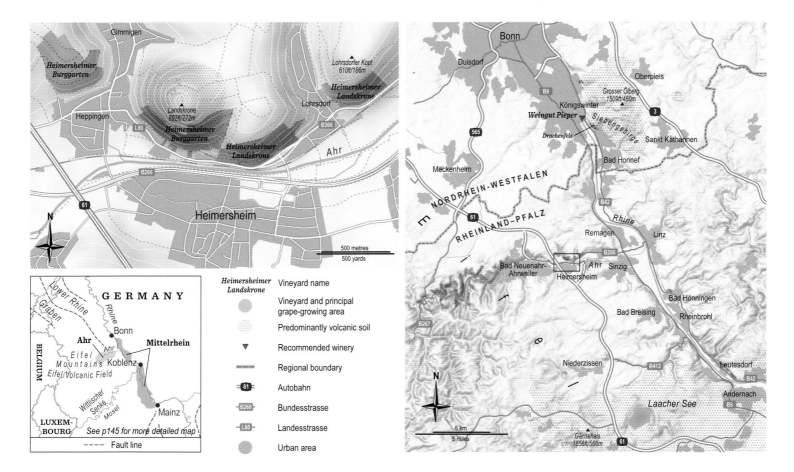

The following map legend items appear:

Heimersheimer Landskrone — Vineyard name

Vineyard and principal grape-growing area

Predominantly volcanic soil

▼ Recommended winery

— Regional boundary

61 Autobahn

B266 Bundesstrasse

L80 Landesstrasse

Urban area

(Inset map labels: GERMANY, Lower Rhine Graben, Rhine, Bonn, Ahr, Mittelrhein, Eifel Mountains, Eifel Volcanic Field, Koblenz, Wittischer Senke, Mosel, Mainz, BELGIUM, LUXEMBOURG, See p145 for more detailed map, Fault line)

(*rotliegend*) soils of the Birkweiler Kastienenbush in the Pfalz (two-hours south). Although there are dozens of factors that contribute to a wine's profile, Dr. Fischer establishes a clear connection between vineyard geology and wine style, a solid bit of scientific bedrock supporting what wine drinkers have observed for centuries.

Ahr & Mittelrhein: The Eifel Volcanic Field

The Eifel Volcanic Field is a vast area of now-dormant hotspot volcanism containing over 200 volcanoes in western Germany, north of the Mosel River. It runs roughly from the borders of Belgium and Luxemburg to well east of the Rhine River. It's Germany's youngest volcanic area; the last great eruption occurred just 12,000 years ago, an event large enough to spread pumice and ash over thousands of square kilometres (miles) from Sweden to northern Italy. Although the eruptive phase seems to have subsided, there are clearly still chambers of hot magma beneath the earth's surface, revealed by numerous geysers.

Isolated parts of the Ahr and Mittlerhein wine regions lie within this field. The **Ahr Valley**, protected by the Eifel Mountains to the north, has a small percentage of basaltic rocks and tuff – just a handful of hectares out of the region's 550. Landskrone, one of the most distinctive landmarks in the valley, is an extinct, slow eruption volcano on the north side of the Ahr River opposite the town of Heimersheim that projected basalt and pyroclastic material through older Devonian sediments. It lends its name to the Heimersheimer Landskrone vineyard, and its basalts also underlie the neighbouring Heimersheimer Burggarten, both designated Erste Lage by the VDP. Pinot Noir is the most planted variety in the Ahr, though terroir expression is for the time being overridden by overly ripe grapes and enthusiastic use of new wood.

At the northern gateway to the **Mittlerhein**, south of Bonn and north of Koblenz where the Mosel meets the Rhine, lies another area of Eifel volcanics around the Laacher See, a crater lake created by an explosive eruption that covered a wide area of the Rhine

---

OPPOSITE ABOVE *The town of Bad Münster under the imposing pink-tinged Rotenfels, 'red cliff', composed of porphyry rock, volcanic vestiges in the Nahe.*

OPPOSITE BELOW *Extinct Landskrone volcano on the north bank of the Ahr River.*

Bastei Vineyard name

⬤ Vineyard and principal
    grape-growing area

••••• Wine region boundary

    Predominantly volcanic
    soil

▼ Recommended winery

🔲41 Autobahn

🔲B428 Bundesstrasse

🔲L412 Landesstrasse

⬤ Urban area

2 km

2 miles

GERMANY

Mosel   Rhine   Rheinhessen

LUX.   Ürzig   Mosel
    Witticher
    Senke   Bad Kreuznach
            Nahe   Nahe
    Saar-Nahe Senke   Oberrheim Graben
FRANCE   Saar   (Upper Rhine Graben)

See p145 for more detailed map

- - - Fault line

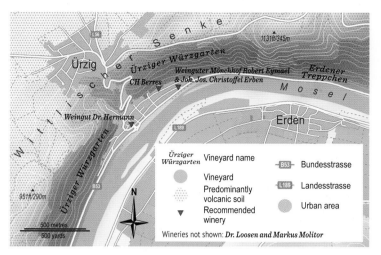

especially around nearby Leutesdorf, and the Siebengebirge (Seven Hills). The hills were formed by a hotspot of magma that rose from deep beneath the earth's surface, swelling the ground above like a pimple, but never quite breaking through in an eruptive phase. The magma cooled slowly into trachyte, a potassium-rich, alkali volcanic rock type between basalt but closer to rhyolite in composition, which is unique to this area of Germany.

Drachenfels (Dragon's Cliff) is the name of one of these seven hills, as well as a perilously steep vineyard rising up to 321 metres (1053 feet) on the east side of the Rhine, opposite the town of Königswinter. In some south-southwest facing sections the slope angle exceeds 50 per cent. High potassium serves to buffer acidity, which, here at the extreme northern latitude of 50.6 degrees, is a welcome phenomenon. 'Riesling from Trachyt is always very well balanced in acidity and opens early on the palate,' describes Felix Pieper of Weingut Pieper, one of just three estates with vineyards in the Drachenfels along with Blöser and Broel-Blöser. The vineyard is a fraction of its medieval size due to the difficulty of farming such a steep site, but it's ripe for discovery.

Mosel: The Wittlischer Senke

Volcanics in the Mosel are much older then Eifel basalts, in fact over 280 million years older. The meandering Mosel River loops northward at the village of Ürzig into the Wittlischer Senke, a shallow depression, like a trough on the earth's surface named after the village of Wittlisch. The trough marks where the earth was pulled apart along a fault, causing a section of crust to sink. Fissures along the edges allowed underlying magma to spill out onto the surface forming silica rich lavas, rhyolites, tuff and ignimbrite. Ürzig is the only Mosel wine-growing village on the rift line, and the spectacular amphitheatre-shaped, ludicrously steep Würzgarten is the only vineyard where volcanic flow mixes with older Devonian slate and sandstone to form blazing red, iron-rich soils. The Ürziger Würzgarten ('spice garden of Ürzig') is a GG planted only to ungrafted Riesling, distinguished from other Mosel Riesling by its typically deeper colour and exotic flavours of mango, peach/apricot, honey, smoke and spice. It's made in all styles from off-dry Kabinett to luscious Trockenbeerenauslese (TBA).

Nahe & Rheinhessen: The Saar-Nahe Senke

South of the Mosel is another area of rifting known as the Saar-Nahe Senke, which runs roughly from the Saar River in the west to the Nahe River and beyond in the east. It resulted in volcanic flows from about the same period: 285 to 290 million years ago. An area of some 200 hectares in the **Nahe** wine region is planted on these volcanic soils, giving rise to many of the region's finest wines, and little else. In fact, you'll only find vineyards, or forests or quarries in this volcanic zone, as the soil is too infertile for other forms of agriculture.

The most spectacular vestige of volcanism is around Bad Kreuznach, where an immense subterranean volcano collapsed during a period of uplifting and covered the region with rhyolitic rock, known locally by its more ancient name, porphyry. The Rotenfels (Red Cliff) is a spectacular outcrop of this reddish coloured rock, which rises imposingly above the towns of Bad Münster am Stein-Ebernberg and Traisen, with several famous vineyards at its feet such as the Traisener Bastei and Rotenfels.

A little further up the Nahe volcanic formations are more varied, ranging from dark andesites to younger, pale-rose-red rhyolites the colour of German *fleischwürst*, or black pudding (blood sausage), with larger rocks mixed with fine particles. A number of celebrated vineyards on the north side of the Nahe River between Bad Münster and Schlossböckelheim, passing through Norheim, Hüffelsheim, Niederhausen and Oberhausen, as well as Altenbamberg, have volcanic influence. Riesling from these areas is prized for its laser-sharp acids and longevity. Felsenberg, Kupfergrube and Hermannshöhle are some of the best vineyards.

Just east of Bad Münster, across the border into the western extreme of the **Rheinhessen**, is a geological continuation of

OPPOSITE ABOVE *Vertiginous view from Würzgarten vineyard, one of Mosel's only volcanic vineyards.*

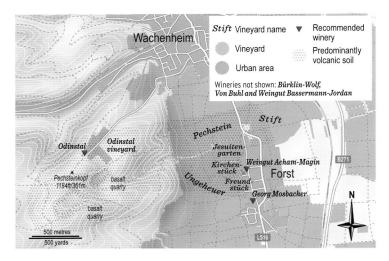

Stift Vineyard name
Vineyard
Urban area
Recommended winery
Predominantly volcanic soil
Wineries not shown: *Bürklin-Wolf, Von Buhl and Weingut Bassermann-Jordan*

Georg Mosbacher. It's among the most expensive vineyards in the country, and produces almost exclusively dry wines. 'The vineyard is special for dry wine,' states *kellermeister* Ulrich Mell of Weingut Bassermann-Jordan matter-of-factly. Adjacent Wachenheimer Gerümpel and Forster Jesuitengarten and Ungeheuer have some basalt influence but are not purely volcanic.

An old basalt quarry near the summit of the Pechsteinkopf is adjacent to the isolated vineyards of Odinstal, first planted in 1820 by Johann Ludwig Wolf. At the time villagers considered him mad, believing that grapes would never ripen in his vineyards at 350 metres (1100 feet) But Wolf came for the soil. The outstanding, majestically concentrated wines of Odinstal today more than vindicate his hunch.

Baden: The Kaiserstuhl Volcanic Complex

Baden is Germany's southernmost wine region and also the most obviously volcanic, in particular the Kaiserstuhl *massif* in southern Baden. The name derives from its roughly horseshoe-shaped ridge open to the southwest that resembles an emperor's chair. The Kaiserstuhl is the only large volcanic complex that rises like an island out of the Rhine Graben up to 557 metres (1830 feet) at the Totenkopf, on the east side of the river, about 20 km (12 miles) northwest of Freiburg, atop the junction of two major faults where periodic eruptions occurred from about 18 million to 16 million years ago. The heavily eroded remnants of a stratovolcano are visible today, surrounded by several smaller parasitic volcanoes such as the Limberg in Sasbach or the Humberg in Burkheim.

Despite its purely volcanic bedrock, a large percentage of the Kaiserstuhl's vineyards are covered in a thick layer of loess, deposited by winds sweeping up the valley from Burgundy, up to 30 metres (100 feet) thick in places. The loess accumulated on the leeward side of hills, mostly on the northeast facing sites, while southwest-facing vineyards, fully exposed to the scouring winds, display their igneous origins. Some of the most highly regarded volcanic vineyards include the Winklerberg of Ihringen, the Kirchberg, Henkenberg, and Eichberg of Oberrotweil, the Kirchberg of Schelingen, the Schlossberg of Achkarren and the Bassgeige of Oberbergen.

In Baden, Riesling's supremacy is finally challenged by the Pinot family: Weisse-, Graü- and Spätburgunder (Pinots Blanc, Gris and Noir), where the notably warmer climate results in Germany's finest examples.

volcanic Nahe. A massive porphyry rock quarry is carved out of the hill southwest of Neu Bamberg, and slightly further east near Siefersheim lie two of the Rheinhessen's finest vineyards, the warm, shallow Höllberg, and the cool, steep and stony Herrkretz, both classified Erste Lage. 'Planting here is a true horror,' relates Oliver Müller of Wagner-Stempel, in reference to the Herrkretz. This distinctively hilly hinterland, referred to locally as the Rheinhessische Schweiz (the Switzerland of the Rheinhessen), has so far remained in the shadow of the more famous wine villages along the Rhine. But considering the quality of the Rieslings from the likes of Wagner-Stempel, and the similarity in style to the justifiably famous wines of the neighbouring Nahe, this will soon change.

Pfalz: The Upper Rhine Graben

Further south, the **Pfalz** lies on the western side of the Oberrheingraben (the Upper Rhine Valley), yet another fault system, albeit on a much, much larger scale. As discussed in the chapter on Alsace (see p.134), the sinking valley through which the Rhine runs has been the site of volcanism for many millions of years, with isolated volcanic formations scattered along its margins. Pechsteinkopf is a basaltic volcano above the town of Forst, which gives its name to one of the village's most revered vineyards, the gently sloped, east-facing GG Forster Pechstein. The name derives from *pech* (pitch), and *stein* (stone), in reference to its abundant pitch-black basaltic stones. Nearly 20 wineries share the Pechstein, all Riesling, including respected names like Von Buhl, Dr. Bürklin-Wolf, Weingut Bassermann-Jordan and

---

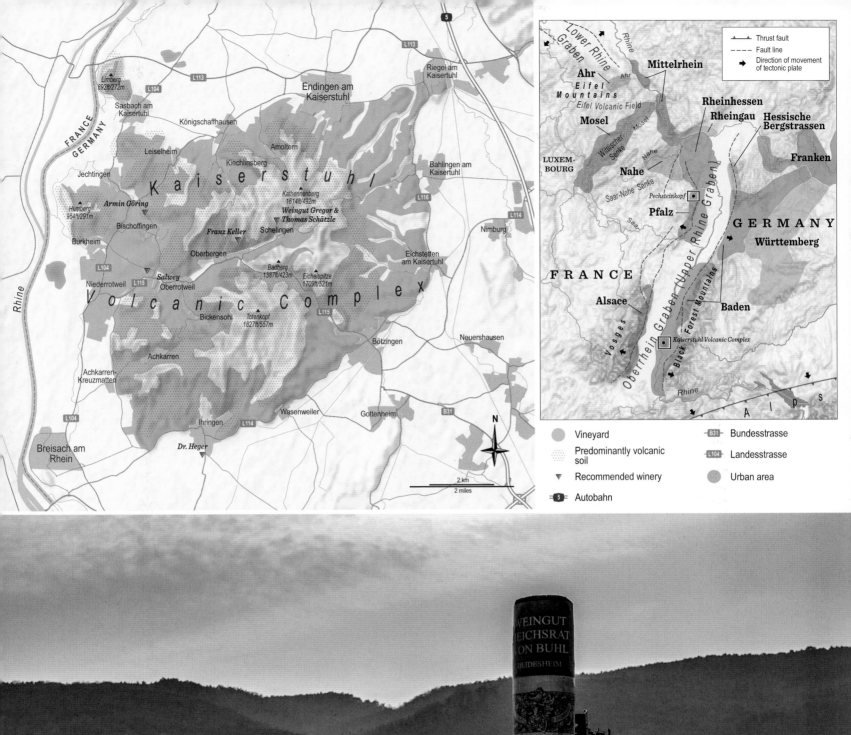

GERMANY – THE WINES & THE PEOPLE

Armin Göring

Bischoffingen
Amthosfstraße
79235 Vogtsburg-Oberbergen
Baden
goering-wein.de

A small operation run by Armin Göring and wife Ulrike Lenhardt (who works for the German Wine Institute) making infinitely drinkable Weiss, Grau and Späburgunder, from several parcels on varied volcanic Kaiserstuhl soils. Designed for pleasure, not competitions. Also top-notch, pot-distilled Pinot Noir.

CH Berres ★

Würzgartenstraße 41
54539 Ürzig-Mosel
Mosel
berres.de

Markus Berres is the 21st generation of the Berres family to make wine from the red-tinged Rotliegend soils of the Würzgarten, from fruity Kabinett to luscious TBA. Versions at the drier end of the spectrum are neither flamboyant nor subdued, often with a typical herbal note and brown spices like clove and nutmeg.

Dönnhoff ★★★

Bahnhofstraße 11
55585 Oberhausen
Nahe
doennhoff.com

Acknowledged master Helmut Dönnhoff crafts the Nahe's, and some of Germany's, most revered wines. 'I express myself clearly and so do my wines,' says Dönnhoff frankly. The majority of production is devoted to Riesling from a collection of top vineyards, largely volcanic. Riesling Felsenberg GG from a very steep, south-facing site on pure weathered porphyry

(rhyolite) is stunningly racy and flinty-mineral; also south-facing Niederhausen Hermannshöhle, with its rhyolite/black slate/limestone mix is the benchmark Nahe vineyard, and Dönnhoff's Riesling the example against which all others are judged. Everything from Dönnhoff is recommended without reserve.

Dr. Bürklin-Wolf ★★★

Weinstraße 65
67157 Wachenheim an der Weinstraße
Pfalz
buerklin-wolf.de

An exceptional, 400-year-old property, now one of the EU's largest Biodyvin-certified biodynamic wine estates. Dry Rieslings from 15 VDP-classified sites are uniformly outstanding, especially Riesling Pechstein GG from a parcel planted in 1978 on the vineyard's pitch-black basalt soils.

Dr. Heger ★★

Bachenstraße 19/21
79241 Ihringen
Baden
heger-weine.de

VDP Baden chairman Dr. Joachim Heger is a top Kaiserstuhl reference, improving on the work of founding grandfather Dr. Max Heger. Entry-level wines are produced from loess sites, top wines from volcanic GG vineyards, especially the exceptionally steep and stony Ihringer Winklerberg in the warm, southwest corner of the region. All wines are dry. Winklerberg Gras Im Offen Grauburgunder hails from a sub-parcel so hot and rocky the grass dries out (literally: Grass in the Oven); Winklerberg Weissburgunder GG v.B. is the most 'volcanic' tasting of the Pinot Blancs, from the Vorderer Berg sub-parcel with the oldest vines and the lowest natural yields. Häusleboden is the top Winklerberg sub-parcel for Pinot Noir, grown on terraced slopes under a wall of lava.

Dr. Loosen ★★

St. Johannishof
54470 Bernkastel-Kues
Mosel
drloosen.de

From entry-level Dr. L, to single-vineyard bottlings from an enviable collection of the Mosel's finest sites, Ernst Loosen produces wines of unwavering quality. Riesling from the Würzgarten comes in Kabinett, Spätlese and Auslese styles, but dry Alte Reben Riesling GG is particularly special, from a small parcel in the heart of the vineyard on the blazing red, volcanic-derived soils gifted by the Wittlischer Senke, with vines approaching 120 years, Loosen's oldest. This old-vine Riesling is seriously firm, beautifully etched and exotic.

Franz Keller ★★

Badbergstraße 44
79235 Vogtsburg-Oberbergen
Baden
franz-keller.de

Indefatigable Fritz Keller operates a hotel and three restaurants, and is chairman of SC Freiburg Football Club, in addition to a hands-on role in this leading Kaiserstuhl estate. A stunning new winery above Oberbergen blends into hillside terraces, completed in time for the 2013 vintage when quality took another leap forward. Fifty labels are made, most are dry; top wines hail from sub-parcels of the volcanic ash and tuff-based Bassgeige vineyard of Oberbergen, the Kirchberg and Eichberg of Oberrotweil and the ultra-stony Schlossberg of Achkarren, all VDP-classified sites. Riveting, waxy and honeyed Bassgeige Weisseburgunder 'Im Leh', smoky Schlossberg Grauburgunder and ultra-refined Bassgeige Spätburgunder stand out in an elegant, understated range, at the top level.

Georg Mosbacher ★★

Weinstraße 27
67147 Forst an der Weinstraße
Pfalz
georg-mosbacher.de

Third generation VDP members Sabine Mosbacher-Düringer and husband Jürgen Düringer are Riesling specialists. Their Pechstein parcel was replanted after the excellent 2012 vintage, so it will be several years before Mosbacher produces this GG. Freshly planted vines go into the Forst Riesling 'Basalt' for now, along with declassified Ungeheuer GG Riesling. Quality in any case is exemplary.

Markus Molitor ★★★

Haus Klosterberg 1
54470 Bernkastel-Wehlen
Mosel
markusmolitor.com

One of the unquestionable stars of the Mosel, Molitor produces wines from 15 meticulously farmed vineyards, each distinct. A rigorously non-interventive, natural approach gives wines of multiple layers and singular character. Capsule colour indicates sweetness: white for dry wines, grey-green for off-dry and gold for sweet/botrytis affected. Molitor's Würzgarten Riesling Spätlese is dramatic, opulent and full-bodied even at low alcohol, replete with honey, tangerine and luscious orchard fruit.

Odinstal ★★★

Odinstalweg
67157 Wachenheim an der Weinstraße
Pfalz
odinstal.de

Thomas Hensel purchased this isolated estate near the forested summit of the Pechsteinkopf volcano in the Pfalz above Wachenheim and Forst in the 1990s, from which Andreas

Schumann produces an outstanding range from Demeter-certified biodynamic vineyards next to an old basalt quarry. Though not all parcels are volcanic; wines are labelled by geological origin: Basalt, Buntsandstein (sandstone), Muschelkalk (limestone) and Keuper. Schumann relates some differences, 'sandstone warms much faster, vines start growing earlier and have access to copious nutrients. The wines ferment faster and are more open when young, with an impression of high acid. Basalt soils have fewer nutrients, vines start growing later, and ripen more slowly and steadily. Wines from these soils are less aromatic, but have more sheer weight and density, and are more harmonious.' Riesling Basalt is consistently roasted and smoky over multiple vintages, a typical basalt signature, also dramatically concentrated, Baroque-style. Weissburgunder Basalt is the class of the Pfalz, pure and intense.

Salwey ★★★

Hauptstraße 2
79235 Oberrotweil am Kaiserstuhl
Baden
salwey.de

Konrad Salwey was thrust into heading the family winery after the unexpected passing of his father in 2011, even if he had already been involved since 2002. With tragedy came opportunity, 'very often we left the grapes out too long. 2011 was the first vintage I was "allowed" to harvest earlier. Spätlese [late harvest] was still very important for my father. I like red wines when they show more elegance than body,' Salwey affirms. Wines have taken a decided turn towards freshness, elegance and less wood, putting Salwey at the pinnacle of Kaiserstuhl wine-growers. Henkenberg, Eichberg and Kirchberg are the estate's volcanic GGs, all in Oberrotweil, the latter a radically stony parcel with pitifully low yields originating the most complete Spätburgunder and Grauburgunder in the range, though all are excellent.

Schäfer-Fröhlich

Schulstraße 6
55595 Bockenau
Nahe
weingut-schaefer-froehlich.de

Perfectionist Tim Fröhlich crafts subtle, classy wines from the volcanic Felsenberg and Kupfergrube GG along the Nahe River. Schloss Böckelheim village blend 'vom Vulkangestein' (the volcanic stone in this case is rhyolite) from parcels up to 320 metres (1000 feet) offers great linearity and drive.

Von Buhl

Weinstraße 18-24
67146 Deidesheim
Pfalz
von-buhl.de

Since 2013, this estate belongs to the same family who owns von Winning and Bassermann-Jordan (in the 19th century they were all one estate). This brought a dramatic change in style, shifting from beautifully ultra-traditional to curiously woody, which can be explained by newly appointed winemaker Matthew Kauffman (formerly of Champagne Bollinger) having to start from scratch – all old casks had been removed and new ones had to be purchased. Though recent releases are unrecognizable to fans of the old style, this is a story to follow.

Wagner-Stempel ★★

Wöllsteiner Straße 10
55595 Siefersheim
Rheinhessen
wagner-stempel.de

The leading estate in 'volcanic' Rheinhessen (and the only VDP member in this far western slice of the region – the rest are all in the more famous villages bordering the Rhine in the east). Daniel Wagner farms organically and production is mostly dry. Top Rieslings hail from the rhyolite-based GG Höllberg, all power, exotic fruit and spice, and Herrkretz, a slimmer, more contained and composed, minerally wine. Excellent Siefersheim 'village' wine blends the young vines from these two sites. In suitable vintages, a small section of the Herrkretz called Turm is bottled separately – the highest acid parcel but harvested very late, yielding Riesling of uncommon density framed by electric freshness.

Weingut Acham-Magin ★

Weinstraße 67
67147 Forst an der Weinstraße
Pfalz
acham-magin.de

A small, under-the-radar, VDP-member winery aiming for finesse and refinement rather than dramatic concentration and opulent fruit. Pechstein Riesling GG from the estate's certified organic parcel is among the livelier, racier and more immediately fragrant examples from the pure basalt site, priced between the basalt-influenced Jesuitengarten and Kirchenstück, two other Forst GGs.

Weingut Bassermann-Jordan ★★★

Kirchgasse 10
67146 Deidesheim
Pfalz
bassermann-jordan.de

A storied and widely respected estate producing a large range of traditionally styled wines from 20 vineyard sites. Pechstein Riesling GG is genuinely concentrated, complete and harmonious – and one of the vineyard's best examples.

Weingut Dr. Hermann ★★

Moselufer 22
54539 Ürzig-Mosel
Mosel
weingut-drhermann.de

Dr. Hermann created this estate in 1967 from his part of the inheritance of the Joh. Jos Christoffel estate. Now managed by son Rudi and grandson Christian, these are robust and intense wines, harvested at the upper level of ripeness for each category, as in the opulent Ürziger Würzgarten Riesling Spätlese, fermented and aged in steel.

Weingut Gregor & Thomas Schätzle

Heinrich-Kling-Str. 38
79235 Vogtsburg im Kaiserstuhl
Baden
weingutschaetzle.de

An up-and coming family estate run by Thomas and daughter Franziska Schätzle. Focus is on Pinot Gris, Pinot Noir and Chardonnay. Estate and Village wines are blends of mainly loess parcels; while the top wines hail from the basalt and tephrit-based Schelinger Kirchberg vineyard, the highest and coolest in the Kaiserstuhl, up to 400 metres (1300 feet). Spätburgunder Schatz von Vulkan, playing off the family name, which means little treasure, balances power with drinkability, made from young Kirchberg vines; Kirchberg Grauburgunder is serious and exotic. Some wines are works in progress.

Weingut K.H. Schneider

Meddersheimer Str. 29
55566 Bad Sobernheim
Nahe
weingut-schneider.com

Karl Heinz Schneider favours slender but expressive, highly mineral wines, as in the Schloss Böckelheim Vulkanstein Riesling Porphyr (rhyolite bedrock), the estate's calling card, with fine tailoring. Also excellent Felsenberg GG from this top weathered rhyolite site in the Nahe.

Weinguter Mönchhof Robert Eymael & Joh. Jos. Christoffel Erben ★★

Mönchhof
54539 Ürzig-Mosel
Mosel
moenchhof.de

One of the Mosel's oldest, former monastic properties dating to 1177, the Eymael family purchased the beautiful baroque manor house called Mönchhof in 1804; Robert Eymael leased the Joh. Jos. Christoffel Erben estate in 2001, and bottles it separately. Würzgarten Riesling Spätlese is multi-dimensional, a reference for the Mosel's only volcanic-influenced (and insanely steep) vineyard. Mönchhof label Würzgarten Riesling is equally compelling and dramatic.

Weingut Pieper

Hauptstraße 458
53639 Königswinter
Mittelrhein
weingut-pieper.de

A small family estate, one of only three with vineyards on Mittelrhein's Drachenfels hill and its trachyte bedrock, unique in Germany. Top Riesling Siegfried Selection is grown under an exposed cliff of trachyte that radiates heat, pushing ripeness and power, yet this is every bit a steely, smoky, north German Riesling, with tart green fruit.

ITALY
AT THE MARGINS OF EURASIA & AFRICA

Italy is not only one of the world's most prolific wine-producing nations (first or second depending on the vintage), but is also one of its most volcanically active. Italy contains the only active volcanoes in mainland Europe, notably Vesuvius and the Campi Flegrei, as well as plenty of island-bound volcanoes, including the island of Vulcano itself – the origin of the western world's word volcano.

The country's impressive contribution to world volcanism arises from its geographic location near the boundary between the Eurasian and African tectonic plates and associated micro plates. The endless jostling, crunching, scraping and subducting of these plates has pushed up the Alps and the Apennines, and caused a chain of volcanism of every kind, from effusive to explosive, from Soave to Sicily. Some of the volcanic areas are long extinct, while others are still alarmingly active. But one thing is clear: without volcanism, the very nature of Italian wine would be profoundly different. Phylloxera-free volcanic soils have helped, in no small measure, to preserve Italy's unparalleled collection of indigenous grapes and its ancient and rich wine-growing culture.

To cover every volcanic wine region in Italy would require several volumes alone. For this work, the focus is on some of the more prominent ones, the volcanic centres known to geologists as the Alpone-Chiampo Graben, which runs through the wine region of Soave, the Vulsini District in southern Tuscany and its corresponding Bianco di Pitigliano/ Sovana DOC, the rich Campanian Volcanic Arc that has touched virtually every wine-growing corner of Campania, Monte Vulture in northern Basilicata, the only volcano east of the Apennines and the Calabrian Volcanic Arc, which includes the still-fermenting magma chambers under Sicily's magnificent Mount Etna, as well as the collection of volcanic islands that surround it.

OPPOSITE *Mount Vesuvius and its two peaks, Monte Somma, left and Vesuvius itself, right (see p.172).*

MOUNT ETNA, SICILY

Between Sicily's two mountain ranges – the Nebrodi along the north coast and the Sicilian Apennines through the centre of the island – Mount Etna rises in solitary grandeur, like an island on the island framed by the Alcantara and Simeto Rivers. To Sicilians, Etna is better known as Mongibello, a combination of the Arabic Gibel, and the Italian Monte, both meaning mountain. It's such a pervasive feature of the island they named it twice.

Etna is a classic stratovolcano, built over the last 600,000 years from successive eruptions that began on the seafloor and have now reached 3350 metres (10,990 feet) above the sea. And it's still growing. Etna is, after all, Europe's, and one of the world's, most active volcanoes. It's existence is associated with the subduction of the African Plate under the Eurasian Plate, though a number of theories have been advanced to explain the details of Etna's particularly active eruptive history, including

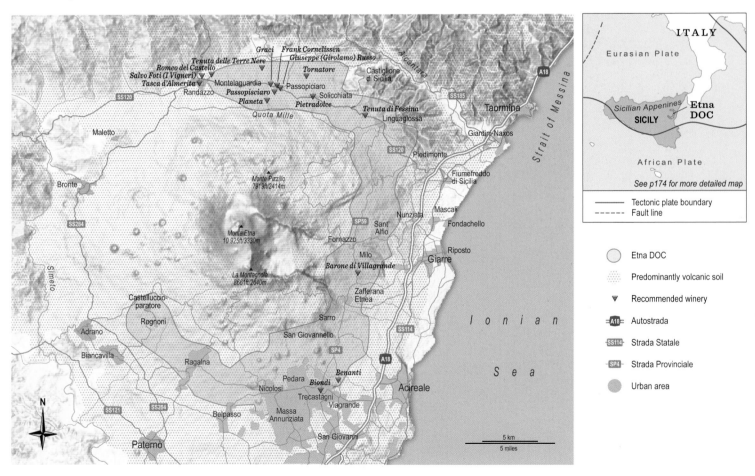

See p174 for more detailed map

OPPOSITE (LEFT TO RIGHT) *Alberello Etneo, Fessina; Archineri Bianco, Pietradolce; Frank Cornelissen, pruning; old casks, Fessina; Biondi's terraced vineyards; Graci; Contrada Barbabecchi; Castiglione di Sicilia; looking north to Etna; old well and terraced vineyards, Terrazze dell'Etna; menu del giorno; old bottles at Barone di Villagrande.*

rifting, a hotspot and an intersection of structural weaknesses in the earth's crust.

Although it appears uniformly conical in shape, Etna has several eruption centres, and literally hundreds of minor cones, vents and fissures on its flanks, adding to its unpredictable nature. Over time, many of these have been obliterated or filled in by subsequent lava flows from above. It's near impossible to predict which side of the mountain will rip open next; the intense seismic activity that usually precedes eruptions provides little more than a few hours' warning.

Throughout recorded history, lava flows have threatened or destroyed many of the heavily inhabited areas of the volcano. Vineyards, too, have come and gone. But their legacy is an amazingly intricate patchwork of volcanic soils, whose nuanced variations are being rendered ever more articulately by a new generation of terroir-obsessed winemakers.

ETNA – 'THE ISLAND ON THE ISLAND'

Mount Etna is both a giver and a taker. Its rich volcanic soils have attracted civilization and provided sustenance to nearby inhabitants for millennia. The quality of Etna's produce has been prized for centuries. But farming these slopes is no rural idyll. The mountain demands backbreaking manual labour, and all too frequently eruptions have obliterated the work of generations in a scorching flash.

Wine has been grown on Etna since Phoenician times, for at least 3500 years. Indeed, the name Etna is believed to derive from the Phoenician word *attuna*, meaning, appropriately enough, furnace. In its hey-day, Etna was among the most prestigious wine regions in all of Magna Grecia and the Roman Empire, and up until the end of the 19th century, vines blanketed its flanks from as high as grapes would ripen down to the Straits of Messina. But a series of uncontrollable circumstances in the 20th century would relegate the wine of Etna to a footnote in the modern Italian wine industry. That is, until the 90s.

The silver lining from that period of darkness is Etna's remarkable collection of old vines. Part of the explanation is the loose, free-draining sandy ash and rocky lava soils with practically no clay, which make the volcano inhospitable to phylloxera; several

---

OPPOSITE ABOVE *White smoke is a good sign – it means mostly harmless water vapour is escaping from Etna; blue or black smoke signals more dangerous activity.*

OPPOSITE BELOW *Old, high-density, chestnut-wood stake-trained vines planted in the* alberello Etneo *system, at Tenuta di Fessina.*

ABOVE *Workers break up volcanic rocks to (re)build kilometres (miles) of walls and terraces at Tornatore; such retaining walls are common across the mountain.*

parcels planted in the 19th century are still producing. Vines also grow very slowly. There's just enough organic matter to keep vines going, and excessive vigour is rarely a concern. And historically vines have been pruned short to reduce yields and increase the chances of ripening, so energy is conserved and vines develop at a tortoise's pace, but travel a long distance in time.

But also, critically, many vineyards were either abandoned in the 20th century, since it was not worth the effort of farming and harvesting them (or even ripping them out). Or, they were maintained solely for family and local consumption. Without commercial pressure, there was no need to replace low yielding, old vines with productive young ones. Etna slept through the post World War II industrialization of Italy, when many old vineyards elsewhere were replanted in productive monocultures. The rocky, perilous slopes of Etna, difficult and expensive to farm, would never have been suitable for industrial wine-growing in any case, and unfashionably pale red and acidic white wines failed to attract much attention. In any event, that an entire generation left the mountain to find a living elsewhere inadvertently preserved old vines for the current one.

By the 1980s there were perhaps only three or four serious bottlers of commercial Etna wine. The modern rebirth is generally credited to Dr. Giuseppe Benanti, a pharmacist who in 1988 decided to revive the family winemaking tradition started by his grandfather, and revitalize the region. Benanti embarked on a five-year research programme to re-learn what had been known a century before – studying the soils and native grapes of Etna and trialing winemaking techniques. He brought on young agronomist/winemaker Salvo Foti, who would become the champion of Etna's grapes and wine-growing traditions, and inspire a legion of followers. The results were quickly embraced in Italy and abroad.

It was the spark that reignited the volcano, drawing dozens of others to its slopes – a dramatic renaissance even for Italy. The theme of grandson reviving grandfather's wine business is common. But many without direct ties to Etna have also joined in the archeological dig to uncover and restore the past. The feeling on this 'island on the island' as the locals consider it, is like a gold rush, everyone hastening to stake claims on parcels of ancient, all-but-abandoned vineyards. New vineyards are being planted, but respecting the lessons of the

ABOVE LEFT *Michele Faro of Pietradolce in his prized Barbagalli vineyard.*

ABOVE RIGHT *Patricia Tóth, winemaker at Planeta's Etna outpost.*

OPPOSITE *Old acacia wood casks in the cellars of Barone di Villagrande, where traditional and technical comfortably meet.*

past: native varieties are farmed in the traditional *alberello Etneo* style. *Palmenti*, the traditional stone-press houses using centuries-old technology that were once part of every household and community, are being refurbished. The surging energy on the mountain is palpable. And the reason is simple: the wines of Etna are unlike any others on planet earth, and the world wants more.

Etna's Grapes

Carricante is Etna's principal white variety, defined by stony flavours and salinity. Native Italian variety expert Ian d'Agata describes it as, 'potentially one of Italy's greatest cultivars, white or red; when properly tended to it yields wines of great longevity and intense mineral character.' Acids are surprisingly fresh and vibrant considering the southerly latitude of Sicily. Catarratto, Minella and Trebbiano are complementary blending varieties, usually included because they're mixed in old field blends.

The chief red protagonist, and one of Italy's finest red varieties, is late-ripening Nerello Mascalese. Its pale crimson-garnet colour (*nerello* means 'little black') draws comparisons with Pinot Noir or Nebbiolo, never deeply coloured, as does its ability to reflect even minor variations in terroir. It features high acids and significant tannins, which can be somewhat fierce if not fully ripe, and marvellous perfume, full of wild strawberry, sour cherry and currants and plenty of savoury herbal and tobacco notes. Given

enough time it develops a magical profile of nearly pure umami-driven flavours, like an essence of dried porcini.

Much of Etna Rosso is pure Nerello Mascalese, though many bottlings, especially from the south side, include a small percentage of companion grape Nerello Cappuccio. The blend is sensible; Cappuccino, being both lower in tannin and deeper in colour, softens and darkens. On its own it generally fails to reach the grandeur of Mascalese.

Etna – the Region, Soils & Wines

The **Etna DOC** covers a semi-circular crescent around the south, east and north sides of the volcano; only the west flank is excluded. Vine-growing starts at around 350 metres (1150 feet) and rises to 1000 metres (3300 feet). The Strade Provinciale Etna Settentionale road, known colloquially as *Quota Mille* ('Elevation One-Thousand'), draws the upper boundary of the appellation for a stretch on the north side. But it's far from a straight line. The delimited zone zigzags up and down; when the appellation borders were drawn in 1968, only 'active' vineyards were taken into consideration, and thus abandoned vineyards at higher elevations weren't included. Many have since been recovered and produce remarkable wines, certainly worthy of the DOC, but are legally only entitled to the **IGT Sicilia** or **Terre Siciliane** designations. Most agree, however, that the sweet spot is between 600 and 800 metres (2000 to 2600 feet).

Many vineyards are terraced to prevent the loose volcanic ash and sand from washing down the mountain. Etna experiences much higher rainfall than the rest of Sicily – a function of its considerable height and bulk. The water-charged Scirocco that blows in from the south drops its moisture on the upper slopes, and considerable snowmelt also contributes to erosion.

Rainfall and average temperatures vary dramatically from year to year, leading to big vintage variation. Southern slopes are notably warmer than east or north-facing slopes, logically, and exposure plays a large role in wine character. But even more important is elevation: rainfall increases, and average temperatures decrease as you move up. There can be several weeks' difference in harvest time between the lowest and highest elevation vineyards. Nerello Mascalese struggles to ripen if planted too high, but fails to shine with all its beauty from a site too low and warm, hence the sweet spot.

Although all volcanic in origin, the soils, too, show considerable differences (and some of the ash is not even from Etna, but rather from a massive explosion of nearby Lipari Island long ago). While some generalizations hold true – such as low clay content, low water holding capacity and a richness in trace elements (particularly iron, potassium, sodium, calcium, phosphorous, magnesium and manganese) soil depth and physical characteristics are as varied as the number of people who farm them.

Elevation also plays a large role in the depth of volcanic soils. The reason is simple: fewer lava flows, and less volume, make it down to the lower elevations. Thus the basalt in vineyards below about 500 metres (1600 feet) is more like a thin veneer over the limestone base on which Etna was formed, and vine roots find their way into an alternate universe from the volcanic world above. In the glass, the wines are clearly different, with more ripe red fruit and less mineral and spice flavour. The age of the lava flow, and the relative mix of ash and scoria also alter chemical composition and, more importantly, soil structure. Every variation from very fine, pulverized volcanic ash to small basaltic pebbles to barely weathered, pure rocky soils can be found, which, of course, have their say on wine style. On this aspect there's still a great deal of work to be done, but investigations are underway, and already exciting differences are observed, especially within a single producer's portfolio.

The Etna denomination provides for the production of sparkling, white, rosé and red wines, all exclusively from indigenous grape varieties. **Etna Bianco** is made predominantly from Carricante (minimum 60 per cent by law, but in practice much more). The finest are grown on the east side, with its gentler morning sun and marine influence from the Straits of Messina, at 700 metres (2300 feet) and above around the town of Milo, which is the only sub-zone entitled the designation **Etna Bianco Superiore**.

Etna Rosso is made from Nerello Mascalese (80 per cent minimum, with possible addition of Nerello Cappuccio), **Riserva** versions require at least a year in wood and four years total ageing before release. **Etna Rosato** is made from the same variety(ies) and, though production is limited, is potentially outstanding – pale in colour, bone dry, sharp and savoury, quite the antithesis to fashionably modern, sweet, pink wines.

Etna Labels: Cru & Contrada

Top Etna wines are often labelled by their *contrada* (plural: *contrade*) of origin – essentially town districts or agglomerated parcels of agricultural land. Now officially obsolete, for wines these function very much like, say, village names in Burgundy, where vineyards are shared, in most cases, by many wine-growers. *Contrada* is used interchangeably with cru (the name of the cru is the name of the *contrada*) ie. Terre Nere's 'Calderara Sottana' or Giuseppe Russo's 'San Lorenzo'. Legally, the wine must come 100 per cent from vineyards in the named *contrada*.

The use of unofficial vineyard names within a *contrada* adds another layer of labelling complexity. An example is Pietradolce's Barbagalli cru, a single vineyard within the *contrada* Rampante. The name comes from the family who farmed the parcel for generations before Pietradolce took it over. 'In Sicily, after many years, an area comes to be known by the name of the family who owns it, at least unofficially,' Michele Faro explains. But there are no regulations around the use of such names. Still others use fantasy names unrelated to either *contrada* or vineyard parcels – Frank Cornelissen's Magma cuvée, entirely from the Barbabecchi *contrada*, or Munjebel from Chiusa Spagnola, are examples. So in the end, how is one to know what the name on the label means? The answer is a little background research. Price, too, is a useful if imperfect guide, as the single-vineyard/cru/*contrada* wines are almost always the most expensive in a producer's range.

MOUNT ETNA, SICILY – THE WINES & THE PEOPLE

Barone di Villagrande ★★

Via del Bosco 25
95010 Milo
villagrande.it

Tenth generation Marco Nicolosi and wife
Barbara head this historic estate, the oldest
still-operating vineyard on Etna, since 1727.
The first vintage bottled, 1940, must be among
the first, if not *the* first commercially bottled
Etna wine. Carlo Nicolosi, Marco's father,
was instrumental in drafting the regulations
for the Etna DOC, granted in 1968. It's rare
to see multi-generational enterprises excel
in an environment as dynamic as Etna's,
often overburdened with tradition. But Barone
di Villagrande manages just that, producing
classically styled yet technically sound wines.
Vineyards are planted in a natural amphitheatre
on the cooler, east side of the mountain at
700 metres (2300 feet). Etna Bianco Superiore
is an archetype: lean, dry, saline. Legno di
Conzo from Villagrande's most elegant,
aromatic parcel of Carricante is a magnificent,
age-worthy white. Savoury Etna Rosso
Lenza di Mannera is aged for six years before
release, a statement on Etna Rosso's ability,
and need, to age.

Benanti ★

Contrada Monte Serra
Via Giuseppe Garibaldi 361
95029 Viagrande
vinicolabenanti.it

Credited with kick-starting the revival of
Etna wine in the late 80s (see p.156), Giuseppe
Benanti and now sons Antonio and Salvino run
this high-profile operation. Pure Carricante
whites are memorable: Bianco di Caselle, and
even more minerally and stony, Pietramarina
Etna Bianco Superiore. The latter, from
alberello-trained vines on the eastern side
in the commune of Milo, is among Etna's finest,
held four years before release. Rounded and
soft Serra della Contessa, from a parcel of
centenary, partially ungrafted vines on the
Monte Serra crater on Etna's lower eastern
flank, and sharper, more chiselled Rovittello
from the north side, planted with old *alberello*-
trained vines, are the estate's two red crus,
both more savoury than fruity.

Biondi *

Corso Sicilia 20
95039 Trecastagni
ibiondi.com

In 1999 Ciro Biondi revived the vineyards once
farmed by his grandfather on Etna's southeast
side. He and English wife Stef apply a traditional
approach, following organic/biodynamic
principles. Simple but engagingly fruity Outis
(*nessuno* or 'nobody' in Sicilian dialect) Rosso
is a vineyard blend. Fresh and salty, steel-aged
Outis Bianco is a blend of Carricante with
Catarratto and Minella. White cru, barrel-
fermented Chianta, made with skin contact, is
golden-coloured, gently oxidative, herbal and
dried orange peel tinged. Of two cru reds,
Cisterna Fuori is the more masculine, savoury
and sturdy, from young (2300-year-old) soils;
delicate and floral San Nicolo is from a much
older crater formed 12,000 years ago with more
weathered, finer volcanic sand.

Frank Cornelissen ★★

Via Nazionale 297
95012 Solicchiata
frankcornelissen.it

Belgian Frank Cornelissen purchased his first small parcel of old *alberello*-trained vines on Etna's north side in 2001, and proceeded to shake the foundations with his radically natural winemaking. Cornelissen spurns 'all possible interventions on the land we cultivate, including any treatments, whether chemical, organic or biodynamic, as these are all a mere reflection of the inability of man to accept nature as she is and will be.' The search for absolute authenticity led Cornelissen to experiment with epoxy-lined clay amphorae – the first in Sicily to do so (at least since ancient times), in an effort to eliminate any outside flavour influence not directly from grapes. His craft has evolved since early releases and these are now wines of beguiling rusticity, graceful and lifted, far from the mainstream. From base Rosso del Contadino (peasant's red), a blend of vineyards and varieties including white grapes in some vintages, to MunJebel Rosso (formerly a blend of vintages but as of 2012 a vintage-dated wine) to the crus Chiusa Spagnola, Monte Colla and Porcaria, the fine and ultra-elegant Vigne Alte blend from Cornelissen's highest parcels of ungrafted vines, and finally the '*grand vin*', Magma, made from the Barbabecchi cru at 900 metres (3000 feet), these are intensely savoury, wild, and earthy, heavily umami-laden wines of unimpeachable authenticity.

Giuseppe (Girolamo) Russo ★★

Via Regina Margherita 78
Frazione Passopisciaro
95012 Castiglione di Sicilia

Trained pianist Giuseppe Russo farms this excellent family estate organically on Etna's north side. Among reds, Á Rina is the (not so) entry-level vineyard blend, exuberantly fruity with classic precision and minerality, acidity and firmness. More brooding Feudo, made from several old parcels, leans towards savoury wild herbs. San Lorenzo is invariably the latest cru to blossom, a mouth-gripping, dark and stormy wine from the lowest yields and oldest vines – some over 100 years old, on particularly rocky soils. Rich Etna Bianco Nerina and purpose-grown, lively Etna Rosato round out the fine offerings.

Graci ★★

Contrada Arcurìa (Passopisciaro)
95012 Castiglione di Sicilia
graci.eu

Trading banking for winemaking, Alberto Graci revived family winemaking traditions in 2004, making pure and refined, elegant wines from mostly old vines farmed organically in the crus of Arcurìa, and the jewel, a pre-phylloxera plot of own-rooted Nerello in *contrada* Barbabecchi (at over 1000 metres/3300 feet). There's not a barrique in site in the winery. Vibrant Etna Bianco (Carricante with 30 per cent Catarratto) is pleasantly saline; younger vines Etna Rosso offers engaging bright red fruit on a light but firm frame. Concentration steps up with Etna Rosso Arcurìa (or Quota 600 until 2012), notably succulent and minerally. Barbabecchi is an Etna reference.

Passopisciaro ★

Contrada Guardiola
95012 Castiglione di Sicilia
passopisciaro.com

Established in 2000, Passopisciaro was the first significant investment by an 'outsider', Roman born, Tuscan-based winemaker Andrea Franchetti (of Tenuta di Trinoro), following a chance conversation with a friend. 'When Andrea saw the terraced vineyards of the Guardiola property for the first time, abandoned since the lava flow of 1947, he knew it was perfect,' estate manager Vincenzo Lo Mauro recalls. Additional parcels on the north side were subsequently acquired. Franchetti, initially sceptical about Etna's indigenous varieties, planted Cesanese d'Afile, Petit Verdot and Chardonnay at ultra-high density, 12,300 vines/hectare. Nerello Mascalese hasn't been entirely abandoned, however, but according to Lo Mauro, 'we're still looking for a style'. The style produced thus far is extreme: late-harvested, with alcohol often surpassing 15% ABV, surely concentrated and carefully made. Only large old wood is used and wines are unfined and unfiltered; all are labelled as Sicilia IGT, even those that would otherwise qualify for the Etna DOC.

Pietradolce ★ ★ ★

Contrada Rampante
95012 Solicchiata
Castiglione di Sicilia
pietradolce.it

A model small estate making top-level, authentically regional wines from mostly old vines, including several pre-phylloxera parcels. Michele Faro's grandfather grew grapes and made wine on Etna, and some of the oldest parcels were in family hands, so he got off to a running start in 2005. Vineyards are on the north side, all above 600 metres (2000 feet): tiny Barbagalli with gnarled centenary bush-trained Nerello Mascalese is the highest and most precious, yielding succulent, spectacularly balanced wines, with endless finish. Cru Archineri is nearly as impressive, also from old vines planted a few metres (feet) below Barbagalli. Steely, flinty-mineral Archineri Bianco is from 100-year-old+ Carricante near Milo on Etna's east side. Infinitely drinkable Etna Rosso from younger *alberello*-trained vines is well proportioned with delicate red fruit. Purpose-made Etna Rosato from 40-year-old trellised vines rounds out the superb range.

Planeta – Cantina Feudo di Mezzo

Contrada Sciara Nuova
95012 Castiglione di Sicilia
planeta.it

A promising venture on the north side of Etna by Sicilian heavyweight Planeta, the latest of six operations on the island. The initial plan was to focus on whites, though potential for reds was soon recognized. Carricante and Riesling, Nerello Mascalese and Pinot Nero were replanted in 2009. Entry-level Etna Bianco and Rosso are easy drinking; Eruzione 1614, named for the memorable ten-year long eruption and lava flow, is Planeta's more serious range. Riesling's powerful aromatics dominate Eruzione Bianco, while Eruzione Rosso shows the typically light-medium body and crunchy acids of Nerello Mascalese. A winery was built right into an earlier 1566 lava flow in 2012 and winemaker Patricia Tóth joined 2013. The best is still ahead.

Romeo del Castello ★ ★

Strada Provinciale 89
95036 Randazzo
romeodelcastello.it

Like many, Chiara Vigo moved back to Etna in 2007 to revive family winemaking traditions, spurred on by Salvo Foti (see next entry), who also consulted in the early years. 'He made me understand that I had a treasure, something I wasn't really conscious of. He gave me the confidence to start making my family's wine again,' states Vigo. But she very nearly had nothing to come back to. The lava flow of 1981 threatened to devour the entire family property between Randazzo and Montelaguardia, but took an unexpected turn to the east, sparing a few hectares of centenary vines. A supremely delicate winemaking touch is applied to just two wines, the graceful and lively steel-aged Allegracore from younger vines and Vigo, from the oldest surviving vines surrounded by the hardened lava flow, a wine of amazing finesse and silky texture, both fruity and savoury, one of the treasures of Etna.

Salvo Foti (I Vigneri)

L.go Signore Pietà 17
95036 Randazzo
ivigneri.it

Modelled on the Winemakers Guild of Catania established in 1435, I Vigneri is an association of producers established in 2000 and led by Salvo Foti, a polarizing figure who has become the unofficial ambassador and safe guarder of wine-related traditions on Mount Etna. Foti has given himself the mission of recovering the volcano's multi-millennial winemaking history by salvaging century-old abandoned vineyards and deserted *palmenti* and, importantly, teaching others how to do it. Among other things, Foti's laudable philosophy insists on farming only traditional *alberello*-trained vines, wild ferments, pressing in *palmenti* and moving wine by gravity. Sulphur is avoided and nothing is fined or filtered. It's a sort of wine-growing that would have been familiar in the 17th century. Wines are dramatic in every sense, reaching inconsistent highs and lows, idiosyncratic, some oxidized, some glorious.

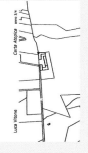

Tasca d'Almerita – Tascante Estate

Contrada Boccadorzo and Contrada Sciaranova
95036 Randazzo
tascadalmerita.it

Giuseppe Tasca d'Almerita's attention was first drawn to Etna in 1999 with 'a 1968 Nerello that was still so fresh after 30 years,' he recalls, and the hook was in. But it would take a decade for the esteemed wine family, anchored in central Sicily at the 500-hectare Tenuta Regaleali, to bring the 'Tascante' project (Tasca and Etna, backwards), to fruition on Etna's north side. Carricante Buonora is simple but crisp, green-apple and citrus-tinged. Nerello Ghiaia Nera is pale and juicy, from young vines. The top selection of old vines is called simply Tascante, followed by the vintage edition; 2008 was the Prima Vendemmia ('first harvest'). The style is light, fresh and savoury, Giuseppe's preference. Wines are processed at the Regaleali Estate, though a winery on Etna is planned.

Tenuta di Fessina ★★

Contrada Rovittello Via Nazionale SS 120
22, 95012 Castiglione di Sicilia
tenutadifessina.com

A jewel of an estate walled in on two sides by lava flows, conjuring up the image of a natural *clos*, producing supremely refined and quietly confident wines. Tuscan Sylvia Maestrelli (of Villa Petriolo, also Ero in Sicily's Val di Noto) and agronomist/winemaker Federico Curtaz from the Val d'Aosta launched Fessina in 2007 with the aim of expressing a place, rather than imposing a style. Curtaz, who worked for two decades with Angelo Gaja, quickly understood the gentle handling Nerello Mascalese needs. Base material is clearly excellent: mostly own-rooted, pre-phylloxera, high-density, *alberello*-trained vines on Etna's north side in *contrada*

Rovittello (650 metres/2100 feet). Particularly fine, black volcanic sand favours finesse over structure. Top Etna Rosso Musmeci is a wine of marvellous finesse, sizzling acids and a gorgeous, silky texture. Musmeci Etna Bianco Superiore, from Carricante planted in 1920 at 1000 metres (3300 feet) on Etna's east side, is lean and angular in the best sense. Erse is the excellent, regionally representative, entry red and white from younger vines.

Tenuta delle Terre Nere ★★★

Contrada Calderara
95036 Randazzo
tenutaterrenere.com

Italian-American wine-importer-turned-producer Marc de Grazia has arguably done more than anyone to put Etna on the international map. Considering his vast connections, it's telling that he chose Etna to establish his first (and only) winemaking venture, first released in 2002. Terre Nere (Black Soils) farms multiple parcels on Etna's north side organically, mostly terraced, traditional *alberello* plantings, including the venerable pre-phylloxera Vigna di Don Peppino speculated to be nearly 140 years old, at the pinnacle of the range. All wines are regionally representative; basic Etna Bianco, Rosso and Rosato are models. Complexity and concentration soar in the four crus: Feudo di Mezzo's volcanic ash and pebbles yield a silky and cedary wine; Guardiola, the highest parcel on volcanic sand and basaltic pebbles, is tight and austere, always slow to open; adjacent Santo Spirito's radically different soils – black volcanic ash as fine as talcum powder – is tender and luscious, the most seductive; Calderara Sottana with the rockiest soils is often the most complete with the broadest spectrum of flavours.

Tornatore

Via Pietramarina, 8A – CAP
95012 Castiglione di Sicilia
tornatorewine.com

A promising estate established in 2013 by successful businessman Francesco Tornatore on the foundations of the family property. Massive investments include a new cellar (built at a speed hitherto unheard of in Sicily), rebuilding kilometres (miles) of lava rock walls and terraces, restructuring and replanting vineyards. When all are in production, Tornatore will be the largest producer of Etna DOC. 2014 tank samples are auspicious, showing uniform structure, tightly wound and expressive of the property's various terroirs.

BASILICATA

Just across the eastern border of Campania in the region of Basilicata stands the 1326 metre (4350 foot) Monte Vulture (pronounced VOOl-too-reh), an extinct stratovolcano. It's unique in being the only volcano in Italy on the east side of the Apennines, and lends its name, and its basalt-derived soils, to the Aglianico del Vulture DOCG – Basilicata's most important wine appellation.

Vulture's eruptive history starts around one million years ago with a violently explosive phase that released massive quantities of ignimbrite, most of which was covered by later volcanic material. The phase that directly affects wine-growing began a half million years ago, when renewed explosive activity – Plinian eruptions – deposited *tufi chiari* (pale tuffs, also called Barile-Rionero tephra after the two towns where the largest deposits fell) across the region.

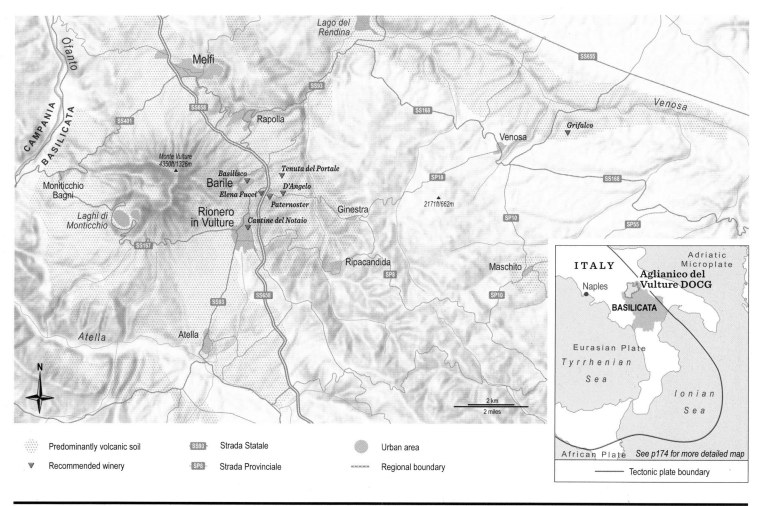

| | Predominantly volcanic soil | SS93 Strada Statale | Urban area |
| | Recommended winery | SP8 Strada Provinciale | Regional boundary |

ITALY
Aglianico del Vulture DOCG
Adriatic Microplate
Naples
BASILICATA
Eurasian Plate
Tyrrhenian Sea
Ionian Sea
African Plate
See p174 for more detailed map
Tectonic plate boundary

OPPOSITE (LEFT TO RIGHT) *Basalt layers, D'Angelo vineyards; Basilisco, Barile; cellar row, Barile; slow traffic; Elena Fucci; Monte Vulture; slow-paced life, Barile; cellar row, Barile; Basilisco, Vigna di Mezzo; Paternoster; basalt with clay layers, Elena Fucci; propagating own-rooted vines, Basilisco.*

164   ITALY

Effusive lava flows during this same period slowly built up the bulk of the volcano, while a further series of basalt lava beds were later laid down. This combination of tuff and basalt forms the parent material on which Vulture's finest vineyards are planted, mostly on the east side of the mountain, between 300 and 600 metres (1000 to 2000 feet). The volcanic material has had plenty of time to weather into heavier clays, much more than the rest of southern Italy's younger volcanic centres. Vulture's last eruptions around 40,000 years ago affected only the uppermost craters, above the vineyard sweet spot.

TIMELESS BASILICATA

Basilicata is a little-visited, almost timeless, bucolic land dominated by agriculture. There are still no *autrostradas* here, the super-highways that link up the rest of the peninsula. The odd car travels on narrow two-lane highways at best, but more frequently on single-lane country roads or unpaved dirt tracks. Shepherds with flocks of sheep might have just stepped out of the Middle Ages. The caves carved out of the lavas underneath the town of Barile might be prehistoric refuges, 16th century wine cellars or contemporary wine shops. Swaying wheat fields, olive groves and stone houses look just as I imagine they have for eons.

Arriving here, it's difficult to pin down the precise year you've stepped into. And as Italy's most sparsely populated region, you can travel for miles without meeting another soul to ask the time.

Basilicata's wine, too, has an ageless dimension. 'It's a land of eternal promise,' muses Vito Paternoster, whose grandfather Anselmo started Basilicata's first commercial winery in 1925. 'But the promise has not yet been fully realized.' Despite small production, styles vary widely, from ancient to post-modern. From the charmingly dried-fruit, pot-pourri-scented wines aged in the antique *botti* of D'Angelo, to the comfortable blend of traditional mindset and hi-tech equipment of Paternoster and the seductive, barrique-informed wines of Elena Fucci made from grapes grown as they were 500 years ago, Basilicata is a constant surprise.

There's still work to be done, but the overall quality potential of the wines from the upper, lava-covered slopes of Monte Vulture is clearly enormous. Here, majestic Aglianico takes on a new and unique dimension. If the Aglianicos of Taburno and Falerno del Massico are the comforting, open-armed grandmothers of the family, and Taurasi the stately aristocratic patriarch, then Vulture at its best would be the sophisticated aunt, full of grace and charm, captivating and refined. Aglianico del Vulture might well be Italy's best, least-known wine.

ABOVE *Majestic Monte Vulture, surrounded by the bucolic charm of Basilicata.*

The Region & the Basalts of Vulture

Given its southerly location, you may be surprised to learn that it snows a half-dozen times a year in the higher elevations of Vulture. The crenellated mountain commands the northern outpost of Basilicata, overlooking the plains that spill over into Puglia and Molise. In contrast to the seaside warmth of the Campanian coast it feels markedly cooler here, the air a little more tense and mountainous. There is also no protective embrace of hills, as in Avellino a short drive away, to hamper the progress of wind; currents from the south whistle unimpeded across the suave landscape, in a rush to meet the vineyards that tumble down the foothills of the volcano. Vulture has a climate of extremes.

Aglianico, the only permitted grape variety, is a late-ripening grape at the best of times. But on Vulture, the harvest stretches regularly into November, at a time when the rest of Italian vintners, save perhaps for those on the upper slopes of Mount Etna, or those precariously close to Switzerland far up the Aosta Valley, have moved on to other tasks in the wine-grower's calendar.

Vulture's ingenious but labour-intensive, traditional vine-trellising method is called *vigna a capanno*, introduced by Albanian immigrants in the 15th century. Three posts are tied together like a tripod over a single vine. One of the posts is fixed, while the other two are moveable. Vines are tied to the moveable posts so that grape bunches develop inside the tripod, under a protective canopy of leaves that shade from the sun and lessen the damage caused by the occasionally fierce winds. The moveable part of the tripod is shifted up to four times during the growing season, as the arc of the sun across the sky changes, and prevailing winds shift. It's not difficult to understand why this system is disappearing, but it's still in use for some of Vulture's top wines.

The soils of Vulture are distinct from other volcanic areas in southern Italy, and much older. Vulture's prolonged eruptive era resulted in a succession of layers of different volcanic materials interspersed with layers of clay that formed from weathering rocks during the quiet periods. Even the youngest layer has already heavily weathered into soil, much as you'd find in, say, Soave, Pantelleria, Oregon's Willamette Valley or Tokaj in Hungary. Much of the mineral content has thus been leached out, making the soils only modestly fertile, much less than in younger Taurasi, for example.

The greatest advantage of Vulture's soil is its selective water-holding capacity; rain filters through the more free-draining rocky deposits into the layers of clay and volcanic tuff where moisture and nutrients accumulate, a useful property in Vulture's dry climate. Vine roots plunge deeply to find these thin layers, where just enough, but not too much, water and nutrients are available. Locals describe these layers as '*il tufo che allatta*', the tuff that gives 'milk' in the nourishing, metaphoric sense. Water stress is rarely an issue, and ripening progresses slowly and evenly.

Yet soil composition varies considerably from parcel to parcel on the mountain, and especially with a vineyard's relative distance to the eruptive craters. This is, in part, the explanation for the disparity in wine styles across the **Aglianico del Vulture DOCG**. It's also the source of internecine strife among growers, arguing

over what should be considered 'true' Aglianico del Vulture. When the appellation was upgraded to DOCG status in 2011, the entire zone, from the highest vineyards on the volcano all the way to the flat, sandy plains bordering Puglia, were given the official benediction. Thus wines grown almost as close to the Ionian Sea as they are to the volcano can legally be called Aglianico del Vulture, even though they have little in common. In reality, Vulture should be at least two separate appellations, if not more. Or, sub-zones should be demarcated to give consumers a chance to better understand these wines.

Logically, volcanic influence diminishes as you move further away from Vulture, and the lower the elevation, the warmer the climate. 'The wines are much softer, less complex,' offers Viviana Malafarina, director of the Basilisco estate owned by Campania-based Feudi di San Gregorio, referring to wines from the plains compared to those on the mountain proper, at higher elevations, on pure volcanic soils. Many echo the description. A proposal by some producers has been put forth to create an Alto Vulture

(Upper Vulture) sub-zone, but so far the effort has been blocked by large interests further down the mountain. Yet it's clear that the area around the towns of Rionero, Barile, Rapolla and Melfi, all hugging the upper eastern flanks of the mountain on bonafide volcanic soil, are distinct. Another zone could be created for the superior wines grown around the villages of Ginestra, Ripacandida and Maschito, villages that are high enough up on their own hills to yield wines with the power and drive one would expect from Italy's highest level of classification. The rest could fall under Basilicata IGT.

But until such sub-zones are drawn up, you'll have to rely on the good name and reputation of the producer, and check the address on the label. It's well worth the effort to track down the best. Aglianico del Vulture at its finest is a grand expression of the sort of perfumed and inviting, savoury and minerally, graceful yet firm style of wine that is becoming ever more rare – the kind you might have enjoyed a century or three ago. You might even say it's a timeless wine.

ABOVE *Basilisco's enchanting Lo Storico vineyard, a small parcel of 80-year-old+ own-rooted vines cultivated* a capanno *on pure lava sand.*

OPPOSITE *Monte Vulture last erupted 40,000 years ago; the effusive discharge that built up this stratovolcano occurred much earlier, about 500,000 years ago.*

BASILICATA – THE WINES & THE PEOPLE

Basilisco ★

Via delle Cantine 22
85022 Barile
basiliscovini.it

The Vulture outpost of Feudi di San Gregorio acquired in 2011, with cellar on the arresting 'Shesh' – Barile's row of grottos carved out of the lava bedrock under the town. Vineyards are certified organic, sited in prime areas between 400 to 600 metres (1300 to 2000 feet), the jewel of which is Lo Storico, a small parcel of 80-year-old+, own-rooted vines cultivated *a capanno* on pure lava sand. Teodosio is the softer, earlier-maturing wine made from younger vines and outcrops of marl that yield more pliable Aglianico. Basilisco is the top, old-vine bottling, firm, savoury and rigid, with pronounced balsamic flavours.

Cantine del Notaio

Via Roma 159
85028 Rionero in Vulture
cantinedelnotaio.it

In 1998 Gerardo Giurotrabochetti took over the vineyards that belonged to his grandfather, an impressive collection in the communes of Rionero, Barile, Ripacandida, Maschito and Ginestra, and an extensive cellar, one of the 1200+ carved out of volcanic tuff under Rionero. Cantine del Notaio was named in honour of his father, a local notary public. Wines are distinguished on style and ripeness rather than vineyard origin. Il Repertorio picked towards the end of October is polished, round but still punchy. La Firma harvested in early November is soft and ripe with sweet fruit and abundant new wood flavours. Extreme Il Sigillo, picked into December after grapes have partially desiccated, has Amarone-like richness and alcoholic warmth, the sort of gentle and velvety wine to slowly contemplate.

D'Angelo ★★

Via Padre Pio 8
85028 Rionero in Vulture
dangelowine.com

Along with Paternoster, Rocco D'Angelo was one of the founders of the Vulture wine business, establishing his company in the early 30s to supply wine to beef up the light reds of northern Italy. Style for the most part remains decidedly traditional, drawing on the strength of vineyards in prime volcanic communes Rionero, Barile, Rapolla and Ripacandida. Arch-classic Aglianico del Vulture fermented in concrete and aged in ancient *botti* is a study in savouriness, like an old apothecary, simmering with dusty-dried fruit and faded flowers. IGT Basilicata Rosso Canetto is Aglianico marginally more fruity and polished. A recent family feud makes the future of the estate uncertain.

Elena Fucci ★★★

Contrada Solagna del Titolo
85022 Barile
elenafuccivini.com

Fucci has quickly risen to the top ranks in Basilicata. In a fateful twist, the property on which her grandfather and great grandfather grew grapes was very nearly sold in 2000. But upon seeing prospective buyers trouncing through the vineyards, the family had a dramatic change of heart. Fucci set off to winemaking school in Pisa, returning in 2004 to launch the business. Prime terraced vineyards in the heart of Barile include some of Vulture's oldest (55 to 70 years) and highest elevation plantings, over 600 metres (2000 feet), organically farmed. A small parcel of ancient vines *a capanno* was preserved. Fucci produces a single-estate wine outside of the new DOCG rules (shorter ageing) called Titolo, a towering monument to the mountain and to Aglianico, a deep, sumptuous and expressive wine that takes many years to unravel.

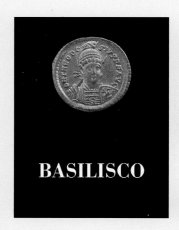

Grifalco ★

Località Pian di Camera
85029 Venosa
grifalco.com

Cecilia and Fabrizio Piccin spent 20 years making wine in Tuscany before uprooting in 2003 to somewhere more peaceful, but with potential to make memorable wine; Vulture seemed ideal. Aglianico is farmed organically in three zones. Light, cherry-scented, entry-level Gricos is grown in the warmer, less volcanic-influenced area around the winery in Venosa. Old-vine Damaschito is the most powerful and muscular, a selection from the village of Maschito on a volcanic outcrop of red, iron-rich soil rising up to 550 metres (1800 feet). Daginestra from 60-year-old vines in Ginestra is contrastingly opulent, seductive and plush, thanks to darker, heavier clay soils. All wines are wild fermented and aged in 300 and 500 litre (79 and 132 US gallons) barrels of mixed origin.

Paternoster ★ ★

Contrada Valle del Titolo
85022 Barile
paternostervini.it

The oldest winery in Vulture established by Anselmo Paternoster in 1925, now run by third-generation Vito Paternoster and siblings, managing a comfortable blend of traditional styling tempered by modern conveniences. Wines were bottled as early as the 1930s, a rarity not only for Basilicata, but all of Italy. The company's early success was based on sparkling wines – at first an accidental, ancestral-method Aglianico that spontaneously re-fermented but turned out rather well. Techniques were later refined and mastered. But reds are the highlight: Synthesi Aglianico del Vulture is a synthesis of several parcels, a gentle but excellent introduction. Single-vineyard Rotundo from 50-year-old estate vines is 'the most modern', barrique-aged, with lightly toasted, cacao-inflected ripe fruit. Traditionalists favour Don Anselmo, made from top vineyards, highlighting the beguiling ash and earth, savoury side of Aglianico, with sumptuous but firm structure and terrific length – among the appellation's best.

Tenuta Del Portale

Contrada Le Querce
85022 Barile

The D'Angelo family (see separate entry) set up Tenuta del Portale in 1990 as a modern counterpoint to the traditional family estate, but it retains definite old world sensibility. Pure Aglianico Starsa IGT Basilicata remains faithful to the variety's spicy, dried-red-fruit character but with a softer touch. Barrel-aged Aglianico del Vulture Le Vigne a Capanno is a gem, made from old, *a capanno*-trained vines, a full and dense, savoury but non-aggressive wine, with great length.

CAMPANIA

The Campanian Volcanic Arc is worthy of a book in itself. It regroups a large number of active, dormant and extinct volcanoes, on land and undersea, along the fault line that runs roughly around the edges of the Campanian plain, and many smaller ones. Although anchored on a bed of limestone and marl, the soils in virtually every corner of Campania are influenced by volcanism. The regular and massive eruptions of nearby Lipari Island, the Campi Flegrei, Roccamonfina, Monte Vulture and Vesuvius have deposited ash and tephra throughout the entire region, enriching the soils with a potent mix of minerals.

Mount Vesuvius is the area's most famous fissure, a 1281 metre (4203 foot) stratovolcano that dominates the horizon from every angle in the Bay of Naples, just east of the city. It's young in geological terms, some 25,000 years old. There are in fact two separate summits; controversy swirls around whether the eruption of 79 AD created the two peaks out of one ancestral cone, or if it has been this way for much longer – conflicting images of the time depict both a single and double peak. In any case, the northern, and older, now extinct peak is called Monte Somma, the southern, younger, taller and still problematically active volcanic cone is Vesuvius itself. Properly speaking, the mountain is referred to as the Somma-Vesuvio volcanic complex.

Vesuvius is comforting in that it follows a fairly predictable pattern of eruptions. A typical cycle includes a major Plinian eruption, as in 79 AD, 472 AD and 1631 AD, with smaller scale, mostly effusive, activity in between, most recently in 1906 and 1944. Volcanologists thus predict the next major eruption will 'probably' happen some time in the next 500 years, earning Vesuvius the title of the world's most dangerous volcano thanks to the three million people living nearby – the most densely populated volcanic region in the world – and its reliable tendency to erupt violently.

The Campi Flegrei, or Phlegrean Fields (Fields of Fire), was the name given by the Greeks to a large area of highly active volcanism on the opposite side of Naples. Unlike Vesuvius, the area has multiple eruptive centres, five maars (volcanic lakes) and up to 90 different volcanic cones and craters that have erupted at some point in the past 37,000 years, on land and undersea. You can't miss the pungent smell of sulphur as you exit the *autostrada* in Agnano, where a geyser spouts a continual stream of hot sulphurous water into the air. The last eruption occurred in 1538, but it's like a ticking time bomb.

One of the most spectacular eruptions of the Campi Flegrei that reshaped the topography of the entire area, as well as the soil composition of much of Campania, occurred 15,000 years ago. During this explosion, 40 cubic km (24 cubic miles) of 'Neapolitan Yellow Tuff' were released, blanketing much of south-central Italy. It is still considered a 'high risk' area, especially the densely populated zone around Pozzuoli. But considering the unpredictable nature of this field of fire, it's just as likely that a future eruption would take place somewhere else along a new vent. Of more immediate concern, however, is seismic activity. The ground is known to heave and swell by up to several millimeters (inches) in a single day, which can quickly amount to many centimetres (inches) or even metres (feet) over the course of a year. 'It's like we're sitting on a balloon that is constantly inflating and deflating,' says Giuseppe Fortunato of Contrada Salandra in Pozzuoli.

The island of Ischia (EES-key-ah) a short, 1.5-hour ferry ride from Naples, belongs geologically to the Campi Flegrei. The island is a study in green, not just from the abundant native flora and grapevines, but also from the uniquely green volcanic tuff visible in many parts of the island. The rare green tint is thanks to Ischia's complex volcanic past, involving periods of building and collapse, submarine eruptions when molten magma met cold water that

CASA D'AMBRA
VINI D'ISCHIA
Fondata nel 1888

CONTRADA
ROCE DEI MONTI
22

PROPRIETA OLIVIERO
AZIENDA FUOCOMUORTO
CASA VINICOLA
BED & BREAKFAST

VITIS VINIFERA
Apiana
FIANO

FRANCESCO DI MARZO
SCOPRÌ LE MINIERE DI ZOLFO
NELL'ANNO 1866

washed out pockets of green minerals, and subsequent upthrust. Many buildings are built out of this moss-green rock, and weather-worn outcrops of green tuff decorate the island like coral formations, most famously Il Fungo, the green mushroom-shaped rock protruding suggestively from the waters on the north side of the island.

The last eruption of Ischia occurred in 1302, leaving behind a lava flow that runs from the Arso crater down to the sea between the Castello Aragonese, which itself sits on a lava dome, and the harbour of Ischia, formed by a volcanic crater lake. According to geologists, Ischia should no longer erupt. But the island is still very obviously volcanically active. Puffs of white smoke and steam billow out of numerous fumaroles on the sides of the mountain, ominous signals that require no degree in volcanology to interpret. And if you dig deep enough virtually anywhere on the island, you'll discover a hot spring; Ischia is famous for its thermal baths.

Roccamonfina is Campania's only (almost certainly) extinct stratovolcano, active from some 650,000 to 50,000 years ago. Its large, isolated cone rises up at the eastern end of the Garigliano River plain (the rift valley which gave rise to the volcano), overlooking Ager Falernus, antiquity's most famous wine region in the northwest corner of the region. The huge central caldera was the centre of both explosive and effusive volcanic activity, though all that remains today are several mineral water springs, occasional minor seismic movements and the volcanic soils of the Falerno del Massico DOC and Roccamonfina IGT.

While there are no volcanoes in **Avellino** and **Benevento** provinces, the soils there have been enriched so often with raining volcanic material that they can rightly be considered for inclusion here.

CAMPANIA FELIX

Campania is a region of singular beauty in the southern Italian peninsula. Abundant sunshine, dramatic scenery, a rich tradition of gastronomy and the south's deepest repertoire of fine wines conspire to make the region a joyful place. The Romans referred to it as Campania Felix, or 'happy country'. Campania is also a stronghold for native grape varieties, many planted for at least 2000 years. The steadfast vision of important figures such as the Mastroberardino family, especially in the post-war industrialization of Italy, and later by others like Leonardo Mustilli, has preserved an enviable viticultural heritage.

So, too, ironically, did the devastating earthquake that rocked the province of Avellino on November 23, 1980. An entire generation fled the ruins, and many ancient vineyards were thus spared the wine boom of the 80s and 90s and the accompanying pressure to modernize and replant with more fashionable varieties. Pockets of wine-growing as it was practiced 200 years ago were preserved.

But Campania's immense viticultural potential is being exploited once again. Since the 90s, the number of producers has increased 20-fold. Unlike southern neighbours Puglia and Sicily, which staked their reputations on impressive volumes, throughout history Campania has always been considered a premium wine region. Today, that reputation is stronger than ever, anchored on some of Italy's finest and most age-worthy volcanic reds and whites.

Exploring Ancient Vineyards

Pier Paolo Sirch, managing director of Feudi di San Gregorio, takes me on a tour to glimpse the utterly original wine-growing practiced a century or two ago in Avellino. First stop is Feudi's Vigneto Dal Rè in the Taurasi appellation. It's like no vineyard I've ever seen, more

ABOVE *The rugged countryside of Avellino from the top of the Castello di Taurasi.*

like a sparse forest of vine-trees. Some of these Aglianico vines actually climb up scattered trees, while others lean on thick chestnut wood posts. Multiple thick and rugged old trunks, grow up from the same spot to high wires stretched between the posts and trees. Arms of the vines run along these wires around two metres (six feet) above the ground with other armlets looping at irregular intervals from them like imperfect seahorse tails. Some vines stretch horizontally a couple dozen metres (feet). The oldest among these, Sirch assures me, surpass their second century. The whole scene is extraordinary, like an antique shop filled with giant, elaborate candelabras by Antonio Gaudì. A pitiable three tons of grapes per hectare are harvested from these ancient relics, about half of a normally low-yielding vineyard.

Next, Sirch takes me on a hunt for what he reckons is the oldest living Fiano vine. It's believed to originate around the hilltop town of Lapio, now within the Fiano di Avellino appellation. Sirch came across what he calls 'La Vecchia di Lapio' (the old mother of Lapio) over a decade ago while quite literally roaming through the forest, looking for old vineyards.

We wander through a maze of green below the town dotted with red and yellow wildflowers – the Campanian countryside exploding with spring life. Finally we emerge in a semi-clearing where the narrow dirt path ends in a field of tall grass beneath an abandoned stone house, and Sirch stops next to a giant vine, with a rugged 200-year-old trunk – it looks more like a hardened piece of rope with multiple strands braided together and must be nearly a metre (three feet) in circumference. 'This is La Vecchia,' he pronounces without unnecessary flourish. We stand in reverential silence for several minutes, staring at the gorgeous old lady. There's little to say. 'You should see the beautiful grapes from this vine,' Sirch finally offers. 'So perfect, translucent, bright green. There's something special about this place.'

ABOVE *Dramatic Sant'Agata dei Goti, Benevento, built on a spur of volcanic tuff.*

OPPOSITE ABOVE *A reportedly 300-year-old Sirica vine in the Taurasi region.*

It's tragic to consider the number of these old vines that have been ripped out in recent times by farmers unaware of their priceless genetic material. These days the ripping out has stopped, 'but alas, much of the damage has already been done, and the patrimony lost,' Sirch laments. 'But at least we have these.' Fortunately, forward-thinking regional leaders like Feudi di San Gregorio and Mastroberardino have been propagating the priceless genetic material from Campania's ancient vines, encouraging many smaller wine-growers to do likewise.

The Vineyards & Wines of Pompeii: Pompeii Lives!

Antonio Dente, chief agronomist for Mastroberardino, takes me even further back in time to see exactly how vineyards in the region looked 2000 years ago. The site is the Roman trading town of Pompeii. In the mid-80s, the archeological superintendence of Pompeii embarked on an ambitious project called Pompeii Viva (Pompeii Lives) to bring the 1st century back to life. The plan was to recreate the gardens and agricultural traditions of Roman times, and wine, it's clear, was a big part of life. Some 200 *thermopolia*, the wine bars of the time (in a city of only some 12,000 people), have been uncovered.

But wine was not only consumed in great quantities in Pompeii, it was also produced. Most of the villas within the walls had their own gardens, olive groves and vineyards. Ancient texts were studied, and many clues gathered from the perfectly preserved ruins in order to recreate a proper Roman-style vineyard. Mastroberardino, the superintendence's chosen partner, set about re-planting in 1996. Dente leads us to the enclosure where the first trials of eight varieties were made: white grapes Falanghina, Coda di Volpe, Caprettone, Fiano and Greco, and reds Aglianico, Piedirosso and Sciascinoso – amazingly still the principal grapes of Campania today – grown on a tall *pergola* nearly two metres (six feet) high. Seven different trellising methods were trialled, covering the known spectrum of techniques of the day. Micro quantities of wine were produced and evaluated, and eventually it was learned that red varieties perform better in the heat and relative dryness of the southern side of Vesuvius. In subsequent phases only reds, including Aglianico, were planted.

Campania's Grapes

Falanghina is the most planted white. Previously considered a blending grape and excluded from DOCs, in the last couple of

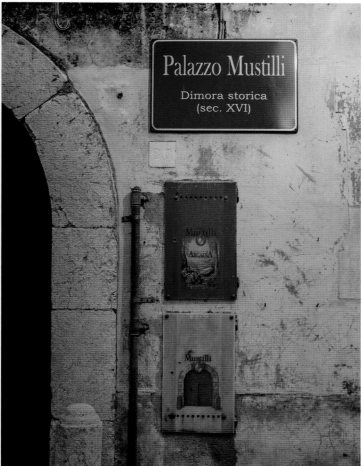

decades it has become enormously successful, now permitted all over Campania. Falanghina is most often fresh and unoaked, and occasionally sparkling thanks to high acids. With notable exceptions, it's in the entry-level price range in a producer's portfolio, though in great terroirs like the tuff of Sant'Agata dei Goti or the poor volcanic sands of the Campi Flegrei, it acquires a grander, sapid, mineral character.

Fiano is southern Italy's greatest white variety, already lauded in the days of Pompeii. It figures most prominently in the Fiano di Avellino DOCG, and was the first white, along with neighbouring Greco di Tufo, to be granted the top classification in the south. Regional hero Antonio Mastroberardino is credited with reviving Fiano's fortunes, bottling his first in 1945. Fiano has a unique flavour, distinctly non-fruity, more like a mix of fennel and fresh herbs, hazelnuts and honey, chamomile and acacia flowers, growing more toasty and smoky with time. It can be full-bodied and vigorous,

and highly age-worthy, especially in the heavier clays around the town of Lapio, but most commonly mid-weight and sharper in the more loosely packed ash and sands in the rest of Avellino.

Greco is another ancient and celebrated grape, brought to Italy from Thessaly by the Greeks in the distant mists of time. Unlike Fiano, Greco is difficult to grow, the wild child. 'It's savage and unfriendly,' says Pier Paolo Sirch, 'low-yielding and sensitive'. It's also very prone to oxidation, requiring careful handling. But when it behaves it can be counted as one of Italy's best and most age-worthy whites, especially from the high-elevation communes within the Greco di Tufo DOCG. If Fiano is not particularly fruity, Greco is even less so. It's marked by its structure – sometimes palpably tannic – with high acids and alcohol, managing the tricky balance between concentration, density and freshness. You won't be long in the region before some winemaker refers to Greco as the 'most red of white wines'. It's said that the huge

OPPOSITE TOP LEFT/RIGHT *Cantina Olivella team/ Serena Gusmeri, oenologist at Giardini Arimei.*

OPPOSITE BELOW *One of Mastroberardino's vineyard parcels within Pompeii's ancient walls under Vesuvius.*

ABOVE RIGHT/LEFT *Doorway in Sant'Agata dei Goti/ Mustilli's historic palazzo and cellars.*

deposits of volcanic-derived sulphur that underlie Tufo (the town grew rich in the 19th century from sulphur mining) are responsible for the wine's particularly flinty and stony character.

Coda di Volpe (*Cauda Vulpium* or 'fox's tail' to the Romans thanks to its curved, tail-like bunches) is a highly productive, widely planted white variety, producing generally soft, fruity and easy-drinking wines (except in cooler sites on stony, free-draining soil like the slopes of Monte Taburno in Benevento where it gains a steely edge). It's been confused for centuries with Caprettone, a distinct, more interesting variety that has historically been planted on the slopes of Vesuvius, enjoying a minor renaissance now that it has been officially recognized as a separate variety. It's naturally higher in acid (though not as acid as Greco or Fiano), delivering marked saline-mineral character and even a touch of petrol (gas).

Catalanesca is a minor but interesting variety grown on Vesuvius, presumably brought from Spain (Catalonia). Revived principally by Cantina Olivella, it's a robust grape with thick skins that can release an overabundance of bitter phenolics if mistreated. It's distinguished enough to have earned its own IGT Catalanesca del Monte Somma.

Ischia boasts two high quality indigenous grapes, Biancolella and Forastera, related to no other known varieties on the mainland. Of the pair, usually bottled pure, Biancolella is paler, more delicate, floral, pretty, like a gentle whiff of spring flowers; Forastera is more perfumed, fruity, imposing and fuller bodied, relatively speaking.

Aglianico (*Vitis ellenica*, or the 'Hellenic' grape) is Campania's headlining red, also considered one of Italy's greatest, capable of extreme complexity and longevity. It's the backbone of the region's only DOCG red appellations, Aglianico del Taburno and Taurasi. The former is made from a distinct biotype known as Aglianico Amaro, which tends to be softer and rounder, less structured and earlier maturing than the Aglianico of Taurasi. But again everything is relative; all versions are on the robust, tannic and acid end of the spectrum, acquiring occasionally a shocking brute force. The best have an unmistakably Italianate character of dryness and austerity, more gravel than sandpaper, with flavours that occupy the savoury pie of the aroma wheel: leather, tobacco, pot-pourri, tar, liquorice, sun-warmed terra cotta and much more. Aglianico is often referred to as the Nebbiolo of the south, sharing similar characteristics, though colour and fruit character are

ABOVE *Sunset over Bay of Naples from Fuocomorto on Vesuvius. Sorrento peninsula, Capri and Ischia (l to r).*

generally much darker and more brooding. Another similarity is the blunting effect of an overlavish use of new wood, which dulls its otherworldly perfume.

Piedirosso (aka Per'e' Palummo) is the next most planted red grape, yet another ancient variety, whose precise character is difficult to pin down. 'It's the most difficult variety in the world, an anarchist,' states Raffaele Moccia of Agnanum in the Campi Flegrei. Most vintners complain of the variety's lack of colour and structure, which led to its historic use as a softening agent for Aglianico. Pure Piedirosso is most successful in Ischia, Campi Flegrei, Taburno and Sannio DOCs, and is generally best consumed young, with a light chill. Sciascinoso is another typical blending partner with Piedirosso, most famously in the Lacryma Christi del Vesuvio Rosso DOC. It's much easier to grow and vinify, yielding fresh, red-fruit-scented wines with modest alcohol and tannins, and lively acids. Pure Sciascinoso is exceedingly rare.

Campania's Volcanic Wine Appellations

Campania is comprised of five provinces; in order of wine production these are: Benevento, Avellino, Salerno, Napoli and Caserta. Salerno and its magnificent Sorrento peninsula, less readily associated with volcanism, is not covered here; the most important volcanic-influenced wine zones in the other four follow.

BENEVENTO produces three times as much wine as the next most productive province, Avellino, over half of the Campanian total. But there are only half as many bottlers of wine, which gives some insight into the industry structure. Bottled wine is a recent phenomenon, though rapidly expanding, as the region takes advantage of the growing interest in Campanian wines, and especially the explosion of Falanghina, most of which originates here.

The Taburno-Camposauro Mountains west of the city of Benevento rise to just under 1400 metres (4593 feet) at the highest peak, Monte Taburno itself. Despite its teasing conical shape, it is not a stratovolcano, but rather a limestone massif, part of the Apennines, though has been regularly blanketed with volcanic fallout from nearby eruptions for eons. **Benevento or Beneventano IGT**, **Sannio DOC** and **Sannio Falanghina DOC** all cover the entire province; the latter two have four sub-zones: Solopaca/Solopaca Classico, Guardia Sanfradimonti (or Guardiolo), Taburno, and Sant'Agata dei Goti, the latter on a spur of volcanic tuff.

The region's reputation leans heavily on Falanghina, Coda di Volpe, Fiano and Greco for whites and Aglianico and Piedirosso for reds. The generally heavier clay-based soils and lower elevations (warmer climate) of Benevento make for fatter, softer wines relative to Avellino.

Aglianico del Taburno DOCG covers 13 communes on the eastern slopes of Taburno-Camposauro, the most heavily planted of which

face slightly north to the Telesina Valley around the towns of Foglianise, Vitulano and Torrecuso, where volcanic influence is more prevalent and the wines denser and more structured. Wines are released after a minimum of two years in the cellar, three for Riserva.

AVELLINO in the Campanian Apennines is a land of extremes – a mountain terroir. The continental climate, ranging from snowy and sub-zero in winter to 40°C (104°F) at the height of summer, elevations from 300 to 650 metres (1000 to 2150 feet) and diurnal shifts as large as 20 to 25°C (68 to 77°F) during harvest, all help explain why such strikingly fresh whites can be produced this far south. It's telling that two of the three DOCG appellations – Fiano di Avellino and Greco di Tufo – are whites.

Avellino's top red is Aglianico-based **Taurasi DOCG**, the first southern Italian wine to be granted the 'G' ('Garantita' or 'guaranteed' that occasionally follows the Denominazione di Origine Controllatta). Centred around the town of Taurasi and neighbouring villages mainly in the Calore River Valley northeast of Avellino, this is surely one of the grandest red wines of Italy, majestic, forceful, sometimes brooding and even brutal in youth, the most structured and age-worthy of all Aglianicos. This is due in part to the particular biotype of the variety grown here, and in part to the deep, iron-rich volcanic ash and clay soils of the zone.

Professor Fabio Terribile of the University of Naples, a soil scientist, classifies the terroir of Taurasi an 'intermediate' type of volcanic soil, between the young soils of Ischia or Campi Flegrei, for example, and the older, more weathered soils of Vulture. 'It's a beautiful category,' he says, though quickly points out that this clay mineral-rich soil would be too fertile in an area with more rainfall. Others, like Antonio Dente from Mastroberardino confirm that the appellation boundaries were cleverly drawn. 'The cooler areas with higher rainfall were reserved for Fiano and Greco,' he says, 'while the Taurasi area is much drier. It's perfect for Aglianico.' Taurasi is aged a minimum of three years (at least one in wood), and four years (18 months in wood) for Riserva. **Campi Taurasini DOC** is a sort of declassified Taurasi, used for shorter-aged Aglianico.

The **Irpinia DOC** covers the entire province of Avellino and includes all of the main grape varieties listed above (except Caprettone).

OPPOSITE *The terraced vineyards of Giardini Arimei on Ischia, with an ominous fumarole visible above.*

ABOVE *Workers tie down Greco vines in the vineyards of Benito Ferrara, above the town of Tufo, Avellino.*

NAPOLI Urban and industrial creep are real problems for the vineyards of Naples, and in particular those of the **Campi Flegrei DOC** due west of the capital. A handful of remaining producers grow grapes in these Neapolitan suburbs, producing small quantities of occasionally astonishing wines from a meagre mix of volcanic sand, ash, pumice stone and, more rarely, larger lapilli and lumps of basalt. Some century-old vines still grow in phylloxera-free safety. The two most important varieties have their own DOCs: **Campi Flegrei Falanghina DOC** and **Campi Flegrei Piedirosso DOC**, both capable of delivering some of the most interesting expressions in Campania .

Vesuvio DOC and its **Lacryma Christi del Vesuvio Bianco / Rosso** sub-categories are Napoli's other important appellations, produced on all sides of the Somma-Vesuvio volcanic complex. The mostly north-facing slopes of Monte Somma have generally older, and much finer, sandy, phylloxera-free volcanic soils, almost like talcum powder. The weather is marginally cooler and wetter than on the south side, which in tandem all yield more refined, fresher, lighter wines, including the speciality **Catalanesca del Monte Somma IGT**. On the southern side of Vesuvius the Mediterranean is in full charge: the sun is that much sharper, the thermometre is nudged up a couple of degrees and less rain falls. Add in the unweathered lapilli and pumice of the 79 AD eruption, (yesterday, geologically) that peppers the soil, with little clay or organic matter, and the same varieties are expressed more forcefully.

Lacryma Christi Bianco is a blend of at least one-third of Caprettone or Coda di Volpe; Greco and/or Falanghina can account

for up to 20 per cent. Lacryma Rosso blends at least half Piedirosso (here called Palummina), with Sciascinoso up to 30 per cent and Aglianico up to 20 per cent. Both the reds and whites of Vesuvio are wines to drink young and fresh, the reds also with a light chill. With rare exceptions, there's little to be gained in the cellar.

Ischia, administratively part of Napoli, deserves its own little section for its staggering beauty, historical importance (it was among the first permanent settlements in Magna Grecia) and mini-collection of vines that grow nowhere else. Recent DNA studies of Ischia's main varieties, Biancolella, Forastera and Per'e' Palummo, reveal no links to other known varieties.

The flanks of volcanic Monte Epomeo that peaks in the centre of the island at 788 metres (2585 feet), and those of Ischia's many other lava domes are dressed with dry stonewalls called *parracine* – built to contain neat terraces, where small quantities of delicate and salty, tense and improbably fresh wines are grown, essences of rock and sea.

Some phylloxera-free vineyards lie close to the sea on particularly gravelly, sandy volcanic soils. **Ischia Bianco DOC** was the first registered appellation in Campania in 1966, and Italy's second white wine DOC overall (after Vernaccia di San Gimignano in Tuscany), revealing the historically high esteem in which the island's wines have been held. **Ischia Rosso DOC**, granted just a few weeks later, is in fact Italy's first red wine appellation. Bianco is made from Biancolella and/or the less-planted Forastera, with a possible sprinkling of other local white varieties. It's more common, however, to find both

---

in their pure form, with names added to the Ischia DOC for clarity. Rosso is made mostly from Per'e' Palummo and sturdier, more tannic Guarnaccia, temptingly but apparently unrelated to, Spain's Garnacha.

The **Pompeiano IGP** is the catchall appellation for the province of Naples, covering all the regions listed here above.

CASERTA is the northernmost province in Campania on the Lazio border. Skirting around the Monte Massico, you'll enter into the horseshoe-shaped Garigliano River basin, capped at the northeastern end by the imposing bulk of the extinct volcano Roccamonfina. You've entered into Ager Falernus, the terroir of antiquity's most sought after wine, Falernum.

The Romans clearly understood the region and its potential 2000 years ago. Falernum was the regional designation, which was further sub-divided into Falerno Dulce (sweet) for the wine produced in the lower (warmer, riper) plains, Falerno Faustiano Tenue for the mid-elevation hills and Falerno Caucino Austero for the more austere, dry wine produced in the highest hills. Some 140 Roman cellars discovered around the town of San Castrese attest to the importance of the production area.

'They had found an ideal spot,' Salvatore Avallone of Villa Matilde tells me, in reference to Roman vintners. The hills encircling the region protect from the inclement weather that rolls in from the north, aside from one small dip in the hills north of Roccamonfina that allows some of the cool morning air through. In the afternoon as the area warms, cool sea air is drawn inland, reversing the airflow. Vineyards are constantly bathed in cool, moving air, which, combined with nutrient-rich, free-draining volcanic ash over limestone soils, meet all of the requirements for fine wine production.

Falerno del Massico DOC is the modern Falernum. Whites are from Falanghina; far more common Rosso/Rosso Riserva is based on Aglianico with a small percentage of Piedirosso. A version with Primitivo (also Riserva) is also permitted, a grape that has 'only' been planted in the region since the mid-1800s. Overall production is a drop in the Campanian bucket. **Galluccio DOC** is Caserta's other appellation, a small area on the border with Lazio in the foothills of two extinct volcanoes, Santa Croce and Roccamonfina itself. The grapes used are essentially the same as for Falerno and it's mostly consumed locally. **Terre di Volturno** and **Roccamonfina** are Caserta's two **IGPs**.

CAMPANIA – THE WINES & THE PEOPLE

Agnanum ★★

Via Vicinale abbandonata agli Astroni 3
80125 Napoli

agnanum.it

Raffaele Moccia is a wine-grower's wine-grower, toiling away alone on vines planted in near-pure volcanic powder on one of the steepest sites in the Campi Flegrei. Terraces are re-shaped by hand at least once a year to prevent the hillside from washing away. 'Why don't you build stone walls?' I ask. 'Look around,' he says. 'Do you see any stones?' It's wine-growing on the lunatic fringe. Some phylloxera-free, ungrafted vines approach 100 years, planted by his grandfather *pratese* (field) style, like wild vines wound around trees or large wooden poles. Dead vines are replaced by layering. These are wild and pure, gravity-defying wines. Falanghina is the calling card, wealthy in salty extract and amazingly just 12% ABV; IGT Campania Sabbia Vulcanica blends Falanghina with a handful of minor indigenous grapes with brighter floral lift and more white-fleshed fruit. Per'e' Palummo takes on a new dimension here, much deeper and darker than the mean, full of wild cherries and crunchy acidity, like authoritative cru Beaujolais.

Antico Borgo

Via Dante Alighieri 18
83030 Taurasi

cantineanticoborgo.it

A small estate making a surprisingly wide range of the typical Irpinian wines (as well as a Falanghina from Benevento). The wine to seek out is the Taurasi, rendered in a traditional style, age-worthy and savoury.

Antonio Caggiano ★★

Contrada Sala 4
83030 Taurasi

cantinecaggiano.it

Former builder and photographer Antonio Caggiano gathered enough discarded 'rubble' after the 1980 Avellino earthquake to construct an impressive museum-like cellar in the village of Taurasi in 1990. He took over an old family vineyard and planted others, and hired celebrated oenologist Luigi Moio, who has helped establish him as one of Avellino's best. Son Giuseppe (Pino) has assumed most of the day-to-day responsibilities. Quality is very near the highest level, in a comfortable space between traditional and modern, favouring precision and purity over sheer weight and extract. Taurasi Macchia dei Goti is one of the appellation's most authentic and expressive. Fiano di Avellino Béchar offers textbook hay and hazelnut flavours; Greco di Tufo Devon is one of the more extreme, pure, stony expressions.

Benito Ferrara ★★

Frazione San Paolo 14
83010 Tufo

benitoferrara.it

Fourth generation Gabriella Ferrara and husband Sergio Ambrosino farm vineyards high in the hills above Tufo in the hamlet of San Paolo, one of the cru-worthy districts in the Greco di Tufo appellation, as well as a small parcel in the Taurasi appellation (some Fiano is purchased). Greco di Tufo is the pinnacle, especially single-vineyard Vigna Cicogna with magical harmony. 'Regular' Greco di Tufo is still impressively substantial, arch-classic and stony-mineral. Fiano di Avellino is also worthwhile, though reds are less successful.

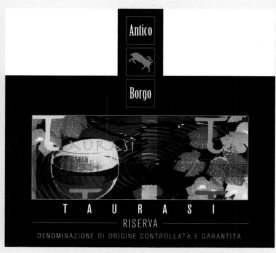

Cantina Olivella ★★

Via Zazzera 14
80048 Sant'Anastasia
cantineolivella.com

A smart, forward-thinking outfit, but with a foot firmly in the past, a model to follow. Partners Domenico Ceriello, estate manager, Ciro Giordano, export manager and viticulturalist Andrea Cozzolino, work to revive lost traditions and grapes on the north side of Vesuvius under Monte Somma. Phylloxera-free, sandy volcanic soils allow cuttings to be planted directly, and can produce grapes in the first year, a sort of layering without the mother vines. Catalanesca is a house speciality, an old Vesuvian variety of Catalan origin that Olivella has single-handedly revived and had re-instated in the official registry of wine grapes (it was mistakenly classified as a table grape after World War II). It now has its own IGT, Catalanesca del Monte Somma, of which, unsurprisingly, Olivella's Kata is the reference, highly mineral, richer and more full-bodied than also excellent and sapid Emblema Vesuvio Bianco (pure Caprettone). Lacrimanero Lacryma Christi Rosso, Piedirosso with 20 per cent Aglianico, is mid-weight with wild-cherry flavour.

Cantina del Taburno

Via Sala 12
82030 Foglianise
cantinadeltaburno.it

A cooperative with some 300 member-growers supplying grapes from approximately 600 hectares, mostly on the slopes of Monte Taburno. Average quality is unusually high, thanks to a dedicated technical team that works with growers to implement rigorous standards. Aglianico del Taburno Bue Apis is the flagship, from a vineyard under Monte Caruso in which some vines have apparently been certified over 200 years old, grown in the old-style high *pergolas* called *ragiera libera*. Lovely dark, ripe, and pure fruit sits on a gentle, plush frame, typical of Taburno. Aglianico del Taburno Delius takes a sharper tack with slightly wilder character, also excellent.

Casa D'Ambra ★★

Via Mario d'Ambra 16
80075 Forio d'Ischia
dambravini.com

The grand old statesman of Ischia, and one of the oldest estates in Campania, established by Francesco D'Ambra in 1888. Bottling began relatively early, in 1956. Casa D'Ambra is by far the largest producer of DOC Ischia, from both estate vineyards and purchased grapes. Biancolella Frassitelli is the gem, from a spectacular west-facing terraced vineyard of green-tinged volcanic dust, suffused with the taste of the sea and summer mist wrapped in tracing paper. Standard Biancolella is only marginally more discreet and transparent, redolent of cherry blossoms; Forastera Euposia is immediately fruity and perfumed. Ischia Rosso Mario D'Ambra, an equal blend of Per'e' Palummo and Guarnaccia, is mid-weight, sea-salt and Mediterranean-scrub flavoured, ideal with a light chill.

Cavaliere Pepe

Via Santa Vara
83050 Sant'Angelo all'Esca
tenutacavalierpepe.it

That Milena Pepe, a Belgian-born, blond-haired, blue-eyed woman with a marked French accent, held the presidency of the Consortium of Taurasi, deep in southern Italy, tells much about her personality: determined, forceful, confident. Father Angelo, a Campanian native, moved to Brussels where he still runs a successful collection of restaurants. He purchased vineyards in the heart of Taurasi and Milena joined as manager; first vintage was 2005. The range reveals ongoing stylistic experimentation to meet local and international demands (around a third of production is sold in Pepe's restaurants). Grecos Nestor and Grancare are the most memorable whites; Irpinia Campi Taurasini DOC the most pleasant, traditional-style Aglianico, herbal-medicinal with judicious wood influence.

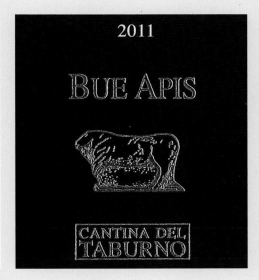

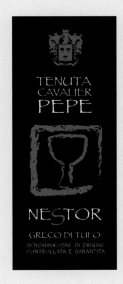

Colli di Lapio di Romano Clelia ★★

Contrada Arianiello 47
83030 Lapio
collidilapio.it

The magic of great terroir and Romano Clelia's attention to tiny details make the difference in this top family-run estate. Fiano is a reference for Avellino, a marvel of sapidity and salinity with terrific concentration. Greco di Tufo Alexandros is typically more parchment coloured, weighty, if not quite with the same drive, but still top notch. Taurasi Andrea is vigorous, with ripeness pushed to just limits before taming in barrique, and Campi Taurasini Donna Chiara an excellent introduction to Aglianico.

Contrada Salandra

Licola
Via Tre Piccioni 40
80078 Pozzuoli

Giuseppe Fortunato runs a small but tidy, fully organic operation on the volcanic hills above Pozzuoli in the Campi Flegrei, which includes honey as well as wine production. 'We're part of nature. I want to reflect this connection between plants and animals, vines and bees. There's no difference.' It was after a beekeeper's fair in Montalcino that Fortunato decided to start bottling wine in 2005. Unusually for Italy, he holds white wines back for two or three years before release. All are spot-on, more confident than dramatic, especially a gently honeyed Falanghina Campi Flegrei with acacia and lemon blossom perfume. Piedirosso is mid-weight and spicy.

Donnachiara ★

Via Stazione
83030 Montefalcione
donnachiara.com

Vineyards have been in the noble Pettito family for 150 years. A winery was completed in 2005, and wines are now made under the guidance of Ilaria Pettito and mother Chiara, granddaughter of Donna Chiara in who's honour the estate is named. Attention to detail is evident, and the range displays restrained elegance and subtlety, leaning more heavily to fresh and reductive rather than open and oxidative. Snappy, wet hay and chamomile-scented Fiano, and lean, tight and stony Greco match their textbook descriptions; Aglianico Irpinia is fresh and flagrantly aromatic. Taurasi Riserva has noted polish but authentically swarthy character.

Femìa Agricultural Holding

Contrada Verzare 9
83030 Lapio
vinifemia.it

A small estate run by the Todisco family with prized holdings in the Campore district of Lapio, in the Fiano di Avellino DOCG, and the Carazita district of Taurasi. Fiano di Avellino DOCG Camporèo is powerful and weighty, underscoring the ageability of top Fianos from great vineyards.

Feudi di San Gregorio ★★

Contrada Cerza Grossa
83050 Sorbo Serpico
feudi.it

Antonio Capaldo established Feudi di San Gregorio in 1986 at a time when much of Campania still lay in ruins after the 1980 earthquake. Wishing to write a new chapter, he commissioned a Japanese architect to design a winery and restaurant unlike anything else in the region – modern, sleek and minimalist. Yet Capaldo eventually realized that Campania's dominant terroir and deep history was the real story, causing a shift in philosophy to safeguard the past rather than reinvent the future. With the help of Managing Director Pier Paolo Sirch, Feudi has become a champion of local varieties and the patrimony of Campania's ancient vineyards. The combination has been potent, and Feudi's success undeniable. With estates also in Puglia (Ognissole) and Basilicata (Basilisco, see p.170), Feudi is among the largest producers in southern Italy. The range is highly reliable, clean and technically sound, if occasionally lacking the edgy personality of the most memorable wines. But under Sirch, the style has edged happily towards leaner, crisper, more minerally wines relative to the more opulent expressions of earlier years. Highlights include terrific Ischia Biancolella (first released in 2014), single-vineyards Pietracalda Fiano di Avellino and Cutizzi Greco di Tufo, dusty and spicy Taurasi and densely-packed single-vineyard Piano Monte Vergine Taurasi Riserva. Flagship Serpico Irpinia IGT, produced from century-old+ Aglianico vines in the Dal Rè vineyard is a riot of dried cherry, potpourri, liquorice and leather – suave and hugely satisfying. An innovative, traditional-method sparkling wine programme initiated with the consulting aid of Champenois Anselme Selosse includes versions from Falanghina, and more successfully, Greco and Aglianico rosé.

Fontanavecchia ★

Via Fontanavecchia
82030 Torrecuso
fontanavecchia.info

Libero Rillo runs one of the oldest and best private estates in Taburno, bottling wines since 1990. He's a pragmatist, subscribing to no particular wine-growing dogma: 'Organic, biodynamic, natural…. These terms mean nothing to me. I believe that wine is food, and food should be as natural and healthy as possible. That's it.' Rillo continues to adjust harvest times and other small details, and is moving away from barriques to larger wood *botti*. Quality has risen steadily. From the entry level, fragrant and fruity Falanghina del Sannio to the dense, highly concentrated yet firm and chiselled Aglianico del Taburno Riserva Vigna Cataratte, the range is excellent.

Fuocomorto

Contrada Croce Dei Monti 22
80056 Ercolano NA
fuocomuorto.it

When Vincenzo Olivieri finally re-excavated the ancestral cellar, he found an etched inscription '12 Luglio 1780, Vincenzo' marking the date (July 12, 1780) that his forebear, also Vincenzo, had finished carving lava deposited from the eruption of 1631 to create a cellar, now the oldest (non-Roman, working) on Vesuvius. It had been buried by a lahar in the eruption of April 5, 1906 in which Vesuvius lost 170 metres (558 feet) off its summit, and remained so for exactly 100 years until the current Vincenzo retired as head of the Consortium of Mozzarella Producers and moved back to the family property. Today, Olivieri farms a tiny west-facing, terraced vineyard, producing artisanal-farmhouse wines,

with character. Delicate, crisp, and salty Caprettone is the speciality, given a short time in 500-litre (132-US gallon) chestnut barrels (Olivieri was the first to bottle and label a pure example). Mid-weight Rossomagma IGT Campania (50/50 Piedirosso/Aglianico blend), has fine stuffing and succulent acids.

Galardi (Terra di Lavoro) ★★★

Strada Provinciale Sessa Mignano
81030 S. Carlo di Sessa Aurunca
terradilavoro.it

The Galardi estate of Arturo and Dora Celentano produces just one wine, the magnificent Aglianico/Piedirosso blend Terra di Lavoro, from organic vineyards high in the foothills of the Roccamonfina volcano. From a hobby in the early 90s to international cult following, the style has remained fiercely artisanal, majestically concentrated without heaviness; the range of savoury, fruity, spicy, mineral flavours is astonishing. Abundant but polished tannins confer exceptional longevity.

Giardini Arimei (Arcipelago Muratori) ★

Pietra Brox 51bis
80075 Forio d'Ischia
arcipelagomuratori.it

Francesco Muratori's Ischian outpost, added to estates in Suvereto (Tuscany), Sannio (Campania) and company headquarters in Franciacorta, hence 'archipelago'. This is a project of love – Francesco was born on Ischia – rather than profit, oenologist Serena Gusmeri assures. Gusmeri, who also runs the Sannio winery, reveals that labour costs on Ischia are more than double, pointing out thousands of metres (feet) of dry stone walls in need of constant maintenance. A formerly abandoned, renovated 19th-century cellar excavated out of

volcanic tuff serves as the winery, surrounded by terraced vineyards on the west coast above Forio. *Palmenti* have been remodelled and put into use. Passito was the initial focus, a medium-dry, smoke, peat and salty dried-apricot flavoured blend of partially dried Biancolella, Forastera and small amounts of Uva Rilla, San Lunardo and Coglionara. Dry white Biancolella-Forastera Pietra Brox was added from 2009, more deeply coloured, sapid and weightier than most.

Joaquin ★

Contrada Carrani
83030 Montefalcione
joaquinwines.com

Raffaele Pagano left the family wine business
in Salerno to strike out on his own in 1999.
A meticulous search for vineyards led him
to Montefalcione in the Fiano di Avellino
appellation and, more recently, a parcel
of very old Aglianico in Paternopoli (Taurasi).
Production is supplemented with purchased
fruit, including grapes from selected villas
and gardens of Capri. 110 Oyster Greco IGT
Campania has uncommon richness and density,
suffused with stony flavours.

La Fortezza

Località Tora 20
82030 Torrecuso
lafortezzasrl.it

Enzo Rillo is the entrepreneur behind this
relatively recent start up in Torrecuso, with
vineyards on the prime hillsides of Taburno
overlooking the Calore River valley. The
Aglianico del Taburno Riserva is unusually
soft and silky, almost Burgundian in style
with lacy, delicate tannins, refined and elegant.

La Guardiense

Località Santa Lucia 104/105
82034 Guardia Sanframondi
laguardiense.it

A 1000-member cooperative winery with
half a century of history – one of the three largest
wine operations in southern Italy. During the
last decade the company has undergone an
ambitious re-structuring and re-design to raise
quality, and has brought on famed oenologist
Ricardo Cotarella. The full range, technically
impeccable, offers fine value. Large emphasis
is on sparkling wine; Quid Falanghina Spumante
Brut would give many Prosecco producers
a run for their money. Experimentation
continues; recent novelties include an
impressive Aglianico Sannio Coste Del Duca,
made without sulphites.

La Rivolta ★

Contrada Rivolta
82030 Torrecuso
fattorilarivolta.it

Third generation Paolo Cotroneo created
Fattoria La Rivolta in 1997 from family
vineyards and launched his first wine in 2001.
Organic wines from Taburno and Sannio
DOCs are clean, detailed, textbook expressions,
especially the entry range. Mid-weight Aglianico
del Taburno is properly spicy and leathery, with
characteristic tenderness (relatively speaking).
More concentrated but less regionally distinct
Terra di Rivolta Aglianico Riserva is treated
to French barriques, sometimes overly so,
but gains in concentration.

Manimurci

Contrada Casale 9
83052 Paternopoli
manimurci.com

A partnership between six wine-lovers
established in 2002, led by Carmine Aliasi,
making slightly idiosyncratic but memorable
wines. Greco di Tufo Zagreo is deeply
coloured and highly perfumed, with fine
depth and complexity.

Mastroberardino ★★★

Via Manfredi 75/81
83042 Atripalda
mastroberardino.com

The grand old wine estate of southern Italy, heavy with history and significance, both creators and defenders of tradition. Mastroberardino was registered in 1878, and Don Piero Mastroberardino the 10th generation to head wine-growing that stretches back to at least 1760 – the year the arches that still support the barrel cellar were constructed. Antonio Mastroberardino, grandfather of Piero, made the conscientious decision after World War II to champion Campania's indigenous varieties in a period when the rest of Italy was industrializing fast and planting more fashionable French grapes. Piero describes the family business as contemporary without forgetting tradition, comfortable as a regional leader without wanting to call too much attention to themselves. The remarkable Pompeii project (see p.177) is a perfect example of this quiet leadership. A family split in 1994 left Antonio and Piero with the family name, but almost no vineyards, and acquiring land and planting began anew. According to estate agronomist Antonio Dente, it was an opportunity to replant with better vine material and vineyard architecture. The portfolio covers all important appellations in Avellino, Benevento and Vesuvius. Taurasi Radici Riserva is one of Campania's (and Italy's) top volcanic wines, a majestic Aglianico equal to the solid ancient arches and wood-panelled splendour of the house. Bottles back to 1934 are still very much alive in the family cellar. Taurasi Radici Black Label is rarely more than a step behind; both are crafted in the upright, stony, fully savoury tradition, best after a decade. Redimore Aglianico Irpinia IGT from clonal selections of centenary vines planted in 2004 at the Mirabella Eclano estate is relatively softer and fruitier; Naturalis Historia Taurasi, from 40-year-old vines in the volcanic clay soils of the same estate is more modern, adding dark cacao bean to Aglianico's usual savouriness. Top whites are no less impressive, especially organic Fiano di Avellino Radici with great longevity from the estate's highest vineyards, and strikingly salty-mineral NovaSerra Greco di Tufo from the Serra vineyard in Montefusco. Villa dei Misteri, the only wine from the Pompeii vineyards, disappears quickly into the cellars of collectors and select restaurants, even if the company has never taken advantage of its rather remarkable story to charge a senator's ransom for it.

Mustilli ★★

Piazza Trento 4
82019 Sant'Agata dei Goti
mustilli.com

Leonardo Mustilli was the first to bottle a pure Falanghina in 1979, considered until then a blending variety. The wine was the result of a detailed study of 30 local varieties, which led Mustilli to plant and propagate Falanghina, now among the most popular of Italian whites. Daughters Anna Chiara and Paola now run the estate. Until 2002, wine was made in the spectacular cellars under the family's ancient palazzo in the centre of Sant'Agata dei Goti, carved out of the volcanic rock on which the entire town is built. Production has since moved to a modern facility on the edge of town. Mustilli remains a reference for Falanghina, especially Vigna Segreta, a vineyard selection of the top Beneventana biotype. Excellent Greco del Sannio is particularly stony and minerally; Piedirosso is juicy and fruity. Aglianico is also crafted in a ready-to-enjoy, fruity style, including the Cesco di Nece vineyard cru, planted in the 1970s.

Pietracupa ★★★

Via Vadiaperti 17
83030 Montefredane

Few discussions about great Campanian wines end without a mention of Sabino Loffredo and his Pietracupa estate, established in 1993. He is notoriously difficult to visit, not because he is unaffable, but because he simply has nothing to sell; his highly-sought-after wines disappear quickly after release, and production is tiny. The cellar is in Montefredane, a small commune between Fiano di Avellino and Greco di Tufo DOCGs. Loffredo's Greco has marvellous purity, awash in lightly salted pear flavours, creamy and densely knit. Highly reputed Fiano di Avellino, Aglianico Quirico IGT and Taurasi are also made. It's worth the effort to track down Pietracupa wines.

Salvatore Molletieri ★

Via Musanni 19/BIS
83040 Montemarano
salvatoremolletieri.com

A family estate established in 1983 making well-respected, traditional-style wines. The Cinque Querce vineyard in the village of Montemarano, one of Taurasi's finest crus, is the source for Irpinia Aglianico IGT, Taurasi and Taurasi Riserva. Wines are dense, powerful and highly age-worthy. Grapes for fine Greco di Tufo and Fiano di Avellino are purchased, though farming is supervised by the Molletieri family.

Scuotto

Via Campomarino 2–3
83030 Lapio
tenutascuotto.it

A family enterprise established by Eduardo Scotto in the heart of Avellino. Fiano from the commune of Lapio is a highlight, made in stainless-steel and barrel-fermented (Oi Nì) versions, on the fuller and creamier side of the spectrum.

Sorrentino

Via Fruscio
80042 Boscotrecase
sorrentinovini.com

The Sorrentino family is the largest vineyard owner on Vesuvius, commanding a spectacular view from the south side over the Bay of Naples and the Sorrento peninsula. Most intriguing wines in the large range come under the Prodivi label, a project started in 2000 to identify special vineyards and produce more consequential, age-worthy wines. Lacryma Christi Bianco Vigna Lapillo (Coda di Volpe with 20 per cent Falanghina), grown on lapilli soils, has palpable tannic structure and generous proportions. Top red Frupa IGT Pompeiano, pure Piedirosso grown at the upper limits of viticulture on very stony soils, features wild strawberries, taut tannins and perky acids.

Terredora ★★

Via Serra 2
83030 Montefusco
terredora.com

Terredora di Paolo, or simply Terredora, was established in 1994 after a split in the Mastroberardino family between Antonio and Walter. Antonio kept the name, but Walter took many of the family vineyards for Terredora. It didn't take long for the company to become a leading producer and exporter, among the most recognized names in Campania. Some 200 hectares are spread in enviable locations throughout Avellino. Overall, the range tends to a more international style: wines from the Campore district of Lapio are considered the Grande Reserves: a well-structured and aromatically dense Fiano di Avellino and a modern, ripe and smoky Taurasi. Greco di Tufo Loggia della Serra is the top, an excellent example of its kind under the Vineyard Collection.

Torrecino

Località Torricino 5
83010 Tufo
torricino.it

Stefano di Marzo runs this mid-sized cellar in the heart of Tufo, and despite a dozen vintages behind him, he's still experimenting, but the path he's on is exciting. From a stylized, international approach fresh out of school, di Marzo has moved to crafting wines he prefers to make: sharper, brighter, more articulate and individual. Greco di Tufo is solid, but di Marzo's eyes twinkle more brightly as he shows a tank sample of Greco Raone – later harvested, wild-fermented, free-run juice only, with full malolactic (all rarities in the region) – with drive and tension, quivering on a string of acids, like a mineral mouthwash. Cask samples of Taurasi indicate the future direction to fragrant, ethereal, savoury, genuinely succulent.

Villa Dora

Via Bosco Mauro 1
80040 Terzigno
cantinavilladora.it

A small family-run, organic operation on the southwest side of Vesuvius launched in 1997 by Vincenzo Ambrosio and wife Dora – among the more serious in the appellation. Lacryma Christi Bianco Vigna del Vulcano is a pure stony essence, like liquified volcanic rock. Lacryma Christi Rosso Gelsonero is the lighter, lightly tarry version, Forgiato the more structured and age-worthy.

Villa Matilde ★

SS Domitiana 18
81030 Cellole
villamatilde.it

Francesco Paolo Avallone was a Roman history buff, and embarked on an ambitious project to recreate Falernum (see p.187). Villa Matilde was thus born in Caserta in 1965, when there was only one other wine producer in the region. The company, now run by Avallone's children Salvatore, Maria Ida and Francesco Paolo, has expanded considerably; Villa Matilde accounts for about 85 per cent of white Falerno and 60 per cent of total red production. Original San Castrese and Parco Nuovo vineyards are in the ancient Roman cru; two additional estates outside of Caserta were added (Rocca dei Leoni in Benevento and Tenuta Altavilla in Avellino), to complete the company's offerings. Oenologist Ricardo Cotarella consults, giving the wide range a friendly, international profile, of above-average quality. Modern Falernums are highlights, now under the Falerno del Massico DOC that Avallone helped create, especially white Vigna Caracci, a single-vineyard selection of Falanghina planted in 1968, unusually aged four years before release. Falerno del Massico Rosso (Aglianico with 10 to 20 per cent Piedirosso) is rugged and firm. These wines are well appreciated by today's wine elite.

Villa Raiano ★

Via Bosco Satrano 1
83020 San Michele di Serino
villaraiano.com

Very fine, highly concentrated and mineral Greco, Fiano, Falanghina and Aglianico from certified organic vineyards. Production falls under 'classic' and single-vineyard selections.

PITIGLIANO, TUSCANY

The medieval hilltop towns of Pitigliano and Sovana in southern Tuscany lie within the Vulsini District, an area of multi-centre volcanic complexes covering over 2200 square-km, (1400 square-miles), most active from 600,000 to 150,000 years ago, even if volcanic activity was recorded as recently as the 1st century BC and some speculate the complex is still active. The largest and most obvious vestige of volcanism is Lake Bolsena, Europe's largest, roughly circular volcanic lake (aka maar) known to the Romans as Lacus Volsiniensis *just over the border in Lazio.*

It was created by the cataclysmic Plinian eruption of Monti Volsini 300,000 years ago, which shot millions of tons of ash and pumice into the air before collapsing into a caldera that later filled with water. Ash from this and other eruptions settled in the surrounding arc from Orvieto to Montefiascone and Pitigliano, eventually compacting and cementing into the hard tuffaceous rock called the Pitigliano Formation, underlying Pitigliano/Sovana DOC (as well as part of Orvieto and Est! Est!! Est!!! di Montefiascone). The tuff, several hundred metres (feet) deep in some areas, is easily carved, as witnessed by the deep network of cellars under virtually every house in Pitigliano. It's also useful for quarrying the whitish building blocks out of which the town is constructed, as indeed is much of Rome.

LOST & FOUND

Seemingly lost in time, the ancient Etruscan town of Pitigliano floats atop a ridge of volcanic tuff, the foundations of its medieval houses carved quite literally into the bedrock. Sheer cliffs fall away into deep, wooded valleys to the north and south, framing the town and making for one of the most spectacular vistas in central Italy.

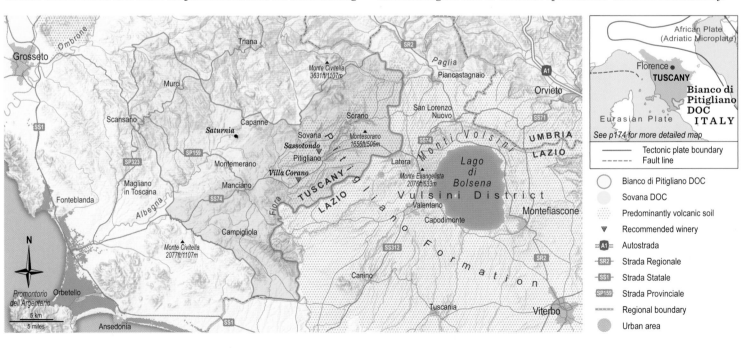

OPPOSITE (LEFT TO RIGHT) *Pitigliano (three times); Carla Benini, Sassotondo; the modest sign of Sassotondo; Pitigliano; 'Tasting Room' at Sassotondo; Pitigliano; open air hot springs, Saturnia, Tuscany (twice); Pitigliano (twice).*

An intact Roman aqueduct mutely speaks of Pitigliano's distant past, while Etruscan tombs carved into the cliffs reach even further into remote history. The town seems as much like an open-air museum as an inhabited Tuscan town.

Pitigliano is remote in space, too. The nearest train station is 50 km (31 miles) away in Orvieto. Grosseto by the coast is further still; this is the proverbial backwater of Tuscany, an area known as the Maremma Toscana. 'Pitigliano's isolation is both a blessing and a curse,' Carla Benini of Sassotondo tells me as we skirt the north shores of Lake Bolsena on the only main road into town, the Strada Statale 74, passing endless potato fields, one of the prized local crops from the region's nutrient-rich volcanic ash soils. The only way to reach Pitigliano without a car is by public bus, though it runs only twice a day, or by bicycle, which requires the stamina of a Giro d'Italia rider to pedal in and out of the steep valleys and slender spurs that radiate out from the lake like the ridges of a scallop shell.

'On the one hand, Pitigliano's location has allowed it to retain its medieval charm,' Carla continues. 'But it has also frozen the region in time. The mentality of farmers has barely moved beyond the feudal era.' This observation goes a long way to explaining why the Cantina di Pitigliano still accounts for 95 per cent of wine production. Private estates number less than a half dozen, which is all the more surprising in a region like Tuscany where the last 30 years have seen a veritable gold rush of vineyard acquisition

and multi-million euro estate development. In Pitigliano, vineyards are still looked upon in a medieval way: almost as a curse, a burden, not a benefit. He who owns land is a slave to it, destined to toil away for a lifetime for somebody else's profit.

While quality has been modest in recent times, there are signs the region is re-awakening with the generational transition. Several prominent companies have also established vineyards in the area, such as Antinori and the 200-hectare Fattoria Aldobrandesca. The Veneto's venerable Tommasi family has two estates within the Pitigliano DOC, Poggio al Tufo and Doganella. Though neither Antinori nor Tommasi produce a Bianco di Pitigliano, preferring instead to produce mostly red wines from non-Tuscan varieties (Malbec, Cabernet, Merlot) under the more general Maremma Toscana DOC.

It's clear that Pitigliano/Sovana need a critical mass of good producers to gain name recognition and penetrate the already crowded market. And good wine is evidently possible. The Romans, and even earlier the Etruscans, made celebrated wines from this tuffaceous rock.

Pitigliano's Appellations & Grapes

The **Bianco di Pitigliano DOC** was created in 1966, on the same day as Brunello di Montalcino. The zone overlaps with part of Morellino di Scansano DOCG in the less volcanic northwest corner, and encompasses the Sovana DOC entirely (though there's a current proposal to fold this red/rosé only appellation into a single Pitigliano DOC). Bianco di Pitigliano is white, made from a minimum of 40 to 100 per cent Trebbiano Toscano, plus up to 60 per cent, combined or separately, of Greco, Malvasia, Verdello, Grechetto, Ansonica (aka Insolia), Chardonnay, Sauvignon, Viognier, Pinot Bianco, Riesling. The **Superiore** mention requires lower yields, higher alcohol and slightly longer ageing. There are also spumante and sweet Vin Santo versions. Red wines (minimum 50 per cent Sangiovese plus up to 50 per cent other red grapes authorized for cultivation in Tuscany) are labelled as **Sovana DOC** or more general **Maremma Toscana DOC** or **Toscana IGT**.

Considering the long list of grapes, a typical style is hard to pin down. But from a grapevine's perspective, the region's soils derived from volcanic tuff are acidic and high in potassium, magnesium and sodium, which could be the source of the saline character often reported in these wines.

ABOVE *Cellars carved out of volcanic tuff are found under virtually every house in the town of Pitigliano.*

OPPOSITE *Stairways in the town of Pitigliano.*

PITIGLIANO – THE WINES & THE PEOPLE

Sassotondo ★

CS Pian Di Conati 52
58010 Sovana

sassotondo.it

Carla Benini, an agronomist from Trento, and husband Edoardo Ventimiglia, a documentary filmmaker from Rome, moved to an abandoned rural paradise in 1990. The property came with vines, though winemaking wasn't the motivation; until 1995 they sold most of their grapes to the Cantina Sociale, as did everybody else. But praise from a friend after sipping their homemade wine changed the course of their lives. The first release was 1997, and Sassotondo has quietly been making the region's best wines since, regionally distinct and charmingly rustic. Vineyards are farmed biodynamically and are two-thirds red, including the flagship pure, peppery Ciliegiolo Maremma Toscana IGT, and an uncommonly big and tannic, old-vine Ciliegiolo San Lorenzo. Bianco di Pitigliano Superiore Isolina (mostly Trebbiano with Sauvignon and a portion of Greco), is markedly saline. More experimental is Numero Dieci Maremma Toscana Bianco (a subtle nod to AC Roma's star no.10 player Francesco Totti, an idol of Edoardo's), a pure 'orange' Trebbiano, fermented and left on skins until June, cleaner and fresher than most in the genre, gently floral and stone- (pit-) fruit flavoured – surely one of the most intriguing versions around. Pure Greco Numero Dieci is made in the same way, with even deeper colour and more exotic herbal, fennel, honeyed aromas.

Villa Corano

SR 74 Maremmana Ovest Km 46+760
58017 Pitigliano

villacorano.it

Stefano Formicone, former director of the Cantina Sociale di Pitigliano, launched his own operation at the turn of the millennium. He is one of the most knowledgeable viticulturalists in the zone. His business model is predicated on selling to large tour groups, who come by the busload from Pitigliano and surrounding towns, accounting for nearly 80 per cent of wine sales. The range is competently made, with Bianco di Pitigliano Superior Cor Unum (Trebbiano blend) a standout.

SOAVE

Standing in the town of Soave today you'd need to be an informed geologist to read the volcanic origins of the land. But there were volcanoes, and many of them, and they've left their mark on many of Soave's best vineyards. Standing where the town of Soave is, 65 million years ago you'd have been underwater in a shallow tropical lagoon. In fact, most of northern Italy was underwater in the period before the Alps formed. But as the African Plate ran up against the Eurasian Plate, the Proto-Alps began to crumple up.

Vast subterranean pools of magma were created as Africa sank and melted beneath Europe. But it was a game of both push and pull, and the seafloor was eventually torn apart along a rift zone. The growing pressure of deep magma pools found release through fissures on the margins of the collapsing trench, and volcanic activity erupted across the top of the peninsula, lasting for 50 million years. The lagoon was soon punctuated by hundreds of volcanic peaks growing out of the water like islands in the South Pacific, and the entire depression slowly filled with lavas and marine sediments over millions of years.

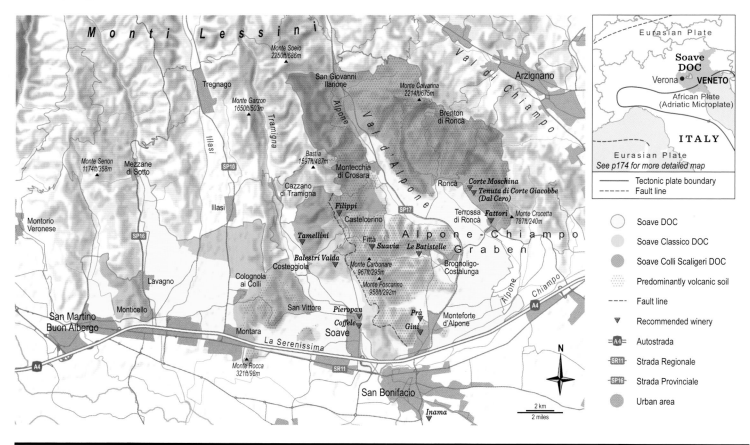

OPPOSITE (LEFT TO RIGHT) *Cantina Filippi, Castelcerino; Capitel Foscarino; Suavia; Pieropan; ripe Garganega; signpost outside of Soave on the SP39; road to Soave; Monte Carbonare; pergola vines at Inama; Gini cellar, cut in basalt; Monte Carbonare vineyards; Castello di Soave.*

This is the area called the Alpone-Chiampo Graben after the two rivers that now frame it, and how it formed explains the dual nature of the soils of Soave: a clearly coloured mix of white limestone from marine sediments, and black basalt. The ancient lagoon eventually drained as the *graben* (trench) was later thrust up and driven against the Alps, causing it to crinkle and form the hills above Verona that are blanketed with vines today. Considering that the volcanic activity in the area ended some 25 million years ago, the soils of the Soave zone have had plenty of time to weather, a fact that makes all the difference to vines.

THE INDUSTRIAL POWERHOUSE

It's a short drive east from Verona to Soave along La Serenissima *autostrada*, the highway that connects northern Italy from Turin to Trieste along the Po River Valley. On either side of the road, row upon row of neatly tended vineyards stretch across the vast plain and up into the foothills north of Verona, the first wrinkles of the mighty Alps not yet visible from this distance. Compared to the chaos of southern Italy, the north looks and feels positively genteel and orderly. It's like a different country, as in fact it once was.

The modern wine-production area for Soave was mapped out in 1931, one of only two to be recognized by the Italian government at the time (Chianti was the other). Some 1500 hectares of hillsides were included in what's now referred to as the Classico zone, between Monteforte d'Alpone and Soave itself, long known for its superior wine. But with the creation of the Soave DOC in 1968, at a period when Italy was transforming from rural agricultural economy to post World War II industrial powerhouse, Soave was expanded almost five-fold with an eye to increasing production and exports of wine. Much of the flat, fertile land through which the highway runs was granted appellation status. The plan worked brilliantly, and cheap, cooperative-produced Soave soon conquered export markets.

Quality producers in the era were exceptions: Pieropan, Anselmi, Suavia and Gini were among the few. But growing pressure from competition, both international and especially domestic, eventually eroded cheap Soave's market share. It was clear that the only future would be quality wine. The 1990s mark the beginning of the turnaround, when others such as Stefano Inama, Graziano Prà, Gaetano and Pio Francesco Tamellini and Antonio Fattori contributed to significantly raising the bar. It's no coincidence that their vineyards are all in the hills, predominantly

volcanic, in the original production area, but also in the surrounding hills called the Colli Scaligeri and the Monti Lessini above the Alpone Valley where the finest wines have always originated. The stories of these wine-growers are similar: the family had vineyards, but sold their grapes to one of the local cooperatives. Yet now the new generation is firmly established and has regained full control of the family assets from grape to bottle. And the quality of Soave has never been better.

The Dual Nature of Soave: Land of Basalt & Limestone

I get a first hand view of Soave's split geological personality when Giovanni Ponchia of the Soave Consortium stops his car mid-way up the hill on the switchback road that leads from Soave up to Fittà. 'There,' he says, pointing to the exposed strata of rock where the hillside was cut away to build the road. 'You can clearly see the limestone.' Two very distinct layers are visible (see above): the bottom layer is a thick strata of yellowish-amber soil that looks

like a kind of sedimentary sand, easily scraped by hand. Above is hard, calcified greyish-white rock – limestone – that formed here when the warm, shallow Adriatic Sea stretched all the way to Piedmont.

We're very near to the invisible fault line that neatly cleaves the Soave Classico zone into two parts. It's invisible because it runs right through the sides of hills – there's no obvious visible surface fracture as with many other faults. This is a much more subtle fracture that occurred long before these hills were uplifted; only the footprints of bedrock and soil mark its existence and trace its path beneath the vines.

Back in the car and around a couple more bends up the hill and Ponchia stops again and points at the hillside underneath another vineyard. 'And there is the lava,' he says with great gusto and satisfaction. In that short stretch of road we crossed the invisible fault and entered into the zone where the bedrock is pure basalt. The difference is stark. No amber sand, no white limestone. Just layers of hardened 'pillow lava', a clear sign of effusive underwater eruptions, and the black earth derived from it (see p.203).

The differences do not go unnoticed by vines, and wines reflect their geological roots. Those from the sedimentary alluvial soils, in the flat lands and valley floor, are consistently the simplest, crunchy and cheerful, but not profound. Soave from limestone-rich soils is the most expressive and aromatic straight off the top, floral, with lots of finesse and elegance. The volcanic wines,

in contrast, are aromatically unyielding. There's riper, more abundant orchard fruit – apricot, pear, nectarine – and tropical fruits (from compounds in the norisoprenoids family of molecules) and, after a few years, the appearance of flint and diesel/petrol/gas aromas and marked graphite-like character. The texture is more viscous and oily, and there's a sense of a darker, more inward-looking personality that takes time to express. 'Volcanic wines are more closed in youth, they need more time to open,' Claudio Gini confirms. 'But in time there's more character, more longevity. Minerality takes time to emerge in Garganega.' Intriguingly, this mirrors some of the differences observed in German Rieslings from volcanic and non-volcanic vineyards (see p.138).

Andrea Pieropan offers a possible scientific explanation, based on long observations of the estate's two principle crus grown on opposite geologies, 'they're born from soils with different pH, which means that the availability of trace minerals is different. For [volcanic] Calvarino, with a pH close to neutral around seven, there's more available zinc, molybdenum and sulphur. For [limestone] La Rocca with its higher pH (alkaline), there's more calcium and potassium. These are measurable differences.'

Professor Attilio Scienza is one of Italy's, and the world's, foremost experts on wine grapes and soils, with a particular fascination for volcanic wines. He has conducted much research

---

ABOVE *Vineyards in* contrada *Salvarenza, source of Gini's exceptional cru from century-old vines.*

OPPOSITE ABOVE *Castello di Soave, unmistakable landmark, first stones were laid in the high Middle Ages.*

OPPOSITE BELOW *Vineyards of the Monte Foscarino cru, firmly anchored in basalts (see pp.208–9).*

into the subject and shares his views with me. 'There are two particular aspects of the volcanic soils of Soave that have an important impact on wine profile,' Scienza explains. 'One is the high proportion of clay, on average much higher in the Soave zone than in other volcanic areas of Italy [because these are relatively old soils], which confers structure and longevity. The other is the high percentage of active limestone, which is not usually found in volcanic terroirs. This brings finesse and elegance.' Such is the magic of Soave, a land blessed with the best of both worlds.

Soave's Grapes & DOC(G)

Soave is Italy's largest white wine appellation with 6500 hectares; its sheer size has made it one of the best-known Italian wines – surpassing even Chianti in the 70s in sales. Though the distinction is dubious; much of what the world knew as Soave was innocuous, mostly harmless white wine made from overproductive vineyards. How things have changed. Soave is one of Italy's greatest white wines, but, as a bonus for wine-lovers, the heavy weight of the past has kept the price of even top cru Soave from soaring, making these some of Italy's best-value white wines.

Garganega is Soave's grape – one of Italy's finest white varieties. Like, say, Chardonnay, it's not boisterously aromatic, but highly reflective of its origins, as noted above. It's also remarkably structured and age-worthy, especially old vines from volcanic soils – 20 years for the best crus is not a stretch. In all of Soave's

various appellations, Garganega must make up at least 70 per cent of the blend, with up to 30 per cent of Trebbiano di Soave and/or Chardonnay. But in practice these make up a much smaller percentage, and Chardonnay has all but disappeared.

The Soave appellation is admittedly a bit of a mess, incorporating confusing mentions and overlapping areas and the willy-nilly appearance and disappearance of the 'G' (as in DOCG). It's a classic case of the authorities trying to appease all factions. But in essence, **Soave DOC** is the most basic mention, used for still or sparkling wines produced in the flatlands and valleys of the region.

Wines produced in the central hills entirely within the communes of Soave and Monteforte d'Alpone, can be labelled as **Soave Classico DOC** or **Soave Superiore Classico DOCG** (for those with slightly lower yields, ten tons vs. 14 tons/hectare, and higher potential alcohol, 11.5% vs. 10.5% ABV) or **Recioto di Soave Classico DOCG**, for the sweet, air-dried grape versions. Wines from the rest of the hilly areas within the greater Soave DOC, but outside of the Classico zone, are entitled to the **Soave Superiore DOCG** or the **Soave Colli Scaligeri DOC** (no 'G') mentions. Sweet versions from this area are called **Recioto di Soave DOCG**. Additionally, several dozen crus (single-vineyards) have been identified and mapped out within the Classico and Colli Scaligeri areas on both limestones and basalts (for the volcanic crus see individual producers on pp.207–9).

ABOVE LEFT *University of Milan professor Attilio Scienza, Italian, and world, expert on vines and wine, with a particular affinity for volcanic wines with the Castello di Soave in rear.*

ABOVE RIGHT *Valentina and Meri Tessari of Suavia, with the Monte Carbonare framed in the winery's window.*

ITALY

SOAVE – THE WINES & THE PEOPLE

Balestri Valda ★

Via Monti 44
37038 Soave
vinibalestrivalda.com

In 1994 Guido Rizzotto purchased 13 contiguous hillside hectares in Soave – a rarity in the region, and built a new winery in 2000. Standard Soave Classico (20 per cent Trebbiano) is pretty and floral with real depth and texture. Vigneto Sengialta is the flagship; the cru name derives from *sengio* (basalt stone in dialect), many of which are littered across the soil's surface above limestone outcrops. The wine is discreet and non-fruity, certainly very rocky, dense and dark.

Coffele ★

Via Roma
37038 Soave
coffele.it

In 1971, Giuseppe Coffele and Giovanna Visco gave up teaching to exploit the Visco family vineyards in Castelcerino, where limestone meets basalt, and make wine in a centuries-old building in the heart of medieval Soave. Alberto and Chiara Coffele carry on the family business today. Alzari and Ca' Visco are the two important crus; the former a substantial wine from limestone subjected to partial drying, the latter a superior cru selection from red volcanic soils in which white-fleshed fruit mingles with flinty minerality on a grippy frame.

Corte Giacobbe (Dal Cero)

Via Moschina 11
37030 Roncà
vinidalcero.com

Brothers Giuseppe and Dario manage Dal Cero together with their sons. Vigneto Runcata, on the ridge of lavas and tuffs between Monte Crocetta and Monte Calvarina, is the origin of the top cru, offering impressive smoke and ash, honey and cold-creosote flavours and a typically gritty texture.

Corte Moschina

Via Moschina 1
37030 Roncà
cortemoschina.it

Patrizia and Silvano Niero farm vineyards in the volcanic Lessini hills. Soave I Tarai is the reference, a satisfying and succulent late-harvested Garganega. Outside of the Soave DOC but also volcanic, sparkling Lessini Durello Riserva '60' Metodo Classico is a classy, dry bubbly, still fresh and vibrant after five years ageing on the lees.

Fattori ★★

Via Olmo 6
37030 Terrossa di Roncà
fattoriwines.com

Antonio Fattori and family produce top-tier, gritty and flinty wines from sizable holdings on the basalts of Monte Calvarina, northeast of the Classico zone. Iron oxide-rich red soils inspired the name of the hamlet Terrossa at the foot of Calvarina where the winery stands. Three Soaves highlight Garganega's versatility: standard-bearer, early-harvested Runcaris is crisp and crunchy; excellent mid-range Danieli has balanced power and intense minerality; extreme cru Motto Piane from late-harvested, partially-dried grapes is deep-coloured and full-bodied. Sauvignon Blanc Vecchie Scuole, dark, savage and mineral, defies easy comparison, neither grassy nor tropical, but layered and textured in its own singular way.

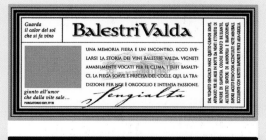

Filippi-Villa Visco ★★

Via Libertà 55
37038 Castelcerino di Soave
cantinafilippi.it

In 2003, Filippo and Alessandro Filippi took the old family property into their own hands, quickly establishing one of the region's most convincing estates. The isolated hilltop property in Castelcerino, just beyond the northern limit of the Classico zone in the Soave Colli Scaligeri DOC, straddles the transition zone between volcanic and limestone soils – the different characters of which are transparently rendered thanks to the Filippis' organic farming and minimalist approach, wild ferments and low sulphur. Purely volcanic cru Castelcerino is a marvel of precision, tightly wound and smoky. Mixed basalt-limestone cru Vigna della Brà is supremely elegant and flinty, with the acid twang typical of great volcanic Garganega.

Gini ★★★

Via Giacomo Matteotti 42
37032 Monteforte d'Alpone
ginivini.com

A deed from 1852 bears witness to Giuseppe Gini's purchase of a vineyard in Contrada Salvarenza, from which Claudio and brother Sandro still produce the estate's top cru. The Ginis boasts an amazing collection of old vines; the youngest of their organic vinyards averages 70 years, as they prefer to replace individual vines rather than replant entire parcels. Soave Classico is a benchmark, a wine of evident old-vine concentration and capacity to age, as an 18-year-old bottle showed. According to Claudio, old vines allow later harvest without losing acidity, while alcohol rarely exceeds 13 per cent. Cru Froscà is dynamic, creamy yet intense, thanks to one of the highest diurnal temperature shifts in the region. Cru Contrada Salvarenze Vecchie Vigne, from further down the same slope is made from own-rooted, century-old vines on basalt over limestone, a wine of massive extract and palpably tannic texture underscored by salty, ashen, flinty minerality. Both need at least a half-decade to show their true character.

Inama ★★

Località Biacche 50
37047 San Bonifacio
inamaaziendaagricola.it

Giuseppe Inama bought considerable acreage in the volcanic Monte Foscarino cru during a difficult economic period in the late 60s – a gamble that has paid off handsomely. Bottled wine came when son Stephano entered the business in the early 90s, becoming one of the motors behind the quality revival of Soave. Vineyards are farmed organically. Precise, stony, pear-scented Vin Soave Classico is the estate's calling card. Vigneti di Foscarino is a selection of old vines facing southeast, a powerful style with evident low yields and high concentration. Vigna du Lot, from the west side of Foscarino, is fermented/aged in French barrels; the warmer afternoon sun and new wood yield deeper colour and baked-fruit flavours – notably woody and leesy. These are extreme, weighty, highly concentrated Soaves.

Le Batistelle ★

Via Sambuco 110
37032 Brognoligo di Monteforte d'Alpone
lebattistelle.it

A small estate in the hills near Brognoligo on all-volcanic soils, run by Gelmino and Cristina Dal Bosco. Lean and racy Montesei Soave Classico blends several parcels; cru Roccolo del Durlo, a steep sub-parcel on the Monte Carbonare with its pure basaltic soil, is dramatically stony and well-chiselled.

Pieropan ★★★

Via Camuzzoni 3
37038 Soave
pieropan.it

Established in 1880 in the heart of Soave by Leonildo Pieropan, this is one of Italy's grand old estates, still performing at the highest level under fourth generation Andrea and Dario. Two crus, bottled since the 1970s (among Italy's first single-vineyard white wines), count among the country's greatest: the deeply volcanic Calvarino ('small ordeal') on the lower slopes of Monte Foscarino earned its name thanks to the difficulty of working the stony soil; it has worn out muscles in the family since 1901; 30 per cent Trebbiano is blended in and fermented in glass-lined concrete and aged on lees for a year. Nearby La Rocca is anchored in the calcareous-clay of Monte Rochetta overlooking Soave's medieval castle; pure Garganega is given a short skin maceration before fermentation and ageing in casks ranging from 500 to 2000 litres (132 to 528 US gallons). In Andrea's words, 'Calvarino gives more linear, crisp salty character, while La Rocca is more round, smooth and soft.' I find La Rocca distinctively chalky; Calvarino's acids are more finessed, still lively and steely but riper, and the nose more discreet, with more compact and tightly wound structure overall. Fine and filigree Soave Classico from old vines on predominantly volcanic soils is lightened by a dash of Trebbiano. Grapes from volcanic hillsides are dried for five months to make pure Garganega Recioto di Soave Le Colombare, with two years ageing in cask to lend a decidedly nutty, caramelized appeal.

Prà ★★

Via della Fontana 31
37032 Monteforte d'Alpone
vinipra.it

Graziano Prà was a key early figure in the revival of Soave Classico, repurposing family vineyards for commercial bottled production in 1990. Today, his enviable collection of crus in the Classico zone, mostly basaltic – Monte Grande, Foscarino, Froscà, Monte Croce, Sant'Antonio and Ponsara – give rise to some of Soave's finest wines. Even the standard Soave Classico Otto is rich and substantial. Staforte gains additional flesh from extended time on the lees in tank. Cru Monte Grande, which includes a dash of Trebbiano di Soave, is broadened and softened by ageing in cask.

Suavia ★★

Via Centro 14
Frazione Fittà
37038 Soave
suavia.it

In 1982, Giovanni Tessari and wife Rosetta established Suavia, the ancient name for Soave. Daughters Meri, Valentina and Alessandra now manage the estate in the heart of volcanic Soave Classico at one of the highest and most northerly points in the zone. Basic Soave from up to 50-year-old vines is beautifully flinty and smoky, while the top cru Monte Carbonare – visible from the winery and named for the coal-like colour of its pure basalt soils – is more extreme and mineral, turning to petrol (gasoline) and peat bog with age. Delicate and floral Massifitti from massale selections of Trebbiano di Soave is also notable, and Recioto di Soave, a mesmerizing interplay of pears, nectarines and salted caramel, is one of the region's best.

Tamellini ★

Via San Matteo 22
37038 Soave

Gaetano Tamellini thought he had something special with the 1997 Recioto di Soave bottled for family use. So he contacted Italian-American wine importer Marc de Grazia through a mutual friend, who saw the potential, too – he still represents them today. A new facility was built in time for the 1998 harvest. Brother Pio Francesco, chemical engineer, manages the cellar with the oversight of oenologist Paolo Caciorgna. Estate vines grow in in a mix of limestone and basalt below Castelcerino near Costeggiola, producing a particularly elegant and delicate Soave. Cru Le Bine di Costiola from predominantly limestone offers grand finesse and refined stoniness.

SANTORINI
THE SOUTH AEGEAN VOLCANIC ARC

Picture-perfect Santorini, or Thera to the Greeks, is part of the Cyclades, a south Aegean archipelago of some 220 islands that also includes Naxos, Mykonos and Paros. The islands are the limestone peaks of a submarine mountain chain, with the exception of Santorini and Milos, which are volcanic peaks that formed along the South Aegean Volcanic Arc. Santorini has been a prolific wine producer for at least 3700 years, as witnessed by winemaking artifacts unearthed at Akrotiri, a late bronze-age city preserved under a thick layer of ash from the island's legendary eruption in the 17th century BC. The cataclysmic blast created one of the world's largest and most striking water-filled calderas (a cauldron-shaped depression caused by the collapse of land following a volcanic eruption), as well as the islands of Thirassia and Aspronisi. It also altered Santorini's terroir forever with its pyroclastic fallout – it might be argued for the better, given the utter uniqueness of the wines grown on the island today.

OPPOSITE *The unique, basket-shaped vine pruning of Santorini,* gyristi, *this vine is likely 80 years old+.*

ABOVE *Vineyards on Santorini's southern end, where the majority of vines are planted.*

Tectonic plate boundary
Fault line

Santorini PDO covers the entire island
All soils are volcanic

▽ Recommended winery
— Asphalt road
⬭ Urban area

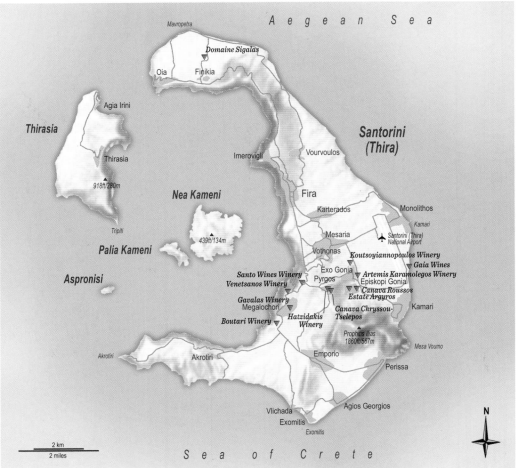

A CHAIN OF PROBABLE EVENTS

Santorini is one of the peaks formed along the South Aegean Volcanic Arc, a string of volcanoes aligned along a 500-km (300-mile) long semi-circular sweep from just offshore of Athens, south through Santorini and west to the Turkish coast. Nisyros, Milos, Egina and Poros are the other main volcanic centres of this zone, also known as the Hellenic Volcanic Arc. It's the most seismically active area in the entire Mediterranean and western Eurasia, lying along a highly stressed meeting point of the African and Eurasian Plates – also responsible for Italy's volcanic geography. Just south of Crete, the African Plate is vigorously subducting under the Aegean Sea Plate (a fractured portion of the larger Eurasian Plate), giving rise to a parallel volcanic arc some 140 km (85 miles) north of the subduction zone where magma from the sinking and melting African Plate finds its way back up to the earth's surface.

Earthquakes are frequent, and Santorini is still highly volcanically active. Historical activity in 196 BC and 1950 AD caused an upthrust of the caldera floor to form Palea Kameni and Nea Kameni, the 'old and new burnt islands' respectively, in its centre.

The Science of Probability

The tension in the air was palpable when Yiannis Paraskevopoulos, co-owner and winemaker of Gaia Wines, arrived at the Heliotopos Hotel in the village of Imerovigli in February 2011 for one of his frequent visits to Santorini. On this occasion, the small lobby of his usual lodgings overlooking the spectacular caldera had become the ad hoc headquarters for a group of volcanologists. The group was huddled around a screen monitoring seismic and volcanic activity on the Aegean seabed. Paraskevopoulos could see a large red blip. It was a full red alert.

OPPOSITE (LEFT TO RIGHT) *Cliffs of wind-sculpted ash; church with caldera behind near Imerovigli; caldera sunset from Imerovigli; Hatzidakis' organic vineyards;* *Hatzidakis Winery; diversity in Santorini's volcanic rocks; Canava Roussos' old cellar; broken steps at Akrotiri revealing the earthquake that struck before* *the great eruption; terraced vineyards on Mount Profiti Elias; old vine in Kavaliere vineyard; old bottle of Canava Roussos; 3000-year-old wine jars, Akrotiri.*

'We're quite sure it's going to blow,' said one of the volcanologists as he entered the room. For some days now, pressure had been building beneath the mid-caldera islands of Nea Kameni and Palea Kameni, which experience small but regular upheavals that cause them to gain a few centimetres (inches) with alarming regularity. The seabed was bubbling up, and this time it was reaching critical levels. Pressure sensors embedded on the seafloor and satellite imagery were drawing the red blip on the monitor that was riveting the attention of the scientists, and now Paraskevopoulos too. The small island of Thirasia had moved several centimetres (inches) away from the northern tip of the main island as the seabed cracked and uplifted between them from gas pressure and the injection of fresh magma into the chamber a couple of miles beneath. The scientists were visibly concerned. 'It's time to call the mayor,' another said grimly.

Within minutes the mayor was on the phone as the scientists explained the gravity of the situation. 'We think it's time to distribute the gas masks.' The mayor paused long and hard as he processed the information. Nothing could be worse for the island then a false alarm for a volcanic eruption. Tourism is the engine that drives Santorini, and without tourists, the economy collapses. The chain of probable events flashed through the mayor's mind. Then, calmly, with characteristically Greek pragmatic, philosophical reasoning, the mayor responded, 'we won't sound the alarm and distribute the masks. If this turns out to be a false alarm, the entire tourist season will be lost and we're all screwed. On the other hand, if the volcano does erupt, we're all screwed anyhow. So I prefer to do nothing and take my chances.'

The mayor's gamble paid off, this time. But the science of probability calls for at least a minor eruption in the next three decades. Another major Plinian event is due in the next 10,000 to 20,000 years.

There was certainly ample warning before Santorini's last great Plinian eruption around 1620 BC. The cracked steps and partially crumbled walls uncovered in the ruins of Akrotiri show the effects of a sizable earthquake that rocked the island just before the calamitous explosion, still being cleaned up when the end came. The sign was understood, and unlike Pompeii, only a single perished soul has been found within the city itself. It's clear that the monumental eruption – the largest on the planet in the last 10,000 years calculated to have emitted 60 cubic km (nearly 40 cubic miles) of pyroclastic material – would have decimated everything within dozens of miles on land or sea. A low surge of toxic gas would have instantly killed anyone fleeing by boat, that is, if the tsunamis caused by the eruption didn't. Destructive waves reached the shores of the Peloponnese, and the Minoan civilization on Crete was dealt a decisive blow from which it never recovered. Up to 15 cm (five inches) of ash even fell in distant Asia Minor, and the climate of the entire Eastern Mediterranean was disrupted for several years.

ABOVE *Santorini's picture-perfect caldera; the two islands in the middle – Nea Kameni and Palea Kameni – grow regularly from volcanic activity.*

The eruption occurred in several phases, as the visible tephra horizons in many parts of the island reveal. In some areas up to 60 metres (200 feet) of debris accumulated above the older volcanic bedrock (compared to Pompeii's six to seven metres (20 to 25 feet), ranging from fine ash to lapilli to larger volcanic bombs. And the shape of the island itself was dramatically altered. Where once the island was circular, with a fully contained, smaller caldera, the eruption caused the northwest and west sides to collapse and large parts of the island to sink into the emptied magma chamber below. Other parts of the island gained landmass from the accumulation of raining pyroclastic fallout.

It was nearly four centuries before Santorini was re-populated by Phoenician traders in the 12th century BC. But they would discover that the apocalyptic eruption had had unexpected benefits for Santorini's future wine-growers – it left behind soils eminently suitable for high-quality wine production.

Santorini's Volcanic Soils & Viticulture

The climate of Santorini is extreme. Very little rain falls, and almost only in winter months. Winds can be ferocious and blow for weeks on end. The summer sun is relentless, and away from the sea temperatures soar. Humidity ranges from near saturation to very low, dropping suddenly as the sun rises and winds pick up. Little plant life has adapted to these harsh conditions. But what does survive – broad (fava) beans, tomatoes and capers, for example, and of course grapes – has ferocious intensity as a result of the suffering. Hardened like a Spartan warrior, each is suffused with forceful flavour, an archetype of its species.

Soil is not really the right term for the surface material of Santorini. Being a mere 3700 years old, and in an arid climate, the upper horizon is made up of unweathered, coarse-textured sand, pumice, ash and rock. The environment is inhospitable to phylloxera, and grafting vines is unnecessary. In many areas, layers of volcanic ash have fused together into a very compact soil locally called aspa. Although very hard to till, aspa, like many forms of tephra, has the useful property of being able to absorb and retain water. In the dry climate of Santorini, this property is what makes grape-growing possible. Scarce rains are held in the ground and released throughout the long dry growing season. But those rare winter gifts from Zeus above would not be sufficient alone; the kindness of Poseidon is needed to supplement moisture during the summer, in the form of sea mists. Each night humidity from Santorini's immense caldera creeps up the high cliffs onto the island where it cools and condenses on vine leaves and seeps into the open pores of the absorbent pumice. Even in the height of summer, scratch just below the surface and you'll find moisture. However, vines must still be widely spaced to allow root systems plenty of room to stretch out in search of water.

Aside from useful physical properties, the soil's chemical properties also influence the wines of Santorini. Although volcanic ash is generally rich in mineral elements, in such a young undeveloped form, Santorini's is dramatically poor in organic matter and clay, resulting in low fertility. The lack of organics is perpetuated by the fact that very little grows in such a hostile environment, and the cycle of plant growth, death and re-absorption of organic material does not occur. Nitrogen, phosphorous and potassium – the three big macro nutrients required by all plants – are in short

bud-burst and flowering. Santorinian wine-growers have learned to adapt over centuries by developing a unique form of training vines called *gyristi*. Each winter/spring, shoots from the previous year are woven into a circular shape, which, over several years begins to resemble a basket, posed right on the ground (see p.210). No posts or wires of any kind are used. Grape bunches can thus grow within the basket, protected from wind-borne projectiles, while a canopy of leaves protects grapes from excessive sun exposure.

After several decades, the yields of these basket-vines, seemingly haphazardly littered across the moon-like landscape, drop to uneconomical levels, in part because of the tremendous distance nutrients must travel through the coiled canes to reach grapes. But rather than replant, at around 70 to 80 years old the vines are instead cut at the surface, and a new shoot is allowed to grow from a dormant bud on the root system, and the coiling begins anew. This renewal has been performed at least four or five times on certain vines, making the root systems of the island's oldest vines hundreds of years old, even if on the surface the vines appear to be young. Santorini can thus lay claim to having some of the oldest vines in the world under continuous cultivation. A petition to join the list of UNESCO-protected living landscapes is being prepared.

But Santorini's winds bring benefits as well. During summer, the cool, refreshing north wind called the Meltemia lowers night-time temperatures to below the dew point, allowing precious drops of water to condense and be absorbed by vines. Daytime winds have the opposite benefit of stripping atmospheric humidity, which, coupled with heat, would otherwise create an ideal environment for moulds, mildews and fungi to flourish. As it stands, most growers farm essentially organically, whether declared or not, needing only an occasional dose of copper to keep vine disease at bay.

supply, keeping vine vigour down and yields pitifully low, giving wines with astonishing concentration and inimitable character. But considering the yield per hectare and the prices paid for Santorini wine, the industry lives at the margins of economic sustainability. If the island's infrastructure weren't already overtaxed by rampant tourism, most wine-growers I'm sure would open a hotel instead.

The shortage of potassium in Santorini's soils also appears to have another critical effect on wine composition: very low pH/high acid. Without this acid-buffering element, even in this hot and sunny subtropical Mediterranean climate, and with fully ripe grapes approaching 14% ABV or more, Santorini wines have a pH of barely 3.0, or below – the sort of acidity level you'd expect in, say, an acid-rich grape like Riesling grown at its marginal northern limit.

Beyond soil, the constant winds on Santorini shape the environment, being both a menace and a saviour. Wind-whipped sand and shards of pumice tear through leaves, buds and grape skins, damaging plants and reducing yields. The size of each year's crop is heavily dependent on weather during the delicate stages of

Santorini's Grapes & Wines

In the distant past there were as many as 50 varieties grown on Santorini, when grapes were virtually the only commercial crop and blanketed the island. Now just three white grapes dominate production, grown mainly in the south around the villages of Pyrgos, Megalochori and Akrotiri. Assyrtiko occupies three-quarters of Santorini's vineyards, selected over centuries for its thick, resistant skins, ability to retain high acids even at high alcohol levels and chart-topping extract. It's considered one of Greece's finest white varieties, and the wines that made Santorini's past fortunes, able to

ABOVE *Exacting and inquisitive Paris Sigalas, in his Kavalieros vineyard.*

OPPOSITE *Less common but equally unique pruning called* klada *or* kouloura *in less wind-exposed vineyards.*

survive long sea voyages, were based largely on Assyrtiko. By law wine labelled as dry PDO Santorini is at least 75 per cent Assyrtiko, though in practice the percentage is higher.

Athiri and Aidani are the other two main varieties permitted in the PDO Santorini, more occasionally appearing on their own under the PGI Cyclades regional appellation. Athiri's contribution is to soften and lighten the blunt intensity and weight of Assyrtiko, while Aidani is prized for its fruity aromatics, a feature that Assyrtiko lacks. Traditionally these grapes were interplanted, harvested and vinified together, especially for the production of delectably sweet PDO Vinsanto – the original Vino di Santorini as it was known to Venetian traders. Today, Vinsanto is invariably a blend of these grapes (at least 51 per cent Assyrtiko, by law), harvested and left to dry in the sun for up to two weeks before pressing and fermentation. A minimum of two years ageing in wood casks is required, but the most-prized bottlings stay much longer in wood, up to ten or 20 years. Vinsanto can be bottled as either a single vintage, or as a blend, with a minimum age indication in multiples of four: 4 Years Old, 8 Years Old, etc. The finest examples are hyperconcentrated essences of the island, challenging, with dizzying sugar levels countered by forceful acids, notable tannic bitterness and palpable astringency.

Nychteri (Nichteri, Nykteri) is probably the closest in style to the powerful dry wines of centuries past. Made from the same grapes permitted for PDO Santorini, it is late-harvested (usually one to two weeks after those destined for straight Santorini), and often weighs in at 15% to 16% ABV, occasionally with some sugar left over. By law today it must be aged in wood for at least three months, though historic versions spent up to two or three years in cask.

A small quantity of mostly dry red and rosé is made from Mavrotragano (literally 'black crunchy'), a deeply coloured, tannic, high-acid variety considered to be Santorini's best. Mandilaria is another tart and tannic red grape better known on Crete, while rarer still is Voudomato, a relatively pale, soft red often used to make Santorini's increasingly scarce sweet red blends (under PGI Cyclades).

Although crops of tourists are Santorini's economic mainstay today, and land prices have soared to the level where vineyard development is discouraged, the crisis of Santorini wine seems to have passed. There are signs that tourism has reached saturation point, and a new generation has been inspired to return to old viticultural traditions. Investment, steady increase in international interest and accompanying rising wine prices appear to be stabilizing the future of Santorini wine.

SANTORINI – THE WINES & THE PEOPLE

Artemis Karamolegos Winery

Exo Gonia
84700 Santorini

A winery founded in 1952, producing clean, competent modern wines. Barrel-fermented Nykteri stands out, with light tropical fruit and integrated wood spice. An on-site taverna serves excellent local fare.

Athiná Wine Group ★

Athiná Tsoli and partner Ageliki Biba produce wine in Naoussa, Goumenissa as well as Santorini, where they've partnered with grower Nikos Pelekanos to produce a classic, neither overly polished nor rustic Assyrtiko under the Athiná label, made at the Karamolegos winery.

Boutari Winery – Santorini

Megalochori
84700 Santorini
boutari.gr

Santorini's modern success story can be traced to the arrival of Boutari in 1989. The large company, based in northern Greece and with wineries across the country, brought the radical concepts of earlier harvest and temperature-controlled, stainless-steel ferments – single-handedly inventing contemporary white Santorini. Kallisti is the top offering, both in unoaked and less successful barrel-aged versions. At the time of writing there is uncertainty about the future while a new winemaker is sought.

Canava Chrysou & Tselepos

Recognizing Santorini's bright future, respected Peloponnesian wine-grower Yiannis Tselepos (Mantinia, Nemea) partnered with the local Chrysou family to launch this joint venture. 2014 was the impressive first release, made by former Domaine Sigalas winemaker Ellie Tentzeraki, a classic Santorini crafted in a rich, full-bodied, concentrated style, focused more on stones than fruit, an exciting new addition to the island's offerings.

Canava Roussos ★★

M Street
Episkopi
84700 Santorini
canavaroussos.gr

Arch-traditionalists, Roussos wines have changed little it seems since the winery was established in 1836 – the oldest still operating on Santorini. Ancient Russian wood casks fill the small *canava* (underground cellar), untouched for a generation. Mandilaria/Assyrtiko blend Caldera takes on savoury, pot-pourri flavours after a decade. Vinsanto tastes more evolved than its two years in barrel (a sort of solera is created by using ancient barrels that held previous vintages), yet refined and elegant. A sweet, tawny-coloured blend of sun-dried reds Mavrothiro and Mandilaria, and Assyrtiko, is the only one of its kind – an original, marvellous herbal-medicinal elixir.

Domaine Sigalas ★★★

Oia
84702 Santorini
sigalas-wine.com

Paris Sigalas is one of Santorini's most important and dynamic figures. Ongoing experiments with modern trellising methods in the north's only vineyards aim to improve both quality and increase yields. Despite a background as a mathematician, Sigalas' wines show an artistic flair, wild but not savage. A full and fruity pure Aidani is the island's best; Estate Santorini is a flag-bearer, unctuous but firm, with a long track record of cellaring, while the Santorini 'Barrel' (mostly old wood-fermented/aged, from slightly riper grapes) is seamless. Single-vineyard Santorini Kavalieros consistently yield's Sigalas's most austere, tightly-wound Assyrtiko. Nychteri mirrors the island's most traditional style, harvested late (September) and forgotten in cask for two to three years.

Estate Argyros ★★★

Episkopi Gonia
84700 Santorini
estate-argyros.com

Despite a century of history (established in 1903), fourth-generation vintner Mattheos Argyros has his eyes on the future: replanting, renovating and building a new winery. Prized parcels of ancient vines, up to 250 years old, yield the outstanding Estate Santorini, a wine of superior length and depth. The same wine sees wood for the Estate Oak Fermented, best after at least three to five years. A pure Assyrtiko is marvellously briny and crunchy, while Atlantis white, from 'young' up to 50-year-old vines, is one of the island's top values. Vinsanto is memorable, with special lots aged up to 20 years in wood.

Gaia Wines – Santorini Winery ★★★

Exo Gonia
84700 Santorini
gaia-wines.gr

Yiannis Paraskevopoulos and Leon Karatsalos established Gaia in 1994, with sights set on top quality wines from Santorini and Nemea (Peloponnese). Paraskevopoulos, who studied oenology in Bordeaux and teaches winemaking at the University of Athens, applies a rigorous, technical approach to constant experimentation, including trials in amphorae and ageing bottles submerged in the sea. Pure Assyrtiko Thalassitis is precise and focused; Assyrtiko Wild Ferment is a step up in complexity, aged half in steel, half in wood. The Thalassitis in 'Oak Fermented' version has gained in finesse in recent vintages as new wood has decreased.

Gavalas Winery

Megalochori
84700 Santorini
gavalaswines.gr

Faithful to his 19th-century winemaking ancestors, George Gavalas has made a mission of reviving rare indigenous varieties like the nutty and waxy Katsano (blended with 15 per cent Gaidouria) and a light, pleasantly sharp, red-berry scented Voudomato Rosé. Vinsanto is a house speciality from Assyrtiko, Athiri and Aidani sundried up to two weeks, crushed by foot, fermented naturally in 1500-litre (396-US gallon) Russian oak casks, and left untouched for six years. Oenologist Margarita Karamolegou is sharpening up the dry Santorini offerings, including a creamy and saline Natural Ferment.

Hatzidakis Winery ★★★

Kallisti
Pyrgos
84701 Santorini
hatzidakiswines.gr

Haridimos Hatzidakis has been making some of the island's most extreme wines since 1997, from certified organic estate vineyards and additional purchased grapes. Ripeness is pushed further than most, yielding wines of shocking concentration and high alcohol and all wines are given skin contact, wild ferments, and are bottled unfiltered (except entry-level Santorini). Organically-certified Santorini Cuvée #15 is generous, and saline; Single-vineyard Assyrtiko de Mylos is a dry, late-harvested, old-vine cuvée from the village of Pyrgos, topped in density only by the Assyrtiko de Louros, from selected centenary vines grown up to 220 metres (720 feet), aged two years in large old casks, like a white version of Amarone. In 2015 production moved from a decrepit installation to a large cellar carved into a hillside of volcanic ash.

Santo Wines Winery – Union of Santorini Cooperatives ★

Pirgos
84700 Santorini
santowines.gr

Under the watch of chief oenologist Nikos Varvarigos, Santorini's largest producer (c.50 per cent of the island's production) makes a solid range of wines, improving yearly. Only the top half of quality makes it to bottle; the rest is sold locally in bag-in-box to satisfy thirsty tourists. Novelties include a complete and creamy Santorini Assyrtiko 'Organic'; bold and intense, late-harvest but dry Assyrtiko Gran Reserve is aged a year each in wood and bottle. A fine collection of Vinsanto is designated as aged 4, 8 and 12 Years in wood – the latter exquisite.

Venetsanos Winery

Caldera Megalochori
84700 Santorini
venetsanoswinery.com

Set in an old, beautifully refurbished winery built in 1947 by Yiorgos Venetsanos, Santorini's greatest winemaker of his era, this re-opened (2015) operation brings together former Boutari winemaker Ioanna Vamvakouri and the two nephews of Venetsanos. The aim is to farm all estate vineyards organically and vinify by parcel to express terroir variations – unreleased samples are promising.

HUNGARY
THE BAKONY-BALATON HIGHLANDS VOLCANIC FIELD & THE ZEMPLÉN HILLS

Hungary may no longer have active volcanoes, but it does have a spectacular volcanic history. Nestled in the embrace of the Carpathian Mountains, the Pannonian Basin was an area of hyperactive volcanism from shortly after dinosaurs roamed the earth to just a couple of million years ago – you needn't travel far in Hungary to find volcanic rocks. Major arcs of volcanoes run parallel to a presumed subduction zone of the Intra-Carpathian Plate under surrounding continental microplates (or formed along fissures of a stretched and weakened crust, depending on the theory), while other isolated volcanic cones and patches appear here and there. Dozens of mineral springs and natural thermal pools dotting the Hungarian countryside are some of the bubbling reminders of the past.

Hungary also has a glorious wine history. The Hungarian word for wine, *bor* is one of only two in Europe not derived from Latin, testifying to the ancient Magyars already-established connection to wine. During the Renaissance, Hungary produced some of the world's most sought-after elixirs. But the future is even more exciting, as Hungarians rediscover their superb collection of volcanic terroirs, forgotten or mistreated for much of the 20th century. Singular wines are already ageing in thousands of cellars carved out of volcanic rock. This chapter focuses on four of Hungary's finest volcanic regions: Tokaj-Hegyálja, Badacsony, Balaton-felvidék (Bakony-Balaton Highlands) and Somló.

THE BAKONY-BALATON HIGHLANDS VOLCANIC FIELD

The spectacular scenery on the north shores of Lake Balaton in the Tapolca and Kál Basins, and further north at Somló, offers obvious evidence of the rampant volcanism in Western Pannonia. Here, queer, trapezoidal-shaped volcanic monadnocks (isolated, flat-topped hills) rise off the plains of northwestern Hungary like a table full of upside down cakes. Over 50 eruptive centres are documented in what geologists have dubbed the Bakony-Balaton Highlands Volcanic Field, from activity that began some 7.5 million years ago and continued for five million years.

These basaltic volcanic 'necks' formed in several phases. The initial eruptions were extreme and violent, as exploding magma came into contact with water by the marshy shores of the ancient Pannonian Sea, which covered most of Hungary until about 5.5 million years ago. Huge tuff rings surrounding massive craters were created, like pie moulds waiting to be filled. Subsequent volcanic eruptions were more gentle and effusive,

OPPOSITE *Rolling vineyards in the Mád Basin, epicentre of fine Tokaji production.*

of the Hawaiian or Strombolian type, filling the craters with lakes of lava, like pie filling in the crust. When the volcanism finally came to an end, there was plenty of time for more mundane natural landscaping. Wind and water erosion slowly scraped away layers of lighter ash, tuff, and pyroclastic material from the first phase of eruptions, eventually exposing the inner core of rock-solid basalt that had cooled and hardened in its crust during the second phase. These exposed remainders are the strange formations that dot the northern shores of Lake Balaton: Badacsony, Szent György-hegy, Gulács, Csobánc, Szigliget, Tóti-hegy and Vár-hegy to name but a few of the better known *hegyek* (hills) where vines now grow. Just a little further north, the straggling volcanoes of Somló and neighbouring Kissomlyó and Ság share the same volcanic genetics. One of the most striking features of these eroded volcanic necks are the magnificent examples of columnar basalts, like the 'organ pipes' of Szent György-hegy (see opposite) as they are called locally, or the 'stone kitchen' near the top of Somló (see p.230, bottom right).

THE ZEMPLÉN HILLS

On the other side of the country in the northeastern corner, the Zemplén Hills are the first crinkles that rise up above Hungary's Great Plain, framed by the Hernád and Bodrog Rivers that tumble out of the Carpathian Mountains. They lie near a presumed tectonic subduction zone, related to the folding-and-thrusting formation of the Carpathian Mountains, squarely along a volcanic arc that stretches essentially from Budapest to the northeast tip of Hungary. For a volcanologist, the Zemplén Hills region is an amusement park filled with hundreds of complex calderas, single lava domes, volcanic fissures, sub-volcanic intrusions, stratovolcanoes and post-volcanic formations.

The most violent activity on the belt that formed the Zemplén Hills occurred 16 to eight million years ago, although it began much earlier. At first, eruptions were underwater. Later, as the Pannonian Sea began to recede, a new crop of massive volcanoes formed an archipelago of peaks, spewing volcanic material that mixed with the water below. Yet more eruptive activity continued after the sea had fully drained, producing an avalanche of tuff, pumice and more lava that buried the older material. Thus, multiple deep layers of andesitic, dacitic and rhyolitic volcanic rocks, ash and tephra make for a marvellously rich volcanic tapestry, intercalated with marine sediments. The region was further shaped by erosion and the post-volcanic activity of hot springs and geysers, whose hydrothermal action scoured, leached and deposited innumerable minerals. If that sounds complicated, that's because it is. Although the soils of the region are all largely derived from parent volcanic material, their composition varies dramatically. It's all part of the story of one of the world's great wine regions.

OPPOSITE *'Organ pipes', columnar basalt formations near the top of Szent György-hegy in Badacsony.*

BADACSONY & BALATON-FELVIDÉK

Neighbouring Badacsony (pronounced 'bah-dah-choin') and Balaton-felvidék on the north shores of Lake Balaton are two of Hungary's 22 official wine regions. They belong to the same volcanic formation, the Bakony-Balaton Highlands Volcanic Field (see p.220), and feature unique and spectacular protrusions of basalt. For centuries the landscape has been considered the most beautiful in Hungary, and much of the area is now protected by a national park.

Balaton-felvidék is a relatively large appellation that covers the northwestern part of Lake Balaton, with the separate appellation of Badacsony within it; both fall within the larger Balatoni regional appellation (NB: the 'i' ending in Hungarian is possessive, so that Balatoni means 'from Balaton'.) Balaton-felvidék's best wines come from the hills surrounding the Káli Medence (Kál Basin), an official sub-zone east of Badacsony, especially the Fekete-hegy, a promontory of lava that juts into the basin like a volcanic peninsula. Wines legally come in all colours, but this is white wine country. Badacsony is a more tightly delineated appellation, named for the town and vine-covered hill of the same name. Vineyards on neighbouring volcanic hills ('*hegy*' means 'hill' in Hungarian) are also included; some of the best known, Szent György-hegy,

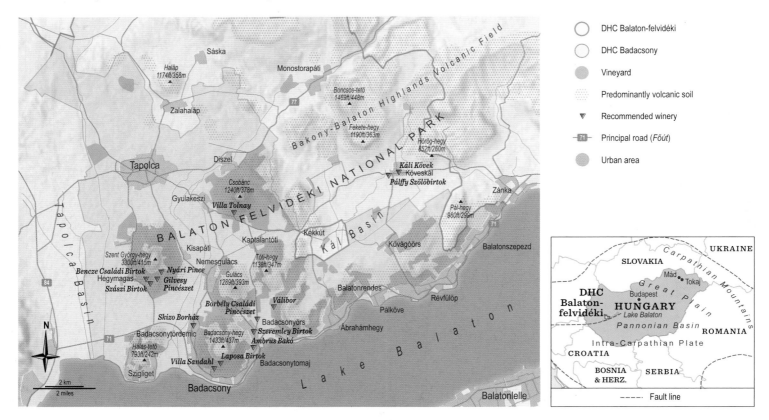

OPPOSITE (LEFT TO RIGHT) *Szaszi vineyards on Szent György-hegy; foggy morning, Szent György-hegy; Badacsony-hegy; view south from Laposa Birtok,* *Badacsony and Szigliget; Kál Basin; Káli Kövek winery; Ödön Nyári; Kál Basin with Badacsony and other volcanic hills behind; looking south* *across Lake Balaton; Badacsony-hegy; Gyula Szabó, Káli Kövek winery.*

Szigliget, Csobánc, Gulács, Hörög and Tóti-hegy, can also appear on labels, although they're not official sub-regions. All of Badacsony is planted on these volcanic plugs, off the valley floors.

A GENERATIONAL TRANSITION

The great Hungarian Sea, Lake Balaton, is the only remnant of the much vaster Pannonian Sea. For winemakers, Balaton has been both a blessing and a curse. On the one hand, its warm, shallow waters create a quasi-Mediterranean climate where olive and fig trees thrive and grapes ripen, in most years, to perfection. People have been drawn to its shores since time immemorial to enjoy benevolent weather, bath in its sun-warmed waters and sip its exceptional wines. But the leap in tourism that occurred from the middle of the 20th century onward created a ready-made, undemanding market that could absorb all the wine the region could produce, and more. Without commercial pressure, quality inevitably slipped.

But a generational transition is underway. Tourism is not what it used to be, and wines must now compete on quality. Sons and daughters have been taking over family wineries, and outsiders have been attracted to the area. There are lots of new names. The terroir is exceptional and there's never been any doubt that fine wine is possible – Badacsony and Balaton-felvidék produce some of Europe's most distinctive whites.

Viticulture in Badacsony & Balaton-felvidék

Distance to the lake makes all of the difference. The southern slopes of Badacsony directly overlooking the lake, for example, are the region's warmest, benefiting from sunlight reflected off the water. Extreme ripeness is easily achievable, and acid levels can drop perilously low. High humidity also favours botrytis, and indeed sweet, late-harvest wines were once a Badacsony speciality in centuries past, even if they are rare today. But Badacsony-hegy wines are still among the most opulent of the region. Further inland, humidity and average temperatures drop slightly, giving the wines of Szent György-hegy and Csobánc, for example, more finely chiselled acids and leaner frames. Soil composition likewise varies between volcanoes, and there's much interest now among wine-growers in understanding their nuanced differences. Endre Szászi from Szászi Birtok points out the particularly complex soils of Szigliget, the most varied in the region. Basalt is of course the base, but post-volcanic geyser activity bound and fused a whole series of additional mineral elements into the soil matrix. And Szászi's Szigligeti Olaszrizling certainly stands out for its extra dimention of flavour. Sándor Mezö of Skizo and Philipp Oser of Villa Tolnay offer up the more pure basalt soils of Csobánc as a potential explanation for the structure, depth and well-defined acids of its wines, which most closely resemble those of Somló. Szent György-hegy tends to have richer, more fertile soils leading to more vigorous vine growth, which surely contributes, along with climate, to the sharper, leaner style. There is still much work to be done.

The Grapes of Badacsony & Balaton-felvidék

After phylloxera had ravaged Balaton's vineyards, new wine legislation in 1893 recommended only white varieties for re-planting, a legacy that lingers today. Red grapes are permitted and grown (including some excellent Pinot Noir), but white grapes tell the story of the region, occasionally in blends, but most frequently pure.

The queen of volcanic grapes, and utterly unique to this region, is Kéknyelű, or 'Blue Stocked', so named for the unusual colour of its stems. It yields a wine of extraordinary character, smoky, flinty, honeyed and floral, with sizzling acids and almost chewable extract. It has measurably more potassium than any other variety grown in Balaton, resulting in the curious feature of high acid and high pH, and dramatically salty taste. Unlike virtually all vinifera varieties, Kéknyelű does not self-pollinate – it's a functionally female plant that needs to be fertilized, and hence is traditionally grown alongside Budai Zöld, a simple, fruity variety that flowers at the same time. But Kéknyelű yields are invariably very low and so only a few dozen hectares remain, though a recent, self-pollinating crossing of Kéknyelű and Budai Zöld called Rózsakő ('Rose Stone'), which shares some of Kéknyelű's remarkable character but with higher, more reliable yields, is gaining ground.

Olaszrizling is the calling card of the region, a full and round, grapefruity wine, gentle and approachable. Rajnai Rizling is the Hungarian name for true (Rhine) Riesling, made here in a mostly dry, medium-full style with characteristic high but ripe acids. Szürkebarát (Pinot Gris) is an historic Badacsony speciality, particularly smoky, fleshy and savoury, increasingly given skin contact. Zöld Veltlini (Grüner Veltliner), Muscat Ottonel and especially steely-sharp Juhfark (more common in Somló) are minor players but worth seeking, while Zeusz is commonly rendered into a plump, sweet wine of modest complexity.

OPPOSITE ABOVE *Robert Gilvesy's new plantings on the lower slopes of Szent György-hegy (see p.228).*

OPPOSITE BELOW *Csobánc Hill: an eerily similar volcanic formation to Szent György-hegy above.*

BADACSONY & BALATON-FELVIDÉK – THE WINES & THE PEOPLE

Ambrus Bakó ★★

H-8258 Badacsonytomaj
Erdős út 23

Ambrus Bakó, a PhD in molecular biology, makes a superb range of wines. It took five vintages to reach a level of perfection that he deemed saleable; 2009 was the first commercial release. He begins with the best sites, which for Bakó means 'vineyards that give intensity and complexity at relatively low sugar.' Results are fascinating: mineral, pale and limpid wines. Late-harvest Olaszrizling Kis Pál Helén, from a 60-year-old vineyard on Köveshegy, has amazing amplitude; Badacsonyi Szőlőskert 039/29 Olaszrizling has staggering intensity and uncommon energy. Badacsonyi Kéknyelű A Villa Mellett is raw and savage, salty, almost chewable, in need of several years ageing. Track these down if you can.

Bencze Családi Birtok

H-8265 Hegymagas
hrsz 1054/18
benczepince.hu

István Bencze credits an Olaszrizling from future neighbor Endre Szászi as his inspiration to leave the IT business in Budapest and launch a winery in 2012, with some family assistance. Many of the old vines purchased have, or will be, rehabilitated or replanted with Furmint, Kéknyelű, Hárslevelű and Chenin Blanc, and plans are to convert to organic/biodynamic farming. As yet unreleased traditional method Bakator sparkling is brisk and linear; lively Pinot Noir is promising.

Borbély Családi Pincészet

H-8258 Badacsonytomaj
Káptalantóti út 19;
www.borbelypince.hu

A mid-sized family operation producing well-priced white wines since 1996 from vineyards spread over four volcanic hills. Badacsonyi

Kéknyelű is the most intriguing, with terrific acidic twang, intensity and pure wet-stone flavour. After a decade, it acquires fine flinty-petrol (gasoline) aromatics like aged Riesling, with beautiful, suave and silky texture.

Gilvesy Pincészet ★

H-8265 Hegymagas
gilvesy.hu

Robert Gilvesy moved from Canada to Hungary in 1994 to start an architectural firm, but after buying an old Esterházy family press house on the southern slopes of Szent György-hegy, was drawn into the wine business. He formally launched his winery in 2012. Only whites are produced (for now), from three vineyards: Mogyorós on the north side of the hill was replanted in 2015. Tarányi on the south side is a parcel of Rajnai Rizling planted in the early 70s, making transparent, bone-dry, lemon-lime versions, as well as barrel-fermented Tarányi Reserve, which has improved as the percentage of old wood has increased. Váradi, a gently sloping parcel on the southeast side of the hill, was fully planted by 2015; some of its old Olaszrizling is used in the Bohém Cuvée, a floral, green-apple and wet-stone-scented blend with Riesling, Sauvignon Blanc and Pinot Gris from Badacsony-hegy. To watch.

Káli Kövek ★

H-8274 Köveskál
Fő út 11
kalikovek.hu

Káli Kövek was established in 2008 by wine distributor Attila Tálos, restaurateur Tamás Molnár, winery owner Robert Gilvesy (see Gilvesy Pincészet) and winemaker Gyula Szabó. White grapes are the focus and the range is very good to excellent, from sharp and appley entry-level Kavics cuvée to strikingly rich, low alcohol, old-barrel-fermented Rezeda Olaszrizling Válogatás (Selection). Firm and minerally Rezeda Rizling blends the top selections

of both Olasz and Rajnai Rizling. Szentbékkálla is the full-bodied, ripe orchard-fruit-scented single-vineyard Pinot Gris from Fekete-hegy and Monoszló Furmint Hegyestú-Csádé Dülö, is both a mouthful to say and a generous mouthful of wine, with the attractive botanical-sage and mint character of the variety.

Laposa Birtok ★

H-8261 Badacsonytomaj
Római út 197
bazaltbor.hu

The Laposa family estate (not to be confused with Laposa Pincészet) is a leading mid-sized operation making sharply focused and technically correct white wines from Csobánc, Köves, Szent György-hegy and Badacsony, as well as Somló, and purchased grapes. Zsófia Laposa, with a master's degree from Bordeaux and experience in California, Burgundy and Alsace, has been in charge of winemaking since 2013. Badacsonyi Kéknyelű and Furmint (from Csobánc and Köves-hegy) are noteworthy. Laposa aims to ramp up complexity and maximize the family's excellent collection of terroirs.

Nyári Pince

H-8265 Hegymagas
hrsz 881
nyaripince.hu

A family-run operation on the south side of the Szent György-hegy run by Ödön Nyári and daughter Emese. Nyári took the reins from his father in 1996 and has enlarged vineyard holdings to be self-sufficient. The varietal range is clean and honest if occasionally rustic, harvested in the slightly overripe spectrum and aged in old barrel and stainless steel. Look for firm and stony Kéknyelű (with 20 per cent Rózsakő), fresh and fruity Olaszrizling and a soft, fleshy Hárslevelű.

Pálffy Szölöbirtok

H-8274 Köveskál
Fő út 40
palffypince.hu

A small, family-run winery, with quality rising through a generational transition. Fekete-hegy and Horog-hegy vineyards are farmed organically. The range is generally solid, with impressive Káli Király Furmint delivering light petrol (gasoline) notes and a fine streak of saltiness. Káli Király Rivalisok Furmint/Olaszrizling, a rare but successful blend of these two 'rival' varieties, marries the salty, wet-stone minerality of Furmint with the soft texture and citrus of Olaszrizling. Káli Király is an official quality category in Kál Basin for use of premium selected grapes only and higher ripeness indication.

Skizo Borház

H-8263 Badacsonytördemic
Szent István út 24
skizobor.hu

From 'schizophrenia', Skizo is a hybrid micro negociant/estate operation run by Balász Sike and Sándor Mezö. The duo has accepted that 'financial independence requires multiple modes of thought,' hence the name. Both also make bulk wine for a large local operation, launching their side business in 2010. 'Fresh' is a range of blended wines from purchased grapes driving volume; passion is driven by the 'Premium Selection', clean, finely detailed, and generally excellent varietal wines from designated vineyards in the Badacsony area. Badacsony-Csobánc Olaszrizling is particularly compelling, a blend of two vineyards with substantial weight, depth and structure framed with crackling acidity. 'We're hoping to become less 'skizo' in the future,' says Mezö.

Szászi Birtok ★★

H-8265 Hegymagas
hrsz 035/7
szaszipince.hu.

Regional leader Endre Szászi farms organically on several volcanoes, producing a range of mostly varietal wines in all colours, and from dry to late-harvest. There's evident care in the densely planted rows of vines that slope gently towards the lake beneath the new cellar on Szent György-hegy. Age-worthy whites are the speciality. Kéknyelű (purchased from the research station in Badacsony) is rendered with terrific intensity and precise minerality (and has inspired Szászi to plant the variety). Kabócás Olaszrizling from Szigliget is one of the most beguiling in the region, showing best after several years.

Szeremley Birtok (Első Magyar Borház)

H-8258 Badacsonytomaj
Fő út 51-53
szeremley.com

The Badacsony region owes much to Huba Szeremley, who began revitalizing and expanding his family's vineyard holdings in 1992, and has been the driving force in re-establishing the region's historic reputation. He's responsible for considerable research into local varieties and terroirs, and was notably the first to replant and make pure Kéknyelű on a commercial scale. Huba's son Laszlo has taken over Badacsony's second largest estate, though quality has slipped into the middle of the pack or rather many others have improved dramatically. The real treat here is the opportunity to taste older wines, something few others can offer.

Válibor ★★

valibor.hu

Péter Váli started this tiny operation in 2000, with a few parcels split between Kisörs-hegy and Tóti-hegy. 'I like the artisan's life,' comments Váli. The wines are uniformly excellent, fermented in both stainless-steel and old acacia barrels. Badacsonyi Budai Zöld is fragrant and fruity; old-vines Badacsonyi Olaszrizling is floral and liquorice-tinged, while Kéknyelű is pure, tightly wound and mineral. Outstanding Pinot Noir would raise eyebrows in Burgundy.

Villa Sandahl ★★

H-8261 Badacsony
Római út 203/1
villasandahl.com

The extreme, uncompromising Riesling-focused vision of Swede Christer Sandahl, his wife Gunnel, and his brother Thord. Sandahl believes Riesling is best suited to this warm terroir on the south side of Badacsony-hegy. He is the last to harvest, yields are frighteningly low, and the wines are ultra concentrated, often with telltale flavours of botrytis and residual sugar. Multiple cuvées are produced, with whimsical name and label changes every year – consult the website to find out what you're drinking. These are striking, highly original and age-worthy wines, easily among the most dramatic in Hungary. Not for casual sipping.

Villa Tolnay ★★

H-8286 Gyulakeszi
Csobánc-hegy 24
villatolnay.hu

Swiss-born entrepreneur Philipp Oser was drawn to Csobánc purely for the quality potential. The property he purchased in 2004 once belonged to Klári Tolnay, a famous Hungarian actress from the 1930s. Wines are examplary. Tavasz (Spring) is the earlier harvested, fresh and crisp range, while the more structured, mineral wines are reserved for the Barrel Selection range, very age-worthy, backed up by several older vintages. Rieslings are top class for Balaton, and Olaszrizlings are uncommonly dense and viscous without losing freshness. Grüner Veltliner is Oser's chosen experimental canvass, playing on harvest time and skin contact in variations labelled Nap (Sun), Hold (Moon) and Föld (Earth).

SOMLÓ

Among the dry white wines of Hungary, those of Somló (pronounced 'shom-low') occupy a special place. The appellation is Hungary's smallest and most vineyards cover a single truncated volcanic cone – Somló-hegy (Somló Hill). But for centuries, these powerful, fiery whites have attracted disproportionate attention, earning wide praise. A famous legend is of their power to increase the conception of male children. No self-respecting 18th-century Habsburg emperor would have been without the nászéjszakák bora, *the 'wedding night wine' of Somló. As unlikely as it sounds, 20 to 25 per cent more boys are born here than in other parts of the country.*

Rising in solitude above the surrounding flat farmland north of Lake Balaton in western Hungary, Somló has been given the nickname of Witness Mountain, alone bearing witness to several million years of history as all else around its hard basalt cap crumbled to dust and eroded away. It has also witnessed wine-growing on its flanks for the last 2000 years. It yields Hungary's, and one of Europe's, most distinctive white wines – singular expressions with uncommon drive and force thanks to a very special terroir, expressive grapes and a centuries-old wine-growing culture with firm ideas on how best to extract the region's potential.

THE WITNESS MOUNTAIN

Despite an extraordinary terroir, Somló has been slow to recover from the era of state-controlled production. Average holdings are tiny, and many weekend growers have no commercial aspirations. Others operate with defiant independence, like their own little islands on this mountain-island, and the useful concept of collective marketing is utterly foreign.

Not surprisingly, it has taken a handful of outsiders to recognize the staggering potential of the region and set it on a path to greater

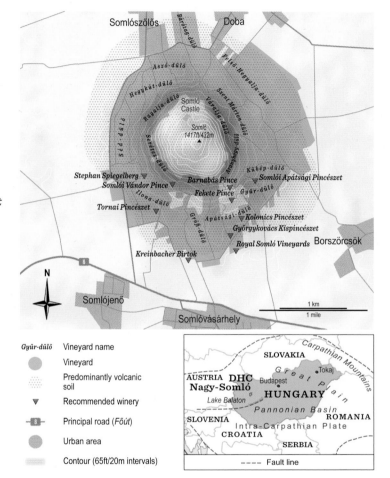

OPPOSITE (LEFT TO RIGHT) *South Somló; Zoltan Balogh, Somlói Apátsági Pincészet; Eva Cartwright, Somló Wine Shop owner; Stephan Spiegelberg's vineyards (twice); misty Somló; Kreinbacher winery; new water drainage channel; old stake-trained vines; traditional dwelling; Arányhegy vineyards; 'Stone Kitchen' columnar basalts.*

worldwide recognition. While quality is not uniformly high, and there is still plenty of rustic winemaking, the path is set, and the number of serious grower-bottlers has grown significantly since the turn of the millennium. The hill is currently witnessing a revitalization of its reputation as one of the most original places on earth to grow wines.

Somló's Soils & Vineyards

Nagy-Somló DHC (Districtus Hungaricus Controllatus), meaning 'Greater Somló', covers exclusively white wines, dry and more rarely sweet, produced on Somló-hegy itself as well as the much smaller Kissomlyó and Ság volcanic hills to the west and northwest (though no commercial wines are actually bottled from these last two areas). The mention of Somló alone on a label is reserved for wines grown above the lower road that circles the hill, considered the best area, though many fine wines even from the prized upper slopes are labelled Nagy-Somló to avoid the extra paperwork required for the more restricted appellation. Vineyards cover all sides of the hill, which reaches 432 metres (1417 feet) at its flattened peak, but few vines grow above 300 metres (1000 feet). The top crus have historically been on the southern slopes, such as the Szent Ilona Dülö (*dülö* means vineyard), Apátsági Dülö and perhaps the most famous cru, Aranyhegy Dülö (Golden Hill).

Soils derive from the basalt bedrock that forms the hill, though there are nuanced differences between them. The east side of the hill has more wind-blown loess, which yields more slender wines. The south and west sides have classically dark, heat-retentive soils that push ripening to the limits, while the west is more stony – it is the site of the last basalt flows – this is perhaps connected to the more dramatic salty minerality of these wines.

Somló's Grapes

Juhfark is the most emblematic variety, and Somló the only region where it occupies acreage of consequence. The name, 'sheep's tail', derives from the elongated, slightly curved shape of its bunches.

It's considered a 'blue collar' grape, like a peasant farmboy, vital, vigorous, hard to prune, with thick canes and big leaves. Juhfark's relatively neutral canvass allows it to faithfully translate nuances of site rather than impose its own varietal character. Acids are the highest in the region, even if it also collects sugars efficiently, and extract is also off the charts. It needs both time and oxygen to take its sting out, and is often bottled with a few grams of residual sugar.

Furmint is arguably Hungary's greatest white grape, and in Somló it delivers a highly articulate, mind-bendingly complex array of savoury and botanical notes, and screaming stony, salty, non-fruit flavours. It's harder to capture then the more direct Juhfark, but when it's right it's a world-beater. Hárslevelű offers a softer, more aromatic, charming expression of the hill, with less cut and obvious mineral character, while Olaszrizling is likewise a relatively soft and fruity expression that turns petrol- (gasoline-) scented with age – a good introduction to Somló before moving on to the more dramatic wines. Aromatic Tramini is a rarity, but acquires a saltiness in Somló like nowhere else.

Somló's Wines

These are wines of consequence; demanding and authoritative. The best can age for decades. The most representative are fermented in wood, usually 500 litre (132 US gallon) casks or larger, rarely new (and often ancient) and left to age on lees for a year or longer, followed by additional time in tank or bottle. 'Somló wines need oxygen, and time, to show their potential,' is a common refrain. Despite their apparent freshness, the wines have relatively low acids. Radiated heat from dark soils, especially on the southern slopes, low yields, and a philosophy of late harvest (in centuries past, growers didn't gather to even begin discussing the harvest until after the third week in October) result in wines with modest total acidity. Add in the acid-lowering effect of high-potassium soils, a feature of many volcanic areas, and the result is generous, full-bodied wine with a satiny, creamy texture. Yet a perception of freshness is driven by enormous extract, giving some 'phenolic drag' – palpable grittiness – and by notable saltiness that contains billowing fruit and ensures balance.

OPPOSITE ABOVE *Somló-hegy transformed – new roads and stone walls built by Jozsef Kreinbacher.*

OPPOSITE BELOW *Ilona Chapel and surrounding vineyards, one of the three main chapels on Somló.*

SOMLÓ – THE WINES & THE PEOPLE

Barnabás Pince ★

H-2094 Nagykovácsi
Berkenye út 18

Barnabás Tóth, retired IT director of the biggest medical university in Budapest, is described as meticulous. He owns a beautifully-sited parcel near the top of the south-facing Aranyhegy vineyard, more of a garden than a commercial vineyard. He has no intentions of expanding; everything is done by hand – his hands, the way he likes it. Excellent Hárslevelű is pretty and elegant, highlighting the charming, honeyed and floral side of the variety, while the Furmint is perfectly balanced and appealingly salty with extreme underlying minerality.

Fekete Pince ★★

H-8481 Somlóvásárhely;
feketepincesomlo.hu

Well past retirement age, Béla Fekete, known as 'the grand old man of Somló' or simply 'Béla bacsi' (Uncle Béla), sold his small parcel in the prized Aranyhegy vineyard to a trio from Budapest in 2013, although he agreed to stay on as consultant. Fekete's minimal intervention and prolonged ageing in old barrels and tank is the traditional gold standard. 'You have to give the wine enough time to show its origins,' Fekete believes. And they are singular, defiantly oxidative, packed with dried fruit, honey and toasted nuts, and anchored on sizzling acids and distinctive salinity. Hárslevelű is palpably tannic – a wine of strong character, while Furmint is a classic, old-school wine, deeply coloured, with a sherry-like whiff and searing volcanic ashy essence on the palate.

Györgykovács Kispincészet ★★★

H-8481 Somlóvásárhely
Somló-hegy Somlai tér 1

Imre Györgykovács is a legend, a micro producer at the top of the quality pyramid who has inspired many. He has farmed his single hectare (acre) on the south side of the hill since 1980, supplemented by small quantities of purchased fruit, bottling the first vintage under his own label in 1992 after the political reforms that swept through Hungary made private labelling possible. Wines are aged several years but kept reductive, as an amazingly fresh and floral, flint and petrol- (gasoline-) tinged four-year-old Hárslevelű shows. Olaszrizling, Furmint and Tramini are also excellent. 'The wines really only start to emerge after a couple of years, and handsomely repay extended bottle ageing,' states Györgykovács convincingly.

Kolonics Pincészet

H-8481 Somlóvásárhely
Somló-hegy hrsz 1273/4
kolonicspinceszet.hu

Budapest-based Károly Kolonics inherited a small parcel of vines from his grandfather in the Apátsági vineyard and bottled his first wine in 2001. The range is classic and traditional, with detail and precision. Juhfark is crisp and mid-weight, while Hárslevelű shows a softer, easier drinking profile from a sandy site. Furmint steals the show, a wine of pitch-perfect balance and terrific length.

Kreinbacher Birtok (Domaine Kreinbacher) ★★

H-8481 Somlóvásárhely
Somló-hegy hrsz 1674
kreinbacher.hu

Starting from scratch in 2002, József Kreinbacher continues to aggressively amass vineyards – he's now the largest producer – and has also invested heavily in structural improvements on the hill (stone terraces, roads, drainage channels, etc.) – single-handedly transforming Somló. A striking, half-buried winery shaped like a curvacious lava flow, was completed in 2011, in large part to produce sparkling wine. Kreinbacher hired an expert from Champagne to consult on the programme, which now represents over half of the winery's sizable production. Each cuvée gets at least 18 months on the lees, the best of which is the balanced and minerally Prestige Méthode Traditionelle from selected lots of Furmint, and the even better Brut Nature from the same base, which shows more purity and unique Somló character without dosage. Kreinbacher produces a wide range of still wines, from an easy-drinking Nagy-Somlói Cuvée blend to a fragrant and pure, exotically spiced Juhfark Selection at the top end, and a deep, stony Öreg Tőkék Bora (Old Vines Wine) Furmint.

Royal Somló Vineyards ★

H-8481 Somlóvásárhely Apátsági Cru
hrsz 966
royalsomlo.com

Royal Somló is a micro estate of less than a hectare (acre), but worth a mention. It's the project of Peter Csizmadia-Honigh, former Education Manager for the Institute of Masters of Wine in London, and his brother, Omar, a London-based branding and media professional, bottled from the family's weekend vineyard. A single Juhfark is made only in 'good years' in a comfortably traditional style –uncompromisingly sharp, mineral, remarkably fruitless and in the end, authentically Somló.

Somlói Apátsági Pincészet ★★

H-8481 Somlóvásárhely
hrsz 1070
juhfark.hu

Zoltán Balogh bought the Somlói Apátsági Pincészet (Abbey Cellar of Somló) that once belonged to the local Abbey, in 2001, and obtained permission to keep the monastic name. He farms organically and tends to harvest late, yielding generally full-bodied, soft and layered wines across his excellent, mostly varietal range. Skin maceration for up to a day lifts aromatics, and fermentation in large old barrels gives wines the micro-oxygenation Balogh believes they need to express terroir fully. Furmint is particularly aromatic, resinous and botanical. Juhfark pits the variety's sharp and driving acids against well-measured sweetness, while crushed wet rock, honey and flowers linger.

Somlói Vándor Pince

H-8483 Somlószőlős
hrsz 2606

Tamás Kis, former assistant winemaker at Szent Andrea in Eger, fell in love with a girl and moved to Somló in 2011. The relationship didn't work out, but he fell in love again, this time with Somló Hill. Inspired, he chose to make wine under the name Somló Wanderer. Kis's wines lean to the austere, reductive, tightly wound side, as exemplified by the Juhfark. But under that uncompromising exterior lie genuine depth, length and citric minerality.

Stephan Spiegelberg ★★

H-8478 Somlójenő
Somló-hegy hrsz 1121

Hungarian/German Stephan (István) Spiegelberg is a self-absorbed artist who accidentally fell into the wine business. He bought the small house where he now lives on Somló-hegy in 1993 as a holiday (vacation) property. 'The problem was that it came with vines,' he laughs. A former DJ and BMW test driver, Spiegelberg began bottling wine in 2004. His tiny parcel in the Szent Ilona vineyard is farmed organically. He makes a bewildering array of unpredictable wines in miniscule quantities, from 'classic' Somló to quirky, extended-barrel-aged 'specialty bottlings'. Low yields and late-harvesting across the board result in wines with weight and texture, but with genuine artisanal variation. Some reach the heights of the region, like the Nászéjszakák Bora, a blend of Juhfark with 25 per cent Olaszrizling that attains massive proportions, demanding bottle age.

Szabó Pincészet

somloijuhfark.hu

A tiny family winery (no relation to the author) producing only Juhfark from high on the west side of Somló-hegy on a prominent lava flow. The wine is decidedly traditional, with no fining or filtration and little or no sulphur. It's full-bodied, powerful, thick and creamy with extract levels more often found in full-bodied red wine. Fruit is secondary to dried-flower, honey and wet-stone flavours, and intense saltiness. It's how I imagine the wines of Somló tasted in centuries past.

Tornai Pincészet

H-8478 Somlójenő
Somló-hegy külterület hrsz 1248
tornaipince.hu

This historic estate was founded in 1946 by Endre Tornai, who was also among the first to bottle wine commercially from Somló in 1984, and is now one of the two largest in the appellation. Friss is the entry-level, stainless-steel-fermented varietal range. Classic is the mid-tier, and Top Selection represents the best lots from Tornai's four vineyards (Ilona, Grófi, Aranyhegy and Apátsági) with lower yields, later harvest and full barrel treatment. Results are mixed; Aranyhegy Juhfark Top Selection is best of the range.

TOKAJ-HEGYÁLJA

Tokaj-Hegyálja (Tokaj at the foot of the hill) is the wine region that covers the now-extinct volcanoes of the Zemplén Hills, named after the town of Tokaj that anchors the southern end of the range, nestled at the foot of Kopasz-hegy (Tokaj-hegy or Bald Mountain), the region's tallest volcanic

remnant at 512 metres (1680 feet). It's here that Hungary's most famous wine, sweet Tokaji Aszú made from beautifully shrivelled, botrytis-affected grapes, has been produced for at least 500 years. (NB: the 'i' ending in Hungarian is possessive, so that Tokaji means 'from Tokaj'.)

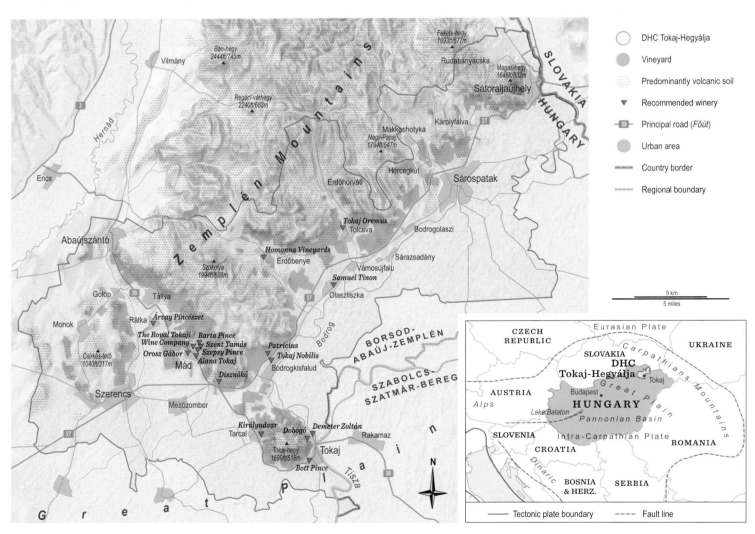

OPPOSITE (LEFT TO RIGHT) Barta Pince, Mád; cellar at Oremus, Tolcsva; Kopasz-hegy from Disznókö; Tokaji Nobilis' vineyards in Bodrogkeresztúr; aszú berries; Samuel Tinon bottles; Mád; Mádi

Udvarház restaurant; Samuel Tinon's organic vineyards, Olaszliszka; aszú berry selection at Samuel Tinon; Mád Basin; Tokaj Trading House cellar.

Far from the administrative centre of Budapest and beyond the eastern industrial outpost of Miskolc, Tokaj-Hegyálja was spared Soviet-era industrialization. Its towns and villages, the cobbled streets, ancient underground cellars, peasant farmhouses and aristocratic manors, its dense oak forests and marshlands, were frozen in a by-gone era. The wines, however, were not so fortunate. Subject to the quantitative demands exacted from virtually all of the country's products, even Tokaji Aszú was stripped of its nobility and made a commodity.

But that's now old news for the history books. Since 1991, Tokaj has fomented its own cultural revolution, now into the second chapter. The initial decade of unbridled euphoria, of embracing foreign investment and encouraging radical change, has given way to a more methodical, introspective and patient period of development. There's little doubt that Tokaj's exceptional terroir – its patchwork of volcanic soils, indigenous grapes, miles of underground wine cellars and centuries-old winemaking traditions – is a worthy world patrimony. UNESCO recognized

as much when it inscribed Tokaj-Hegyálja on its list of World Heritage 'Historic Cultural Landscapes' in 2002.

But in this second chapter, the region's most celebrated producers are relying less on the glories of the distant past, and pointing less to the more recent past for excuses. They've moved on to the serious business of producing great wine, unlike any other in the world. As Gustav Mahler said, 'Tradition is not the worship of ashes, but the preservation of fire,' an appropriate maxim in Tokaj's post-volcanic, post-communist era.

THE PRESERVATION OF FIRE

Tokaj-Hegyálja is an appellation for dry, sweet and sparkling white wine produced in 27 communities in Borsod-Abaúj-Zemplén County in northeastern Hungary. Dozens of hillsides have been named and classified since 1737, the oldest official vineyard classification in the world, yet exciting work still lies ahead. The celebrated vineyards of centuries past were classified based on their sweet wine production

ABOVE *Majestic Király-hegy (King's Hill) dominates the Mád Basin landscape.*

OPPOSITE ABOVE *In Disznókö's vineyards the misty mornings/sunny afternoons encourage botrytis.*

OPPOSITE BELOW *Deep, extensive cellars of Tokaj Oremus, covered with black mould* cladosporium cellare.

(susceptibility to botrytis), but finding and mapping the nuances of the greatest sites for dry wine, a focus of the last decade, is only now underway. With so many ambitious producers in on the research, results have already begun to crystallize.

Soils, as noted above, are complex, but the most important type from which many variations derive is called nyirok, a heavy clay weathered from volcanic rock with varying amounts of rocky debris. It's the most widespread soil in the region, often tinged red from metal oxides, turning darker as organic matter increases. Being a generally cold soil it encourages plenty of acid retention and an occasionally severe salty-mineral character in wines. Many of Tokaj's finest vineyards are variations on nyirok, yielding wines that shift from elegance, as in the more reddish clays of the Király, Nyulászo, Percze and Szent Támas vineyards, for example, to more powerful and broad-shouldered in the brown or black clays of Csontós or Betsek. The presence of more stones mixed in the clay, as at the Úrágya vineyard, encourages an austere, steely-sharp expression.

Non-volcanic loess soils (from wind-blown particles) are also present, especially in the southern part of the appellation, exposed to winds and dust from the Great Plain. The southern slopes of Kopasz-hegy (aka Tokaj-hegy or Bald Mountain) are nearly pure loess, as at the Mézes-Mály, Hétszőlő and Szerelmi vineyards, where both dry and sweet wines take on a much softer, opulent and less edgy character.

Tokaj's Grapes

As in many historic wine regions, the vineyards of Tokaj before phylloxera were field blends of dozens of grapes. Some treasured mixed plantings of old, randomly stake-trained vines in ultra-high density from before World War II still exist, but the majority of vineyards have been replanted to just a handful of grapes in orderly, trellised, monovarietal rows. The recent interest in dry wines features mostly single-varietal bottlings, though classic Tokaji Aszú is most often a blend.

OPPOSITE ABOVE *The village of Erdöbénye and surrounding vineyards.*

OPPOSITE BELOW *Unassuming cellar entrances, like these in Erdöbénye, often lead to vast cellar networks.*

ABOVE *Demijohns of pure eszencia at Disznókő; sugar concentration can top 80 per cent.*

Furmint made the cut over centuries for its capacity to retain high acid levels at high ripeness, and for its susceptibility to *botrytis cinerea*. It's aromatically discreet, tending to vague citrus and white-fleshed orchard fruit, but more often to an intriguing mix of resinous, herbal aromas like bay leaf, dried mint and sage. It makes full-bodied, high extract, densely mineral wines, which in sweet aszú form, can age a lifetime.

Hárslevelű is prized for both its distinctive floral aromatics (the name means literally 'linden leaf') as well as its affinity for botrytis. It's slightly more gentle and softer than Furmint, and in the view of many growers, less mineral, but still highly respected. Sárga Muskotály occupies most of the remaining acreage, better known as Muscat Lunel or Yellow Muscat. It's the earliest ripening of the main grapes, and like all in the Muscat family, has intense, floral aromatics, often used in small quantities to perfume blends.

Zéta is a botrytis-inviting crossing of Furmint and Bouvier created in 1951 mainly to increase aszú production, though lacks complexity, as does the 1970s Hárslevelű/Bouvier crossing called Kabar. Other ancient exotics like Kövérszőlő (fat grape) and Gohér have been the subject of recent experiments to recover the region's lost varieties.

Tokaj's Wine Styles

Tokaji Aszú is the region's most historically celebrated, and one of the world's most multi-dimensional wines, combining extreme levels of sugar, extract and acid with astonishing flavour complexity. Its invention was no accident. Late nights and early autumn (fall)mornings in the region are as reliably misty as afternoons are dry and sunny. The Bodrog River, which runs the length of the southeast side of the Zemplén Hills, and the Tisza River, which

meets it at the town of Tokaj itself, supply the moisture that condenses into thick, pea-soup fog during cool nights. Such a humid environment invites spores of botrytis to settle on grapes and set about their welcome work of shrivelling and concentrating. Yet warm afternoon rays and constant breezes slow its progress, preventing degradation into much-feared grey or black rot.

István Szepsy and his son speculate, however, that there's more than just fortuitous weather patterns that favour great aszú; soils play a role too. Szepsy believes that the richness in mineral elements supplied by Tokaj's geologically endowed soils protect grapes from nefarious moulds. As salt preserves food, so to does the concentration of mineral salts preserve Tokaj's grapes, allowing for shrivelling without rotting.

Tokaji Aszú is made by soaking individually hand-picked, botrytis-affected berries ('*aszú*' in Hungarian) in a base of fresh grape must or wine for a few hours up to a few days, then pressing, (re)-fermenting and ageing at least 18 months in wood. Sweetness varies according the ratio of aszú berries to base must/dry wine, formerly (and still occasionally) labelled in increasing level of sweetness as 5 or 6 **Puttonyos**, but officially categorized by residual sugar. A puttony is a hopper used to collect aszú berries, it holds about 25 kg (55 lb). 5 Puttonyos ranges from 120 to 150 g/l

ABOVE *Sun sets over the extinct volcano Kopasz-hegy.*

(about the same as Port, although higher acidity in Tokaji makes it taste drier), with 6 Puttonyos above 150 g/l. (New laws introduced in 2014 raised minimum sweetness levels, which effectively eliminates 3 and 4 Puttonyos Aszús, and drops the mandatory mention of puttonyos level altogether, though it's still commonly seen on labels.) Extreme wines with more than 450 g/l of sugar, made purely from aszú berries without maceration in base wine, are called Eszencia – a pure essence of botrytis with usually just 3% to 4% ABV.

Szamorodni is made from late-harvested grapes, pressed and fermented without the step of macerating as for aszú. It finishes Száraz (dry) or Édes (sweet), depending on the degree of ripeness/ botrytis at the time of harvest, and is aged oxidatively in wood. Tokaji Késői Szüretelésű ('Late-harvest') is a recent, mid-90s category for sweet late-harvest wines also unmacerated but aged for the most part in stainless steel.

Among the many dramatic, sweeping changes that have re-shaped Tokaj in the post-communist era, perhaps the most significant has been the development of **dry Tokaji** wines. Until the early 2000s, dry Tokaji was largely an afterthought, essentially the leftovers from aszú production. Mád-based grower Orosz Gábor lays claim to producing the first serious single-vineyard dry Tokaji in 1998 from the Király vineyard, while the head-turning quality of high-profile grower István Szepsy's 2000 Úrágya vineyard Furmint set Tokaj on a new path where dry and sweet share equal respect. Many early experiments were disappointing, most notably because of the tendency to oxidize prematurely, but constant refinement of technique, most critically the strict elimination of all aszú (or just rotten) berries, use of larger wooden casks or stainless-steel vessels, less new wood and more careful pressing and handling has made it clear that truly memorable and age-worthy dry Tokaji is a reality.

ABOVE *The pretty village of Mád in its topographic basin surrounded by prime vineyards.*

TOKAJ-HEGYÁLJA – THE WINES & THE PEOPLE

Alana Tokaj ★★★

H-3909 Mád
Rákoczi út 15-17
alana-tokaj.com

Co-owners András and Attila Németh, and András' wife Allison, focus on all-estate grown, top-quality late-harvest and aszú wines from unthinkably low yields. Similar extremes are reflected in the winemaking. There's no attempt to control or adjust, or even analyze the wines at any stage. Alana owns an enviable collection of first-class crus, including sizable parcels of Betsek, Király and Veresek. Base wines for aszús are made mostly from late-harvest Muskotály and Hárslevelű; sugar-rich Zéta is often picked for aszú. Across the range these are wines of singular intensity and monumental sweetness. Even the late-harvest styles often tip over 200 g/l of sugar, while the 2006 Aszú Eszencia (a category that no longer exists) is a balance-defying explosion of orange pekoe tea and essential oil of rose with 316 g/l of sugar.

Árvay Pincészet ★

H-3908 Rátka
Széchenyi tér 13
arvay.eu

János Árvay has been making wine in Tokaj since 1975, initially with the state company, a period which he recalls with horror. In 2009 he moved back to Rátka to the Árvay Family Winery, farming mainly around the village, including the two most prized vineyards, Padi-hegy and Isten-hegy, and shifting focus to dry wines. Quality is variable, even if the top bottles are some of the best in the region.

Barta Pince ★

H-3909 Mád
Rákóczi út 83
bartapince.hu

Károly Barta jumped on a chance to buy a large, partly abandoned parcel on the historically celebrated first growth Király Dülö (King's Vineyard) in Mád, one of the steepest in Hungary. Replanting started in 2003 with high-density, stake-trained vines – mostly Furmint – and he enlisted winemaker Attila Homonna (see Homonna Vineyards, overleaf) from the first bottling in 2008, favouring his artisanal, minimal intervention approach. Vineyards are cultivated organically. Drinkers of Homonna's excellent dry wines will find Barta's more than vaguely familiar, tightly wound and flinty, requiring plenty of air, or ideally, ageing in the cellar. Despite young vines, there's depth and impressive length in both the Furmint and the Hárslevelű.

Bott Pince ★★★

H-3910 Tokaj
Szerelmi Pincesor 0145/19
bottpince.hu

Husband and wife Judit Bott and József Bodó run this small, widely admired, single-vineyard-focused estate, built slowly from the ground up since 2006. Six terroirs are farmed organically, a natural philosophy that follows into the winery where nothing but small amounts of sulphur are used, 'the only way to represent the values of Tokaj with credibility and integrity,' Bott says. Wines are occasionally quirky, but the beauty is in their asymmetrical character. An old-vine Csontós Furmint is considered the top cru, bone dry, broad-shouldered and long-lived. Teleki Hárslevelű from high-density, 70-year-old vines

on the south side of Kopasz-hegy is an atypical loess wine, much firmer, more acid-driven than most wines from this south-facing hillside, thanks in part to shallower loess and thus root access to underlying volcanics. Furmint and Hárslevelű from the Határi vineyard display the site's almost painful flinty-stony character, while a 6 Puttonyos Aszú is excellent but edgy.

Demeter Zoltán ★★★

H-3910 Tokaj
Vasvári Pál út 3
demeterzoltan.hu

Zoltán Demeter is one of Tokaj's loudest, free thinking voices. But he also makes the sort of quality wine that silences anyone opposed to his ideas. Despite considerable success, he remains a one-man operation. 'I don't trust anyone else to do what I do,' he says frankly. He started his own label in 1995 and now farms nine old-vine vineyards in five villages. Over the years, he has rationalized his range, and the wines have become more precise and focused, particularly the dry wines, which are archetypes. Öszhegy Muskotály is an essence of the grape, barely off-dry but sizzlingly mineral. Szerelmi Hárslevelű is generously proportioned but tight; Boda Furmint from Demeter's 100-year-old family vineyard in the far north of the region is breathtaking, with supreme cut and class. But perhaps the most arresting wine is the Birtok Bor, the dry estate blend of Furmint from the Lapis, Betsek and Holdvölgy vineyards. It's half the price of the single vineyards, yet absolutely equal in quality. 'That's the point. I didn't want it to be an inferior wine. It represents my estate after all,' exclaims Demeter. A single-estate aszú is made without puttonyos designation – a massive, extremely sweet but balanced wine, one of the very finest in the appellation.

Disznókő ★★★

H-3910 Tokaj,
Pf 10
disznoko.hu

French insurance giant AXA Millésimes purchased the former imperial Disznókő estate from the Hungarian government in 1992, among the largest properties in Tokaj. Chief winemaker, László Mészáros, focuses on aszús of exemplary finesse. Furmint is used most often as the base, and aszú berries are macerated in still-fermenting must, seeking refinement over power. Finished alcohols are slightly higher than average, meaning lower sugars. The ultimate expression of Disznókő's elegant style is the pure Furmint Kapi Vineyard 6 Puttonyos Aszú, a single, mid-slope, south-facing parcel, with lighter clay soils laced with volcanic pebbles and loess.

Dobogó ★★★

H-3910 Tokaj
Dózsa György út 1
dobogo.hu

An onomatopoeic reference to the 'clippity-clop' of horse hooves on cobbled streets, the Zwack family (makers of Hungary's great Unicum bitters) established Dobogó in 1995. Prime vineyards around Mád in the crus of Betsek, Szent Tamás and Úrágya are farmed without herbicides or pesticides (not quite organic). Winemaker Attila Domokos guides Dobogó's superb range, made from absurdly low yields on average, less than a kg/vine. Estate Dry Furmint is exceptionally dense and pure, combining the power of the Betsek with the elegance and creamy fruitiness of Szent Tamás. A pure Betsek Furmint is austere and savoury, with characteristic resinous notes. Aszús are rendered in a concentrated, sugar-rich style, yet always balanced.

Homonna Vineyards ★★★

H-3932 Erdőbénye
Hunyadi út 61
homonna.com

Every region needs its iconoclast, and Tokaj's is Attila Homonna. He belongs to no associations and plays by his own rules. He makes some of the most precise and finely detailed, stable and age-worthy dry wines in the region, mastering the delicate balance between oxidation and reduction. Production is tiny, the way Homonna wishes to keep it. Even the entry-level Furmint/Hárslevelű is finely tuned on a string of succulent acids, while the Határi Vineyard, a 100-year-old+ field blend of mostly Furmint on the border between Erdőbénye and Olaszliszka (*határ* means border) is dry Tokaji at its savoury, botanical, salty best. Rány Vineyard Furmint-Hárslevelű is slightly more generous and round, though with the same transparency and purity that marks all of Homonna's wines.

Királyudvar ★★

H-3915 Tarcal
Fő út 92
kiralyudvar.com

Former royal property Királyudvar (King's Court) has a history of wine production dating back to at least 1431. American businessman Anthony Hwang (also of Domaine Huet, Loire, France), purchased it from the Hungarian state in 1995, and set about restoring it, initially hiring the region's top winemaker István Szepsy, and later Zoltán Demeter. Responsibility has since passed to Szabolcs Júhász and quality continues to rise. The entire estate is certified organic and is converting to biodynamic. Furmint Sec is an ultra-refined blend of Percze, Henye, Lapis and Betsek. Furmint Demi-Sec hails from the Betsek vineyard and its cool, clay-rich soils, while satiny Hárslevelű Lapis is medium-sweet. Tokaji Aszú 6 Puttonyos Lapis is a strong argument for single-vineyard aszús. Also the most sophisticated traditional-method sparkling in Tokaj.

Orosz Gábor ★★

H-3909 Mád
Táncsics út 4
oroszgabor.com

Mád-based Orosz Gábor is credited with making the first serious dry, single-vineyard Furmint in 1998, four years after officially launching his commercial enterprise from old family vineyards. Orosz works a collection of Mád's most highly regarded crus, including Király, Úrágya, Betsek, Szent Tamás, Hosszúkötél, Veres and Nyúlászó. Wines are as powerful and broad-shouldered as the man himself. Dry wines often close in on 15% ABV, and wood is used to work in additional layers of flavour. Fresh aromatics are sacrificed for texture. Betsek Furmint stands out with its marked stony signature and full, succulent palate. 'Betsek is consistently the most mineral wine in my range,' he confirms. Aszús are likewise intense, rumbling across the palate.

Patricius ★

H-3917 Bodrogkisfalud
Várhegy dulo 3357 hrsz
patricius.hu

Owned by the Kékessy family, Dr. Péter Molnár PhD has managed the estate since the first vintage in 2000, devoting considerable resources to researching old clones and 19th century varieties in the hopes of rediscovering lost genetic diversity. Molnár favours blending over single-vineyard wines to build complexity, and everything from a subtle, ethereal dry Furmint and fragrant dry Muscat, through to concentrated but elegant 6 Puttonyos Aszú and monumental Eszencia, is consistently classy.

Samuel Tinon ★★

H-3933 Olaszliszka
Bánom út 8
samueltinon.com

Samuel Tinon is affectionately known as the mad Frenchman devoted to Szamorodni, of which he makes the best in Tokaj. With a degree in viticulture and oenology and experience in Australia, Chile and Italy, he was initially brought from Bordeaux in 1991 to manage Royal Tokaji (see opposite). A decade later, when 'he finally understood the region', he started his own winery. 'It took me ten years to express in Tokaj what I had in mind,' he reveals. Szamorodni *száraz* (dry) is wonderfully nutty and savoury, like top-notch amontillado sherry with more acid. Szamorodni *édes* (sweet) shares similarly burnished, old-furniture and maple-syrup flavours but with gentle sweetness. Superb aszús are crafted in the traditional, oxidative fashion. Increasing curiosity about dry wines has led to three solid versions of Furmint: an estate blend, and Határi and Szent Tamás crus.

Szent Tamás ★★

H-3909 Mád
Batthyány út 51
szenttamas.hu

Szent Támas is a recently established, ambitious estate belonging to Kovács Károly, focusing mainly on dry wines, confusingly named after the great vineyard in Mád (where he also owns land). Wines from a dozen estate vineyards are made by István Szepsy Jr., son of Tokaj's best-known producer. Mád village blend of dry Furmint is the fine entry. Dongó vineyard Furmint is saline and fruity, while Percze Furmint is more full-bodied and dense. Pitch-perfect Szent Támas Vineyard Furmint is the pinnacle, rightfully considered Mád's *grand cru*, with two bottlings: regular and limited selection '86', referring to the specific sub-plot within Szent Támas, bottled only in magnums.

Szepsy Pince ★★★

H-3909 Mád
Batthyány út 59
szepsy.hu

A living legend, István Szepsy traces his winemaking roots in Tokaj to the 16th century. He has been one of the driving forces over the last quarter century in putting the region back on the international map, and still establishes the gold standard for dry and sweet wines, with prices to match. His vineyards are spread mostly around the Mád Basin, the most complete collection of top crus and old vines in the appellation, farmed in pre-industrial fashion. Dry wines represent over 80 per cent of production, crafted in a typical minimal intervention style and tend towards the reductive side with vast ageability. Aszús are among the most sought-after in Tokaj.

The Royal Tokaji Wine Company ★

H-3909 Mád,
Rákóczi út 35
royal-tokaji.com

Royal was the first foreign-owned company in the region after the fall of communism. It was then, as today, formed by a consortium of British shareholders led by noted British wine writer Hugh Johnson. The original focus on single-vineyard aszú wines from first growth vineyards in Mád, has changed little, even if dry Furmints were introduced much later. Of the vineyard-designated wines, the loess-rich soils of Mézes-Mály yield the lightest softest, most floral-honeyed version. Nyulászó, with its red-tinged volcanic clay gives a robust yet still elegant expression, while Betsek and its heavier black nyirok volcanic clay seems 'cooler', with more biting acidity. Szent Támas is the most complete, with its iron-streaked red volcanic clays delivering elegant acids, loud minerality and expansive flavours. Tokaji Aszú Red Label from estate grapes remains an excellent introduction; Blue Label from purchased

aszú berries is only a minor step down. Single-vineyard aszús reflect similar characteristics as the dry wines from the same crus.

Tokaj Nobilis ★

3916 Bodrogkeresztúr
Kossuth Lajos út 103
tokajinobilis.hu

Tokaj native Sarolta ('Saci') Bárdos focuses on textural richness and mineral character rather than aromatics across her well-made portfolio. Top dry wine is the Barakonyi Furmint, owing its edge in depth perhaps to the vineyard's older vines, planted in rhyolite tuff. In time, the younger Csirke-mál vineyard, and in particular the sub-parcel Bárdos calls Susogó (onomatopoeic for the sound of rustling leaves in this cool, shallow, stony-andesitic corner), may well top it.

Tokaj Oremus ★★★

H-3934 Tolcsva
Bajcsy Zs 47
tokajoremus.com;

The Álvarez family of Spain's iconic Vega Sicilia purchased the historic Oremus estate in 1993, embarking on an ambitious restoration plan, building a modern production facility and investing heavily in vineyards. Massal selection of Furmint from a century-old vineyard started in 2006, critical work to preserve the genetic diversity of Tokaj's most important variety. András Bacsó at the helm has made Oremus one of the most reliable and consistent estates. A single dry wine is made, the broad and powerful Dry Furmint Mandolás vineyard blend, which has gained in finesse as wood influence has waned. Tokaji Late Harvest is gentle, with pear purée and yellow plum; 5 Puttonyos Aszú is a regional reference.

GLOSSARY OF VOLCANIC & GEOLOGICAL TERMS

Aiken: official United States National Cooperative Soil Survey (NCSS) soil series consisting of very deep, well-drained soils formed in material weathered from basic (alkaline) volcanic rocks (*basalts, tuff breccia*).

Alluvium / alluvial soils: accumulation of loose sediments re-shaped and deposited by flowing water, such as a river.

Andesite: predominantly *extrusive igneous rock*, between *basalt* and *rhyolite* in silica content (around 60 per cent). Frequently found in island arc magmatism (*subduction* zones), from both *explosive* and *effusive eruptions*. Term is derived from the Andes Mountains.

Andisol: official United States Department of Agriculture taxonomy term for soils derived from volcanic ash or other volcanic ejecta. The term derives from the Japanese 'black soil'. Also known as Andosols.

Ash (volcanic): tiny fragments (less than 2 mm/¼ in) of pulverized rock expelled during violent volcanic eruptions. Ash is created when suddenly depressurized gases dissolved in *magma* rapidly expand and escape into the atmosphere. The chemical composition of ash is dependent upon the magma that formed it, ranging from basaltic (*mafic*) to rhyolitic (*felsic*). Ash weathers rapidly, releasing a wide range of potential plant nutrients and minerals. See also *phreatomagmatic, tephra*.

Basalt: *igneous rock* that forms both *intrusively*, but mostly *extrusively*, from *lava* rich in iron and magnesium, and poor in potassium and sodium, with less than 50 per cent silica (*mafic*). Basalt's low viscosity leads to more gentle eruptions. Oceanic crust is composed primarily of basalts (or closely related gabbro and peridotite) formed at mid-ocean *rift zones*, making it the most abundant rock type on the earth's surface, even if it makes up only a few per cent of the continental surface.

Breccia: agglomerated rock composed of cemented angular fragments of rocks and minerals. **Volcanic breccias** are cemented rocks made up of bits of *lava* and *ash* often, but not necessarily, from an explosive eruption.

Caldera: a cauldron-shaped depression formed by the collapse of land following an explosive volcanic eruption.

Cinder or Scoria cone: a conical-shaped hill composed of loose *tephra* that accumulates around a volcanic vent.

Colluvium / colluvial soils: accumulation of sediment deposited by gravity (as opposed to *alluvium*, deposited by moving water).

Dacite: predominantly *extrusive rock* between *andesite* and *rhyolite* in *silica* content (*felsic*), often found with andesite.

Effusive eruption (also Strombolian, Hawaiian): a mild volcanic eruption with gentle lava flows.

Extrusive rock: *igneous rock* formed from rapidly cooled *lavas* at the earth's surface (exposed to air or water), in contrast to *intrusive rock*. Because of the rapid cooling, extrusive rocks often exhibit fine-grained crystals. Only soils formed on extrusive rocks are considered in this book.

Felsic: descriptive term applied to *igneous rocks* that are relatively rich in pale-coloured elements like *silica* and potassium. *Rhyolite* is the most felsic rock, also high in sodium. (Ultra-)*mafic* rock is at the other end of the spectrum.

Feldspars: the most commonly occurring group of rock-forming minerals in the earth's crust, accounting for up to 60 per cent of all the world's rocks, *igneous (intrusive* and *extrusive), metamorphic* and *sedimentary*. Technically, they are distinguished chiefly by their potassium, sodium and calcium content.

Fumarole: vent in the earth's crust in volcanic zones, often connected to a subterranean *magma* chamber, which emits steam and gases such as carbon dioxide, sulphur dioxide, hydrogen chloride and hydrogen sulfide.

Graben: from the German meaning ditch or trench, a linear depression of the earth's surface between two parallel faults. As the faults spread apart, the land between them collapses. Volcanoes often form along the faults or within the graben. See also *rift zone*.

Greywacke: type of *sedimentary* sandstone, characterized by having two distinct grain sizes due to how and where it forms. It has a fine, muddy component mixed with much coarser fragments, in roughly equal proportions, and has a generally dark (grey) colour.

Hotspot: in geology, a location on the earth's surface above a mantle plume, where upwelling *magma* breaks through and erupts. The existence of hotspots is not universally accepted.

Igneous rock: rock formed from cooled and solidified *magma* or *lava*. If cooled from magma underground, the rock is termed *intrusive*, if from lava above ground, it is *extrusive*.

Ignimbrite: unconsolidated, or solidified material deposited by a 'fiery hot, rock-dust cloud', a hot suspension of *ash*, particles, gases (also called a *pyroclastic* flow or density current) flowing rapidly from a violently explosive volcanic eruption. Colour and composition varies according to the original *magma*.

Intrusive rock: *igneous rock* formed from *magma* cooled very slowly beneath the earth's surface, often with large crystal formations visible to the eye. Granite is a common example of intrusive rock.

Lahar: Javanese word for a volcanic mud or debris flow containing a slurry of *pyroclastic material* mixed with water and sediment. Lahars occur when hot erupting material mixes with wet mud from heavy rains or rivers, or snowmelts around the summit of high-elevation volcanoes.

Lapilli: Latin for 'little stones', airborne volcanic material (*tephra*) ranging from two to 64 mm (¼ to 2½ in) in diameter, roughly from pea to walnut-sized.

Lava: general term for molten rock (*magma*) after it is expelled from a volcanic vent, and the rock formed from it after cooling. Lava forms *extrusive igneous rocks*.

Loess: soil type composed of deposited windborne sediment.

Maar: from the Latin *mare*, or sea, a crater caused by an explosive *phreatomagmatic* volcanic eruption, which subsequently fills with water to form a lake.

Mafic: descriptive term applied to *igneous rocks* relatively rich in elements like magnesium and iron (ferric compounds), hence MA-FIC, also low in silica. Basalt is a mafic rock, also relatively rich in calcium. *Felsic* rock is at other end of spectrum.

Magma: general term for molten rock beneath the earth's surface. *Lava* is magma that is expelled during a volcanic eruption. See also *extrusive*, *intrusive* and *igneous rocks*.

Metamorphic rock: rock type formed from the transformation of another type of rock, caused by heat and/or high pressure. The physical and or/chemical characteristics of the original rock are significantly altered (eg. slate and schist). **Metavolcanic rock** is metamorphic, recrystallized rock of volcanic origin.

Monadnock: a isolated hill or mountain that rises above a surrounding plain. Volcanic monadnocks typically form when *magma* erupts through, but is contained by, a layer of softer rock like limestone or *tuff*. When the covering layer erodes away along with the surrounding land, the core of hard, solidified *lava* remains standing in isolation.

Obsidian: *extrusive igneous rock*, also known as volcanic glass, formed from rapidly cooling *felsic* rock, without crystallization. Unlike most pale felsic *lavas*, obsidian is most often black in colour.

Phreatomagmatic eruption: a highly explosive volcanic eruption in which *lava* comes into direct contact with external bodies of water such as oceans, lakes or groundwater.

Plinian eruption: a highly explosive volcanic eruption that produces a huge plume of smoke and ash that can rise many miles into the stratosphere.

Porphyry: from the Greek for 'purple', a textural term describing *igneous rock* with large-grained crystals set in finer material, often pink, purple or red. Such rocks form from *magma* cooled in two stages: first slowly, deep underground (*intrusive*), followed by a second, more rapid cooling phase at shallow depths. In Germany, porphyry (*porphyr*) is used interchangeably with *rhyolite*.

Pumice: a typically pale-coloured type of rough-textured *extrusive rock*, formed from highly pressurized, frothy *lava* (mixed with gases and water) erupted explosively, and rapidly depressurized and cooled. Abundant gas bubbles trapped and frozen in the rock give it low density; pumice often floats in water. **Pumicite** is a finer-grained equivalent.

Pyroclasts / pyroclastic material: a general term applied to airborne fragments ejected during volcanic eruptions (also called *tephra*).

Rift zone: an area on the earth's surface where the crust extends and sinks, such as a *graben*, causing a series of parallel fractures and faults. Rift zones may result in volcanism, when underlying *magma* is able to escape through the resulting fissures. Can also refer to smaller fissures – spreading ground in volcanic areas – through which *lava* flows.

Rhyolite: predominantly *extrusive igneous rock*, with more than 60 per cent *silica* (*felsic*), high in potassium and sodium, and low in iron and magnesium. Eruptions featuring rhyolite are most often explosive, thanks to its lower melting point and high viscosity.

Scoria: dark-coloured, low-density, rough-textured *extrusive rock* formed from rapidly cooling *basalt* or *andesite lava* flows or ejected as *lapilli* or volcanic bombs. Similar to *pumice*, gas bubbles become trapped and frozen in molten rock as it solidifies, but scoria has greater mass and sinks in water.

Schist: type of *metamorphic rock* formed at very high temperatures and pressures that cause foliation, the alignment of minerals into thin layers (schist derives from the ancient Greek meaning 'split'). Schist comes in infinite variety, and is often described by its predominant mineral, as in **mica-schist**, a schist rich in mica, a silicate mineral.

Sedimentary rocks: formed by weathered, eroded or precipitated particles, deposited on land or under water, which are subsequently cemented together (eg. limestone and sandstone). These usually contain few different major minerals relative to *igneous* and *metamorphic rocks*, ie. they have a less diverse mineral composition.

Silica: a widespread chemical compound formed from silicon and oxygen, aka silicon dioxide, one of the most abundant in the earth's crust. Silica content is used to distinguish between types of *lava*.

Shield volcano: very broad, low-profile volcanoes, formed by successive mild eruptions of low viscosity *lava* (*basalts*) that spreads over a large distances. Less common than *stratovolcanoes*.

Stratovolcano: a steep-sided, tall, often conical-shaped type of volcano, sometimes called composite volcanoes as they are built over many successive, often violent eruptions, each building up mass and height.

Subduction: the geological process of one tectonic plate getting dragged under another. It occurs at convergent plate boundaries, where plates are drifting towards one another, as opposed to divergent boundaries, and often results in volcanism along an arc parallel to the subduction zone.

Tephra: general term for any fragmented material ejected during a volcanic eruption, also called *pyroclasts*. If tephra is still hot enough when it hits the ground, it can fuse into pyroclastic rock, such as *tuff*.

Tephrite: alkaline (basic) *extrusive igneous rock* close to *basalt* in composition.

Trachyte: a fine-grained, alkaline, (basic) *extrusive igneous rock* rich in *feldspars*, between *rhyolite* and *dacite* in *silica* content.

Tuff: rock composed of volcanic *ash*. Once deposited, it compacts and consolidates into a solid, though relatively soft rock, which is easily carved. Not to be confused with tufa, a type of limestone.

Volcanic field: large areas prone to volcanic activity from multiple vents, including *cinder cones, calderas, shield* or *stratovolcanoes* and *fumaroles*, clustered together.

Zeolite: a type of mineral similar to *feldspar*, but containing water. In volcanic areas, zeolites can form when volcanic rocks and *ash* come into contact with alkaline ground water. Its high ion-exchange capacity facilitates mineral uptake via root systems.

BIBLIOGRAPHY

Alkonyi, László, *Tokaj – A Szabadság Bora* (Budapest, Spread Bt., BORBARÁT, 2000)

Bauer, Andrea; Wolz, Sascha; Schormann, Anette; Fischer, Ulrich, *Authentication of different terroirs of German Riesling applying sensory and flavor analysis* (Neustadt, Department of Viticulture and Oenology, 2011)

Brown, Kenneth A, *Cycles of Rock and Water: Upheaval at the Pacific Edge* (New York, Harper Collins, 1992)

D'Agata, Ian, *Native Wine Grapes of Italy* (Berkeley and Los Angeles, University of California Press, 2014)

Foti, Salvo, *Etna : i vini del vulcano* (Catania, Giuseppe Maimone Editore, 2011)

Frankel, Charles, *Vins de Feu: À la Découverte des Terroirs des Volcans Célèbres* (Paris, Dunod, 2014)

Guerrero, Manuel Méndez; Sanchez Garcia, Isidoro; Sánchez Reyes, Juan Carlos, *Canarias Desde El Mar Hasta El Cielo* (Canarias, Grupo CPC, 2014)

Guilbert, Benjamin, *Caractérisation de la minéralité des vins blancs issus du cépage Riesling par l'étude de la nutrition minérale: variation en fonction du terroir, du millésime et des pratiques vitivinicoles* (Montpellier, Université de Montpellier, 2012–2014)

Gregutt, Paul, *Washington Wines & Wineries: The Essential Guide, 2nd ed,* (Berkley and Los Angeles, University of California Press, 2010)

Kourakou-Dragona, Stavroula, *The Santorini of Santorini* (Athens, The Fany Boutari Foundation, 1995)

Leitão, Cristina, *Madeira The Book* (Funchal, Funchal Publications, 2007)

Metcalf, Charles, and McWhirter, Kathryn, *The Wine and Food Lover's Guide to Portugal* (London, Inn House Publishing, 2007)

Moio, Luigi, *Colori odori ed enologia della Falanghina: Programma di selezione clonale e ampelografica della vite in Campania* (Napoli, Stampa Orpi)

Moio, Luigi, *Colori odori ed enologia dell'Aglianico: Sette anni di sperimentatzione e ricerca enological in Campania* (Napoli, S.T.A.P.A-Ce.P.I.C.A, 2004)

Monaco, Antonella; Mustilli, Anna Chiara and Pignataro, Luciano, *Falanghina* (Sorrento, Franco di Mauro Editore and Azienda Agricola Mustilli, 2005)

Pogue, Kevin R, *Influence of basalt on the terroir of the Columbia Valley American Viticultural Area* (Soave, Proceedings of the 8th International Terroir Congress, Centro di Ricerca per la Viticoltura, 2010)

Reiner-Schultz, Hans *The Future of Riesling, TONG Magazine n°9* (Belgium, Millefeuille Press, 2011)

Saillet, Stéphane, Rapport de stage du Diplôme National d'Œnologue: *Etude sur les éléments minéraux des vins issus de Riesling en Alsace : variations en fonctions des terroirs, pratiques viticoles et œnologiques.* (Montpellier, Université de Montpellier, 2012)

Swinchatt, Jonathan and Howell, David G, *The Winemaker's Dance: Exploring Terroir in the Napa Valley* (Berkeley and Los Angeles, University of California Press, 2004)

Wright, W H (Terry), *Geology, soils and wine quality in Sonoma County, California* (Forestville, Sonoma State University, 2006)

PICTURE CREDITS

Page 20, above left: Domaine Serene
Page 20, above right: Carabella Vineyard
Page 23 Pacific Rim Solstice Vineyard: Pacific Rim Winery
Page 35: Cristom Vineyards: John D'Anna; Soter Vineyards, Eola Amity Hills: Carolyn Wells Kramer; Cristom Vineyards: John D'Anna; Phelps Creek under Mt Hood: Phelps Creek; Cristom Vineyards: John D'Anna; Brittan Vineyards: Thomas Heinser)
Page 36, below: Thomas Heinser
Page 37, above: Carabella Vineyard
Page 38: John D'Anna, Cristom Vineyards
Page 39, above: Phelps Creek
Page 39 below: Anna M. Campbell
Page 42-43: Andrea Johnson
Page 46: Phelps Creek
Page 48: John D'Anna
Page 56: Obsidian Ridge Vineyards
Page 58: Arkenstone Vineyards, Howell Mountain (twice): Arkenstone Winery; Mayacamas Vineyards: Nick Korompilas; Arkenstone Vineyards: Arkenstone Winery
Page 61 above: Terra Valentine
Page 61 below: Cathy O'hagain (NB: photo to be used for promotional purposes)
Page 63 above: Russ Widstrand
Page 64: Philip Togni Vineyard
Page 66: Duckhorn Vineyards
Page 72: Repris Wines, Moon Mountain (first two): Erik Almas; Richard Dinner vineyard: Paul Hobbs Wines
Page 76: Erik Almas
Obsidian, Lake County: Obsidian Ridge Vineyards; Obsidian Ridge Vineyards: Obsidian Ridge Vineyards; Brassfield Estate vineyards under Round Mountain volcano: Brassfield Estate; obsidian: Obsidian Ridge Vineyards; Brassfield Estate Winery: Brassfield Estate Winery; obsidian at Obsidian Ridge Vineyards: Obsidian Ridge Vineyards; red volcanic soils, Hawk and Horse Vineyards: Hawk and Horse Vineyards; Obsidian Ridge Vineyards aerial view: Obsidian Ridge Vineyards; Lake County diamonds; Hawk and Horse Vineyards: Hawk and Horse Vineyards; now what do we do... planting at Obsidian Ridge Vineyards: Obsidian Ridge Vineyards; Obsidian Ridge Vineyards, Mt Konocti: Obsidian Ridge Vineyards
Page 85: Brassfield Estate Winery
Page 86: Obsidian Ridge Vineyards
Page 91: Laberinto Wines, Alto Maule: Laberinto Wines; Cono Sur Rulos del Alto vineyard, Bío-Bío: Cono Sur; Laberinto Wines, Alto Maule: Laberinto Wines; Cacique Maravilla's 200-year-old+ País vines: Cacique Maravilla
Page 121: trenzado vines, Valle de la Orotava, Tenerife: credit: Alec Dorsaint-Pierre
Page 123 below: Alec Dorsaint-Pierre
Page 124 below: Suertes del Marqués
Page 129: Alec Dorsaint-Pierre
Page 134: Domaine Zind Humbrecht (all photos)
Page 141 below: Faber & Partner
Page 153: Frank Cornelissen, pruning: Frank Cornelissen; Biondi's terraced vineyards: Vini Biondi
Page 165: Basilisco, Vigna di Mezzo: Basilisco
Page 168: Basilisco
Page 201: Cantina Filippi, Castelcerino: Consorzio di Soave; ripe Garganega: Consorzio di Soave; Monte Carbonare vineyards: Consorzio di Soave; Castello di Soave: Consorzio di Soave
Page 204-205: Consorzio di Soave (all three photos)
Page 225: Badacsony and Szigliget: Gilvesy Pincészet
Page 227 below: Gilvesy Pincészet
Page 230: South Somló: Eva Cartwright; misty Somló: Eva Cartwright; Kreinbacher winery: Eva Cartwright
Page 237: Samuel Tinon bottles: Samuel Tinon; Samuel Tinon's organic vineyards: Samuel Tinon; Olaszliszka; aszú berry selection at Samuel Tinon: Samuel Tinon.

ACKNOWLEDGEMENTS

The list of people and organizations to recognize and thank in this section is a mini-volume of its own. Without their support, time and graciously shared knowledge, this book simply would not be. I owe a sincere debt of gratitude to (ordered by chapter): the Washington State Wine Commission, Oregon Wine Board, California Wine Institute, Napa Valley Vintners, Sonoma County Vintners, Lake County Wineries Association, Wines of Chile, Filipe Rocha of the Azores Escola de Formação Turística e Hoteleira, SATA Airlines, Adeliaçor, Instituto Do Vinho Da Madeira, Madeira Regional Tourism Board, Alec Dorsaint-Pierre of Harfang Exclusive, Canary Islands, Sopexa and the Conseil Interprofessionnel des Vins d'Alsace, German Wine Institute, Piero Titone of the Italian Trade Commission, Maria Gilli of ICE Roma, ASSOVINI, Giovanni Ponchia of the Consorzio Tutela Vini Soave and the Volcanic Wines initiative, Consorzio Tutela Vini d'Irpinia, Sannio Consorzio Tutela Vini, Giorgio Tinelli of the Italian Chamber of Commerce, Toronto, Sofia Perpera and George Athanas of Wines of Greece and Wines of Santorini, Éva Cartright of the Somló Wine Shop, Robert Gilvesy of Gilvesy Pincészet, Badacsony, Rita Takaró, the Tokaj Trading House and the Government of Hungary.

If the bibliography looks suspiciously light, that's because much of the information that appears here (and what could be several more volumes' worth), was shared directly by so many of the leading minds in the fields of geology and soil science. For their generously given time and collective centuries of research, I'd like to thank: Dott. Attilio Scienza, University of Milan, Dr. Uli Fischer of the Competence Center of Wine Research, DLR Rheinpfalz, Neustadt and Dr. Ernst-Dieter Spies of the Landesampt für Geologie, Mainz, Germany, Prof. Alex Maltman, Wales, Dr. James A. Kennedy, Prof. Thomas Rice, Dr. Jean Jacques Lambert, Daniel Roberts (aka Dr. Dirt) and Paul Animosa of California, Dr. Kevin Pogue, Whitman College, Walla Walla, Washington, Pedro Parra, Chile, and Dr. Lukácsy György, Hungary, not to mention the countless others whose research papers I came across along the way.

I's also like to sincerely thank the wineries and winemakers chronicled in this book for their hospitality and graciously given time to answer my innumerous and sometimes difficult questions, and for the opportunity to taste their volcanic offerings, as well as those wineries I visited but which do not appear in these pages, often because of editorial constraints.

This book may well not have come to be were it not for my publisher, Jacqui Small, who saw some fantasy in my outlandish idea, along with Fritha Saunders, Jo Copestick and Emma Heyworth-Dunn of Jacqui Small Publishing, to who I am indebted. Peter Dawson and Namkwan Cho of Grade Design are responsible for the spectacular layout and eye-pleasing design of the book, for which I am absolutely thrilled and grateful. Many thanks also to expert cartographer John Plumer, whose maps are a rich addition to the text and photos, bringing to 3-D life all of the regions along with many of the geological features that underlie the volcanism therein. And I owe of course a sincere debt of gratitude to copy editor Hilary Lumsden, who managed to untwist the mystery of many of my sentences, and from whom I've learned the value of synthesis and succinctness. Her deep knowledge of the subject allowed for efficient exchanges and guided me to the essential, while her attention to detail is unparalleled.

And finally, the greatest thanks of all are owed to my wife, Alexandra, and my children Esmai and Julius. Their unconditional support of this project, of my regular absences, 5am wakeup alarms and long days at the library made this all possible. I'll mow the lawn tomorrow, darling, I promise.

INDEX

Illustrations are indicated in **bold**.
Map page references are indicated in *italics*.